CONCEPTUAL FRAMEWORKS IN GEOGRAPHY

GENERAL EDITOR: W. E. MARSDEN

The Geography
of Settlement

Peter Daniel B.A.

Head of School of Humanities, Bedford College of Higher Education

Michael Hopkinson M.A., M.Sc.

Senior Lecturer in Geography, Bedford College of Higher Education

Maps and diagrams drawn by Tim Smith

Oliver & Boyd

Acknowledgements

The authors and publishers wish to thank all those who gave their permission for us to reproduce copyright material in this book. Information regarding sources is given in the captions to Figs, Plates and Tables, and in the References at the end of the Book.

Oliver & Boyd

Robert Stevenson House
1–3 Baxter's Place
Leith Walk
Edinburgh EH1 3BB
A Division of Longman Group Ltd

ISBN 0 05 003128 7
First printed 1979
Second Impression 1981

**Printed in Hong Kong by
Wilture Enterprises (International) Ltd**

Contents

Editor's note

An encouraging feature in geographical education in recent years has been the convergence taking place of curriculum thinking and thinking at the academic frontiers of the subject. In both, stress has been laid on the necessity for conceptual approaches and the use of information as a means to an end rather than as an end in itself.

The central purpose of this series is to bear witness to this convergence. In each text the *key ideas* are identified, chapter by chapter. These ideas are in the form of propositions which, with their component concepts and the inter-relations between them, make up the conceptual frameworks of the subject. The key ideas provide criteria for selecting content for the teacher, and in cognitive terms help the student to retain what is important in each unit. Most of the key ideas are linked with assignments, designed to elicit evidence of achievement of basic understanding and ability to apply this understanding in new circumstances through engaging in problem-solving exercises.

While the series is not specifically geared to any particular 'A' level examination syllabus, indeed it is intended for use in geography courses in polytechnics and in colleges of education as well as in the sixth form, it is intended to go some way towards meeting the needs of those students preparing for the more radical advanced geography syllabuses, such as those of the JMB, the Oxford and Cambridge Board and the Scottish Higher Grade.

It is hoped that the texts contain the academic rigour to stretch the most able of such candidates, but at the same time provide a clear enough exposition of the basic ideas to provide intellectual stimulus and social and/or cultural relevance for those who will not be going on to study geography in higher education. To this end, a larger selection of assignments and readings is provided than perhaps could be used profitably by all students. The teacher is the best person to choose those which most nearly meet his or her students' needs.

W. E. Marsden
University of Liverpool.

Preface

In this book we have tried to do three things. Firstly we have traced the development of the towns and villages of England and Wales in a chronological order to give an idea of how the present landscape of settlement came into being. Then we have analysed the theoretical structures which geographers erect to give order to the distributions and interactions within the landscape and have applied them and illustrated them within the context of recent urban growth. Thirdly we have tried to draw out the perceptions that people living in settlements have about their environment and to show how these ideas shape the urban fabric. To try to unite these three geographical worlds of objective reality, idealized models and contemporary perceptions we have relied upon a conceptual framework in which each aspect of the geography of settlement is pegged to a geographical idea that can be expressed relatively simply but developed to levels of complexity appropriate to the reader's interest. Often we have included examples from outside Britain, and some sections of the book are concerned with chronology whilst others are concerned with exemplifying static concepts. We hope, however, that the overall pattern is one of comprehensible, if not comprehensive, explanation of settlement location, functioning and interaction.

We are grateful for the help of many people in producing this book; not least to the urban geographers, historians and sociologists on whose work we have drawn for our material. In addition we owe a considerable debt to Bill Marsden for his guidance on the style and format of the text; and for his meticulous editing and the many helpful suggestions that we have incorporated.

We should also like to thank John Bale, author of a companion volume, for his judicious comments, and Enid Desert for transforming our manuscript into legible form.

Finally, without the patience and support of our wives and families, the book could not have been written.

Peter Daniel
Michael Hopkinson.
Bedford College of Higher Education
January 1979.

1 Introduction

A. Changing Geographical Method

Settlements may be defined as places which are inhabited on a permanent basis, as distinct, for example, from camps or fairs. Although they may be categorized according to their size, status and range of facilities provided, so that hamlets may be distinguished from villages, villages from towns and so on, it is important to bear in mind that, in reality, there exists a *settlement continuum* and each category merges gradually into the next.

Settlement provides a focus for interdisciplinary study. The economist, sociologist, historian, psychologist and geographer are all able to examine a settlement from a clearly defined disciplinary base. Geography acts as an integrator, borrowing from the other disciplines but, at the same time, making its own distinctive contribution, particularly with respect to spatial organization. Looking for patterning both within and amongst settlements provides some insight into how things are organized spatially.

1. Traditional approaches

Traditionally, the geographer was content to describe these relationships while at the same time examining cause and effect in a rather subjective and unscientific manner.[1] Frequently, cause was related to the physical environment. For example, the location of a town might have been explained in relation to its position at the lowest bridging point and head of navigation on a river, or as a springline settlement established at an assured supply of fresh water. Geography was also concerned with the unique. The distinctiveness of a town was stressed; the nature of its site, its development through time, its employment structure, major industries and so on. This in turn led to the classification of settlements according to the characteristics of their site (such as hill top, scarp foot, meander core) and their functions (such as market town, mining town, resort, centre of heavy industry).

2. Quantitative approaches

The search for common characteristics was gradually extended to include a search for order in both the spacing of settlements and their internal organization. At first this was based on careful observations or empirical research, from which generalizations were made and broad principles identified which seemed to have some

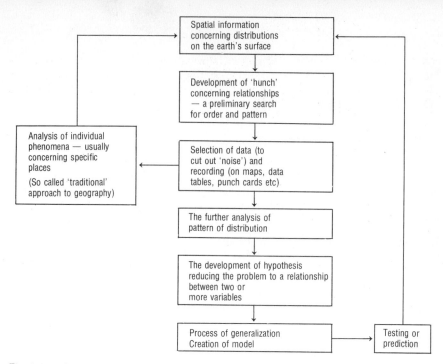

Fig. 1.1 Comparison between the traditional method and a scientific method in geography. (Source: B. P. Fitzgerald, 'Scientific method, quantitative techniques and the teaching of geography' in *New Directions in Geography Teaching*, R. Walford (ed.), Longman, 1973, p.86)

universal application. These concepts and principles were embodied in models which acted as simplifications of reality, enabling a general statement to be made about how things are organized spatially,[2,3] Many of the classical models which throw light on spatial organization within and amongst settlements are discussed in the ensuing chapters. For example, in Chapter 4, you will study the internal structure of towns and discover how a number of models have been developed which purport to give some insight into how different activities or functional zones are arranged within towns and cities. The application of statistical techniques allied to the increasing use of computers (which enable vast volumes of data to be handled) have meant that the generalizations can be tested against the real world, and the models refined and reformulated where necessary. The 'quantitative revolution' as it became known, meant that scientific method was adopted by the geographer in the search for a greater understanding of spatial organization. Hypotheses were formulated and tested to try to discover geographical concepts relating to location, patterning, and spacing of settlement, functional zoning within settlements, rural-urban interaction and so on (see Fig. 1.1).[4] For a fuller discussion of changing geographical method see John Bale's 'Introduction' to the companion volume in this series (*The Location of Manufacturing Industry,* First Edition).

Underlying the quantitative revolution was the belief that problem-solving was a rational process, relying upon logical thought and accurate information for its success. An example of this in geographic terms is Allan Pred's[5] model of the choice of profitable sites. Given that there is a 'best' site for an industry, a shop or a settlement, indeed for almost any sort of human activity, he argues, individual choice will depend upon the accuracy of information available and the wisdom of the decision maker in evaluating that information. True, there may be factors which distract from a logical choice but by and large rational 'economic man' will make a predictable, wise decision.

3. Behavioural approaches

Whilst reliance upon economic theory, mathematically analysed data and a logical approach is attractive and appears eminently reasonable, many geographers have grown dissatisfied with the effectiveness and relevance of such methods when applied to real world problems. They are aware that not all decisions are the result of rational, economic forces but that other factors need to be considered. For example, it may well be that the structure of a town can be understood only when attention is paid to subjective factors. One aspect of this relates to the environment as it is perceived by its population at local levels and through the filters of different cultural traditions.[6] In Chapter 5, you will learn how the pioneering work of Walter Firey[7] in Boston is extremely important in this respect. Firey recognized that certain parts of Boston have acquired symbolic and cultural connotations and this has prevented them from being overtaken by economic forces and developed in a predictable way.

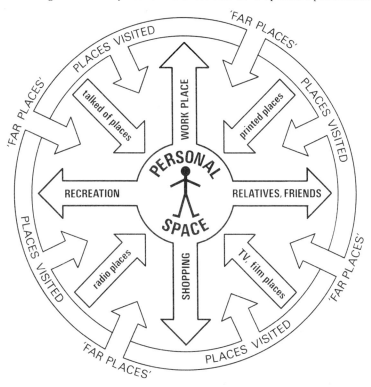

Fig. 1.2   Man's perceptual map. (Source: B. Goodey, *Perception of the Urban Environment*, University of Birmingham, Centre for Urban and Research Studies, Occasional Paper 17, 1971, p.7)

In another important pioneering work, Anne Buttimer[8] argues that space has social as well as purely physical attributes and that these will exert a strong influence on the way in which a settlement develops. In Fig. 1.2, Goodey[9] suggests that people's perception of the environment is arrived at through the interaction of primary and secondary sources of information. Primary sources involve direct personal contact with the environment through work, leisure, shopping trips and so on, and secondary sources are the descriptions of places obtained from the media or in talking with friends and acquaintances. The behavioural approach therefore argues that human decisions cannot be explained in purely rational terms because human actions are greatly influenced by the perceptions people have of their environment.

The search for a greater understanding of the processes which help to shape a town has led geographers towards a greater appreciation of the interaction of economic, political, social and behavioural forces at work. Thus the *friction of distance* may influence land values in a town and, in turn, the manner in which different areas are used, but superimposed on this is a range of *cultural* constraints. The way in which different parts are perceived will also act as a powerful influence on the way in which they are used and the sort of people who live there. Geographers are increasingly interested in the application of the theories of spatial organization in solving urban problems. Research conducted into housing conditions, distribution of socio-economic groups and crime rates has highlighted spatial inequalities which exist within our towns and cities (see Chapter 5). The political implications of social inequality have attracted the attention of a group of radical geographers led by David Harvey.[10]

4. The relevance of settlement geography

Each successive development within the study of geography has enriched it. One approach does not supersede another, but rather each new development builds on what has gone before. There is still a need for the student of geography to have a sound factual basis – to know where places are situated, to have some conception of the relative size of settlements, and so on. But it is equally important for that student to have some sort of historical perspective, to have some insight into the way in which settlements have evolved through time and the historical forces which have helped to shape them. At the same time, there should be some grasp of spatial organization both within and amongst settlements. Students should be able to apply scientific method to gain greater understanding, while remaining aware of the importance of cultural/behavioural considerations. We would hope that after studying the settlement component of an 'A' level geography course, you would know how to begin to structure an investigation of a town which is unfamiliar to you.

Geography is an exciting and dynamic subject, concerned with issues which affect us all no matter where we live. We are all to a greater or lesser extent concerned with environmental quality and social well-being: urban transport policies, the plight of the inner city, patterns of retailing and related topics are relevant to us all. Increasingly, through greater public participation in the planning process, we are all being given the opportunity to contribute to the formulating of decisions which will affect the way in which settlements will develop in the future. It is one of our objectives in writing this book that you will be better equipped to contribute to such discussion and be able to make judgements based on knowledge rather than prejudice.

B. The Layout of this Book

In examining the geography of settlement, the book attempts to synthesize the approaches outlined above. The early chapters are historical in treatment. Chapter 2 examines the sequence of occupation in rural areas from prehistoric times. Chapter 3 continues the sequential development of the town from the medieval period through to the industrial age, and the effect of early attempts at urban planning is discussed. Chapter 4 is devoted to the study of urban morphology, the pattern of settlement growth and zoning of activities; while in Chapter 5 the concepts of social areas and social activity are examined. Chapter 6 investigates the most important of the city's economic zones, the Central Business District, and this is followed in Chapter 7 by an attempt to explain the relationship between the town and its surrounding area through the ideas of central place theory. Chapter 8 is concerned with the linkages which exist between the town and its surrounding area, the urban field. The changes that have taken place in these relationships are discussed – how they can be measured and how they should be controlled and investigated. Chapter 9 examines the effect of settlement planning in Britain in the post-war period, with particular emphasis on new towns, problems of urban renewal and planning strategies in rural areas.

In each chapter we have tried to identify key ideas which are exemplified in the text. For example, in Chapter 2, the description of nucleated and dispersed settlements is related to the factors responsible for these kinds of settlement pattern in England and Wales. Hence, in reading this book you will find the chapters sub-divided into sections, each containing basic ideas which are summarized at the end of each chapter. Each section also contains individual assignments; pieces of work which the student is asked to perform in order to reinforce a grasp of the immediately preceding material. The assignments are accompanied by additional activities and readings at the end of each chapter, which are designed to relate to the chapter as a whole. The assignments and activities vary widely in type and are designed to give a range of experiences to the student. It is important to stress that the summaries of key ideas, readings and assignments are intended to be integral rather than supplementary to this introduction to modern settlement geography.

It is also our desire to emphasize that the sequence of chapters is, in general, progressive rather than arbitrary. We feel that the reader should be careful to ensure, by reference to preceding chapters, that he or she is aware of the ideas which are being built upon and which might be missed if later sections were read in isolation. Throughout the text there is an attempt to balance the chronological study of settlement development with the application of current methods of urban analysis and measurement. The two elements are seen as complementary in explaining the present settlement landscape. In determining whence they should draw their examples the authors have been conscious of the need to keep the length of this volume comparable with others in the series, and have therefore concentrated upon British and, to a lesser extent, other 'first world' cases. It is hoped to include consideration of the 'third world' city along with other aspects of problems of the developing world in a subsequent volume.

Key Ideas

A. Changing geographical method

1. It is recognized that all subjects have characteristic organizing concepts or key ideas. Those of geography are markedly spatial in kind.
2. The traditional approaches of geography as a study of landscape relied heavily on describing man/land relationships, examining cause and effect in a rather subjective and unscientific manner.
3. These were challenged in the 1960s by a more mathematically oriented methodology, based upon data collection and hypothesis testing.
4. The role of individual and group behaviour and perception has increasingly replaced a logical and mathematical approach to geographical study in the last decade.

Additional Activities

1. Read the references listed below by Bale, Walford and Lawton and summarize the main developments in geographical method which have occurred since the early 1960s.
2. Read Firey's and Buttimer's articles. How is it possible for space to acquire social characteristics?

Reading

BALE, J., *The Location of Manufacturing Industry*, Oliver & Boyd, 1976, Chapter 1.

WALFORD, R., (ed.), *New Directions in Geography Teaching*, Longman, 1973, in particular pages 69–106.

LAWTON, R., 'Changes in University Geography', *Geography*, **63,** Part 1, January, 1978, in particular pages 2–9.

JONES, E., (ed.), *Readings in Social Geography*, Oxford University Press, 1975, in particular, BUTTIMER, A., 'Social Space in Interdisciplinary Perspective', pages 128–137, and FIREY, W., 'Sentiment and Symbolism as Ecological variables', pages 138–148.

2 Settlement origins and growth

In the introduction we define a settlement as a place which people inhabit and where they carry on a variety of activities – trade, manufacturing, defence and so forth. This study of settlement will touch upon almost all aspects of human social and economic activity: so that the study of settlement geography provides an introduction to the study of social geography in general.

A. Geographical Concepts of Settlement Location and Morphology

1. The choice of location

In the past, geographers have argued that the physical conditions in an area – rock type, climate, slope and so on – actively determined the pattern and organization of settlement, land tenure and usage as well as the type of crops that could be grown to support the population and the minerals that might be exploited. Today this concept of 'physical determinism' has been superseded by the realization that social factors are also important in the location and developing character of any settlement. Geographers recognize that whilst almost any kind of settlement form is possible in a given landscape, the probability is that certain locations will be chosen in preference to others, and how they are used will depend upon the levels of skill and technology available to the people living there. In this chapter we will examine some basic concepts about rural settlements, and how they are exemplified in the British landscape.

The boundaries of English parishes represent the limits of the area which a village utilized and controlled. These areas vary in size, often as a result of local characteristics of terrain and organization. The air photographs (Plates 2.1, 2.2) illustrate the variety of parish shapes and sizes in different parts of England. An important consideration by early settlers in a new area was the choice of *site* – the actual location upon which to erect their dwellings, stockade and workshops. The size of this original location often became too small and inconvenient as population grew, but the nature of the initial site frequently continues to exert control over the present plan of the settlement.

If physical conditions provide a range of options from which to choose, we can get some idea of what sort of site would seem a suitable one to a group of colonizers if we know the following:

Plate 2.1   Austwick, North Yorkshire. A village in upland Britain. Note the small, stone-walled fields near the village for livestock grazing, the open moorland and the evidence of the effect of relief on land use. There are many individual farms, but no manor house visible. *(Aerofilms)*

(a)   what conditions are needed (in their experience) for an ideal site.

(b)   what degree of choice is open to them; how much they must compromise their ideal version of a site in the face of real constraints.

Obviously *site factors* will change in their relative importance over time. With new methods of transport, improvements in techniques of cultivation, and the simple increase in population, some sites will become obsolete and others will appear more attractive. However, we may assume that for early settlers in an area such as lowland Britain, the site requirements would be fairly simple. It has been suggested by Michael Chisholm[1] that the basic requirements of a group of Saxon settlers would be: defence, water, fuel, building materials, land for crops (arable) and livestock (grazing). The degree of importance which they attached to these would be conditioned by the frequency with which they would need to use them, and their choice amongst settlement sites, though subjective, would reflect their evaluation of these needs.

If we can start to view the landscapes through the eyes of the early settlers we may be able to determine what would constitute good choices of sites for them, bearing in mind that their knowledge of a new district would be imperfect.

14

Plate 2.2   Husbands Bosworth, Leicestershire. A lowland parish. Note the compact site, the absence of farm houses in the fields (a sign of late enclosure) and the fine church showing the former prosperity of farming in this area. Field boundaries are hedgerows, rarely designed to be stock-proof in this arable area, and in the foreground evidence of former cultivation (ridge and furrow) can be seen. The local 'great house' in its park is on the left of the picture. *(Aerial photography dept., University of Cambridge)*

2. Identifying settlement form

The use to which land around a settlement was put frequently influenced building patterns – whether all the farmsteads could be grouped together for defence and sociability, or whether individual houses were built out in the fields, giving the village a more fragmented appearance. The former types are collectively referred to as 'nucleated', indicating a grouping around a central nucleus, and the latter as 'dispersed' settlements. If we consider the whole of England and Wales, we can find a general pattern of settlements which are predominantly of one type or the other.

15

We should note, however, that a similarity of arrangement or *morphology* does not necessarily imply a similarity of origin or rationale behind this pattern on the ground.

(a) Nucleated villages

Villages of the nucleated type are of common traditional pattern, often related to the way in which land has been owned and worked. The following factors may encourage nucleation:

    (i) joint and co-operative working of land (the open field system);

  (ii) defence (hilltop location, sites within a meander);

 (iii) shortage of water (spring line);

 (iv) swampy conditions and a shortage of 'dry point' sites;

  (v) lack of suitable building materials.

For example, Anglo-Saxon settlers who allocated strips of land in 'open fields' to villagers and who farmed their lands on a rotation system tended to have a nuclear village in the midst of their land. A surviving village of this type is Laxton (Plate 2.3) which is studied in Orwin's book *The Open Fields*.[2]

Plate 2.3   Laxton, Nottinghamshire. Three great fields with the village at the centre can still be discerned although some encroachment has taken place. The houses line the street boundaries between the fields with long strips of land running away behind them. There are remains of a common at the top of the street, and of a glebe area around the church, which was originally for the priest's use. *(Aerofilms)*

(b) Dispersed settlement

When the open fields were enclosed (see page 37) it became more logical to build farmhouses out in the fields of the newly established farmsteads, and a dispersed pattern often resulted. Dispersed patterns are also associated with:
  (i) livestock farming (e.g. Scotland and N.W. Lancashire);
  (ii) agricultural specialization (e.g. market gardening in areas of very fertile soils). Such specialization and improvement of crops was not possible if land use was frequently and arbitrarily changed by a decision of all the villagers;
  (iii) very low densities of population (e.g. upland regions, and the crofting settlements in coastal areas where farming is a part-time occupation);
  (iv) dissolution of very large estates (e.g. the break-up of monastic lands at the Reformation).

The entire process may be summarized in the following way. High land, poor soils and much available water help to create dispersed settlement, while lower areas, better soils and shortage of water seem generally to be associated with nucleated settlement. This summary could be qualified, but these environmental factors seem the most important in nearly all areas.

The pattern of settlement and land use was established when land was under common ownership, but during the agricultural revolution of the eighteenth century in Britain, growing migration from rural areas to new towns reduced the numbers of people who were obtaining a living from the soil. Landowners were therefore encouraged to press for the *enclosure* of their lands so that agricultural experiments and increased productivity could be pursued. This process had been going on in earlier days but the rapid spread of 'Parliamentary Enclosures', as they were called, led to the setting up of field boundaries and the evolution of the 'English' style of farmsteads that today we regard as traditional.

The process of enclosure was so called because landlords built enclosing fences around the common grazing land in the villages, and divided up the great fields which had formerly been farmed by the inhabitants as a group. New land holdings were leased out in the form of separate farmsteads, and this often meant that new farmhouses were built at a distance from the old village.

(c) Effects on the landscape

Nucleated villages tend to have survived in arable and mixed farming areas, where land had been worked under open field systems. Equal shares of land of varying quality was ensured by the system of allocation of strips in large fields. Whilst this pattern is retained in Laxton, Nottinghamshire (Plate 2.3), the practice of communal cultivation is rare in Europe today. However, the retention of farm buildings in village streets, and a pattern of field boundaries based upon the old strip system, is still common. Isolated examples of strip holdings do persist in some remote areas where terrain is difficult, although even here the regrouping of land holdings into larger and more economic units in the interests of efficiency is likely to have taken place.

The consolidated farm provides more opportunity to plan land use rationally and independently, and reduces the number of journeys for the individual, but it is commonly the case that the farm buildings are retained in their nuclear form, unless the new farm is too far away for easy access. A compromise which allows the farmhouse to remain in the village centre, is for land holders to 'farm out' from the centre, so that each holder still retains a 'toe-hold' in the community. This is often true of areas of late enclosure when travelling distance was less of a problem. Such patterns are sometimes referred to as *evolved*, whereas those deliberately reformed at the time of field enclosure are more obviously *planned*. Often the two exist side by side, for reorganization was on a parish basis at the whim of local landowners until the later Parliamentary Enclosures.

Enclosure of land is not the only factor which disturbed the evolution of village pattern from a three-field rotation system to an owner-occupier system. When dairying became profitable, serving the needs of growing market towns as communications improved, some land was enclosed to form individual units. Another example is where landowners took a rather rough hold of the economy of farming. Consider this account of the clearance of part of the Scottish Highlands in the summer of 1807 by the notorious Patrick Sellar, to enable the Earl of Sutherland to graze sheep:

> Our family was very reluctant to leave, and stayed for some time, but the burning party came round and set fire to our house at both ends, reducing to ashes whatever remained within the walls. The people had to escape for their lives, some of them losing all their clothes except what they had on their backs . . . The people were driven away like dogs . . .[3]

Although there were cases of extreme hardship where eviction was ruthlessly carried out, in most of the rest of Britain the process of land enclosure was a slower and more orderly process. It might be resisted by some tenant farmers and the poorer villagers, but often the opportunities it provided for improved husbandry were felt to outweigh the disadvantages. The extracts below describe the parish of Oakley in Bedfordshire before and after the greater part of the land was purchased by a large landowner and subsequently enclosed. They are taken from work done by students at Bedford as part of their course on village studies.

> Like most of Bedfordshire's parishes, Oakley was an open field village before the coming of the Agricultural Revolution in the late eighteenth century. This meant that the land was divided into four great fields with farmers working scattered strips within each field.
>
> Before being enclosed in 1803 the parish of Oakley consisted of three large open fields. In addition to the open fields, 266 acres on the eve of enclosure consisted of old enclosed parcels of land, called closes, situated around the areas of settlement in the parish. Within the three fields the strips were grouped together in furlongs, each furlong containing from 30 to 70 strips.
>
> It is interesting to note that in 1737 there were 36 owners of land in Oakley but by 1799 this number had fallen to 24. This was mainly due to the activities of the Dukes of Bedford, who, after the 4th Duke purchased Oakley House in 1737, gradually extended their interests in the parish and soon came to dominate it.
>
> Holdings of owners and tenants in pre-enclosure Oakley were not consolidated into single blocks but were intermingled throughout the fields and furlongs.
>
> The attitude of the farmers towards enclosure varied, some were pleased to take on new leases, but others left their farms rather than carry out instructions as to the crops they should produce and the methods of farming they should employ, which were written into their leases. The

farm houses and buildings were kept in repair by the Duke as landlord. The husbandry was carried out by daily labour. Some annual servants were retained: the horse-keeper who was responsible for the plough team, the cowman if a large herd of cows was kept, and the kitchen maid and the shepherd. These were people with special skills – the shepherd could earn up to 15 guineas a year.

With the exception of the freeholders, all the villagers would have been dependent on the estate, in some way, for their livelihood. Most of them would have been employed as agricultural labourers with a smaller group fulfilling the roles of craftsmen and domestic servants.

According to the 1801 census, 265 people were resident in Oakley. The unemployment situation was particularly bad during the years 1812–13 and 1819–20 when the poor relief rose to its peaks.

Although nucleation and dispersal are useful geographical concepts which we can apply to the landscape features which survive from former times, in individual cases the village is explicable only in terms of its own history. The sequence of landscape settlement is of particular significance in explaining the present landscape, and it is this that we will consider in the next section.

ASSIGNMENTS

1. *Choose two O.S. maps at 1:50 000 scale, of contrasting areas of Britain, and using tracing paper map the parish boundaries and location of villages. In each of the areas studied calculate the average size of parishes and the size of the largest and smallest parishes. Parish size may be calculated by superimposing the map over squared paper on a light-table and counting the number of whole and part squares contained within the parish boundary. Secondly, calculate the ratio between the longest and shortest distances across the parish. This ratio may be expressed by the formula* $r = l/L$, *where* l *is the longest distance across the parish and* L *the shortest.*

   Add the principal streams and rivers and the major contours to your map so as to gain a general impression of the relief of the area. Geology could also be added if you have access to an O.S. Geological Survey map. Can you explain the differences in parish size and shape?

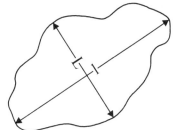

Fig. 2.1   Formula for calculating the shape of a parish.

2. *From the accompanying map, (Fig. 2.2) determine three suitable sites for settlement, having regard to the factors listed by Chisholm (see page 14). Do the sites vary in attractiveness if the importance attached to the factors is changed? Do all members of your group agree upon the locations of the sites? If you 'entered' the map area from the south-west corner which site would you encounter first? Would this have any bearing on your settlement decision?*

3. *The date is 1800. Assume that you are either a large landowner, or a small tenant farmer, and justify the case for or against enclosure of your local parish to a vilage meeting. Useful background information and ideas may be obtained from*

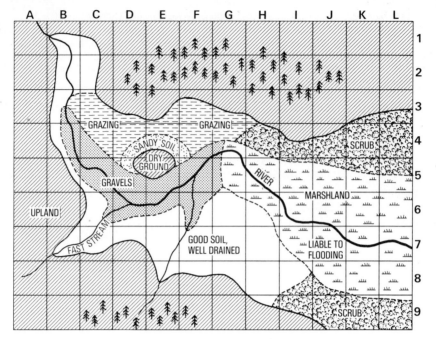

Fig. 2.2   A map showing alternative sites for settlement.

Orwin's book The Open Fields[4], *Hoskin's* Making of the English Landscape[5]
and Ashton's The Industrial Revolution 1760–1830.[6]
Questions that you may wish to ask might include:
(a) *What effect will enclosing the land have upon farm labourers?*
(b) *Will there have to be new building, or realignment of roads?*
(c) *How will the land be apportioned?*
(d) *Will the village support as many people in future?*
(e) *What effect will there be upon community life – the church, inn, local
      tradespeople?*

B. Settlement Evolution in England and Wales

Having considered the morphology of rural settlement in Britain we may now turn
to consider its distribution and how this changed over time. You will see how some
areas experienced waves of immigration which have left evidence in place names of
predominantly one language or period. The effects of farming requirements on the
character of rural settlement at different periods have just been mentioned. Let us
now try to distinguish the residual or relic features in the present rural landscape
and the systems which operated at the period of their establishment.

There is evidence of human occupation in Britain from about 4300 B.C., although
actual settlements are later in date. Table 2.1 illustrates the different physical
evidence of the three main periods of settlement before the Roman Invasion.

Table 2.1. Prehistoric chronology. (Source: P. Lively, *The Presence of the Past*, Collins, 1976.)

Time scale	Period of settlement
c. 4300–2400 B.C.	Neolithic (causewayed camps, long barrows, megalithic tombs)
c. 2400–700 B.C.	Bronze Age (round barrows, hut circles, stone circles)
c. 700 B.C.–A.D. 43	Iron Age (hill-forts, small square fields, villages, farmsteads, brochs)

1. Pre-Roman settlements

Early Bronze Age dwellings form the first examples of recognizable houses, though the earliest dates of settlement in a particular area may range from around 1500 B.C. to 500 B.C. (see Fig. 2.3). Examples of the former can be found on Dartmoor, which may imply that it was in the more exposed upland areas of Southern Britain that these communities developed. Admittedly the subsequent cultivation of lowland S.E. England may have destroyed evidence of early settlements there, but the hill forts were probably more realistically defensible (see Plate 2.4), and although cultivation in Britain dates from about 700 B.C., it is likely that only when specialist mould-board ploughs had been developed could the heavier lowland clays be tilled. Village and hamlet growth required a stable surplus of food so that settled agriculture could be possible. An early Iron Age example is Chysauster in W. Cornwall (Plate 2.5) where eight or more houses, each of several rooms around an open court, line a cobbled street. Each house appears to have possessed garden plots and the hamlet was surrounded by arable fields. This settlement dates from about 200 B.C. and appears to have been continuously occupied until Roman times. These isolated hamlets and farmsteads are mostly identified in the south-west peninsula, although as the Celts retreated westward their settlement names may have been superseded by invaders. In the west country the physical features of hills and rivers have retained the names most successfully (e.g. Axe, Esk, Usk (*isca* – water), Case (*us* – water)) although in parts of the Pennines similar words (including *Dove*– *dube* – black) also persist.

Iron Age huts were commonly located in defensive circles at relatively inaccessible sites. The Holyhead Mountain circles discovered in 1865 on Anglesey are an example of this. In areas where there was no suitable natural eminence to ensure safety, the early inhabitants followed the pattern of the terpen dwellers of the Low countries and built lake villages. There is evidence of one such village at Glastonbury, Somerset.

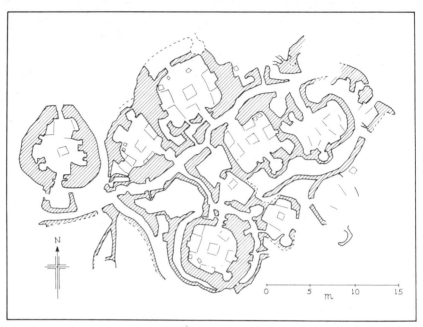

Fig. 2.3   An early Celtic site. Skara Brae, in the Orkneys, may be the oldest domestic site in Europe. Consisting of eight circular huts, of diameters between four and six metres, it was preserved by drifting sand dunes until being rediscovered in 1850. Originally believed typical of Bronze or early Iron Age settlements, it is now thought to date from 2500 BC, and may have been occupied by an elite group of priests or elders, as no evidence of farming has been uncovered. Early sites, often undefended, are particularly common in Scotland, Wales and the West Country and are generally classed as ceremonial (e.g. Stonehenge) or burial sites. The ordinary homes of the people have often perished, being constructed of timber. Some have been preserved in peat bogs in Ireland. (Source: E. Mackie, *Science and Society in Prehistoric Britain*, Paul Elek Ltd.)

Plate 2.4   Maiden Castle, Dorset. The vast extent of this fortification can be seen by the scale of the road running past and the buildings nearby. The height of the earthworks and the depth of the trenches has been greatly levelled over time but the maze-like entrances are still visible. *(Aerial photography dept., University of Cambridge)*

Plate 2.5 Chysauster, Cornwall. In the west country, remains of pre-Roman settlements, with stone walls and comprising groups of semi-circular huts, are to be found. These Iron Age hamlets were supported by the growth of vegetables and tin smelting. In lowland Britain the 'Celtic fields' of terraced cultivation in chalk areas are contemporary. Both represent the larger scale that agriculture reached when Iron replaced Bronze Age techniques of cultivation around 300 BC. *(Crown Copyright. Reproduced with permission of the Controller of HMSO.)*

2. Roman settlement (50 B.C. to A.D. 400)

During these four centuries of foreign occupation the total population of Britain rose to something approaching half a million, and a dualistic economy developed. The Romans as administrators and military lived in villas side by side with indigenous Celtic villagers. In the first phase of the settlement, the new conquerors concentrated on opening up harbours and communications in a manner emulated by all subsequent imperialists. Burke describes the process:

> During the first forty years they constructed some 6000 miles [approx. 9700 km] of highways with six routes radiating from London, which was already recognized as the country's natural gateway. Comparison of the Ordnance Survey Map of Roman Britain with a modern map reveals how closely the routes selected by Roman surveyors for main radiating highways correspond with those chosen by nineteenth-century railway engineers for main-line routes.[7]

The foci of these routeways were the Roman towns, some based upon Celtic settlements and forts, others new (see Fig. 2.4). Derived from Italian models with formal plans and walks, they existed as defensive and administrative centres and hence relied upon a subservient rural landscape for food. They established the pattern of a city-region, though their size was limited by the technology available to cultivate and transport food. Even London could aspire to a population of no more than 30 000. Though smaller than cities located by the Romans in more productive agricultural terrains, these towns still represented a vast increase in complexity, area and scale over anything previously seen in England. It has been suggested that larger settlements such as London covered some 121.4 hectares, and it is noteworthy that until late in the medieval period London had not expanded far outside its northern and eastern boundaries, although building along the Strand to the administrative centre at Westminster had transformed the western edge. Even smaller cities such as Caerwent covered about twenty hectares and must have seemed infinitely superior in technology to the indigenous population when compared to their own structures.

In the later years of the occupation, a local Romano-British upper middle class developed villas, clearing large areas of natural vegetation and building self-contained estates on new sites, especially on the chalks, oolites and gravels of south

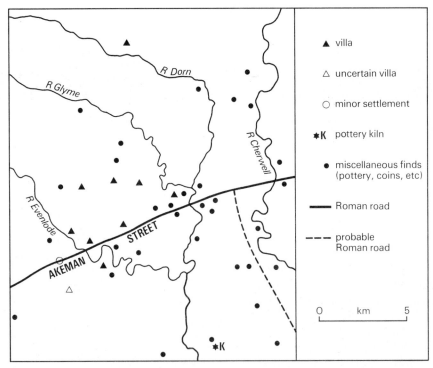

Fig. 2.4   Romano-British settlements in part of Oxfordshire. The concentration of Roman settlements along the Cotswold escarpment is clearly shown in this map. There was a great concentration of settlement where ancient sheep droving routes along the valleys met the newer Roman Akerman Street along the scarp. The importance of obtaining water in this oolitic limestone area was also a locating factor. (Source: W. G. Hoskins, *Making of the English Landscape*, Hodder and Stoughton, 1977)

east of England. As prosperity and security increased, dependence upon the *castra*-camps lessened, and over five hundred of these villas have been located. From them, agricultural districts were administered with a community of workers including the *villacus* or overseer, the *coloni* or freemen and slaves, all of whom lived in the central complex of buildings. Important villas include Chedworth (Gloucestershire), Bignor (Sussex), North Leigh (Oxfordshire) and Rochbourne (Hampshire). Many of these villas are extensive – Rochbourne has over sixty rooms – and some later became centres for industry including metal work, pottery, or cloth fulling as at Chedworth. (See Plate 2.6 and Fig. 2.5.)

Plate 2.6   Chedworth Villa. One of the large villas of the Cotswolds, with well preserved foundations and hypocausts. The house in the centre is a nineteenth-century museum and the roofs in the lower part of the picture are modern to cover excavated mosaics, but the layout is essentially as the Romans left it. Such villas housed both farm workers and their lord so extensive storage and communal facilities were needed. (*Aerial photography dept., University of Cambridge*)

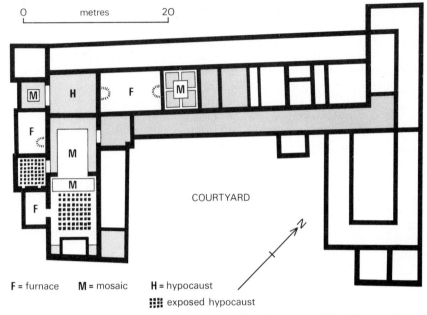

Fig. 2.5   The plan of a house at Verulamium (St Albans) c. AD 160. Many Romano-British houses and villas were built around an open courtyard, facing in a southerly direction to catch the sun, with separate quarters for family and servants. Heating for the apartments and baths was effected by a system of underground air ways (hypocausts) heated by furnaces. The floors of bath houses and public rooms were normally covered in mosaic tiles, many of which have survived. The open layout shows that defence was of little importance for the occupying aristocracy; and the whole plan prefigures later 'ranch type' complexes in Imperial estates (e.g. plantations in India, farms in S. Africa) where workers co-resided with employers in self-sufficient units.

The distribution of villas and of the villages of the indigenous population were frequently separate. The two systems appear to have existed side by side in the less densely settled areas, whereas in more populous areas such as North Oxfordshire there was much more intermingling and contact. In the remoter districts, the effects of Roman culture might have been confined to the use of the pottery and coinage of the new overlords in the old settlements of circular huts and pits surrounded by fenced fields. It is probable that the villas and their estates decayed gradually during the decline of Roman power and were difficult for the Romano-British to maintain after the Imperial withdrawal. The network of roads serving cities with agricultural produce from the estates and in turn providing highways for defence and administration also broke down and the towns were looted for building materials. Whereas the complex and large-scale fabric of urban life was difficult to sustain, village life may have been more durable. There is evidence that these sites continued as local centres in the more isolated and localized agricultural systems which persisted after the fourth century A.D. One example is that of Ashmore in Dorset, and there are others in Hertfordshire and Gloucestershire – regions of relatively dense population and intense land use, inland from the more vulnerable areas which were disrupted by Germanic raiders.

Table 2.2. Pre-Anglo-Saxon place-name endings. (Source: A. Guest, *Man and Landscape*, Heinemann, 1974.)

CELTIC (before fifth century A.D.)		ROMAN (LATIN)	
Place-name ending	*Meaning*	*Place-name ending*	*Meaning*
Avon, Esk, Eye, Dee	river	caster cester chester	fort, camp, (later a town)
hamps	a dry stream in summer	port	gate, harbour
aber	river mouth, or ford	street	paved way
bre, -drum don	hill	fos(s)	ditch
caer	fortress		
coed	wood		
pen	hill; head		
porth	harbour		
tre	hamlet		

3. Anglo-Saxon settlement (A.D. 450–1066)

The Saxon invasions of the fifth and sixth centuries were preceded by raids which penetrated the old Roman colony to test its resistance, and discovering it weak led to more prolonged settlement. 'The Britons fled from the English like fire' (*Anglo-Saxon Chronicle*, A.D. 571). Most Anglo-Saxon villages occupied new sites, often along river valleys in the southern and eastern areas of the country, ignoring the Celtic and Roman settlements (see Fig. 2.6). The newcomers cleared much more woodland with axes and the use of fire, and often this practice is recalled in the names of their new settlements, e.g.

Swithland (Leicestershire)	– 'The land cleared by burning'
Barnet, Brentwood (Essex)	– 'Burntwood'
Brindley (Cheshire)	– 'Burnt clearing'

Timber was valuable for building and for fuel and once removed, the activities of grazing animals destroyed seedlings and prevented regeneration. It is to the Saxons that we owe the characteristic *green village* of lowland Britain, although examples occur westward as far as Devon (see Plate 2.7). In the north east a similar but distinctive form is found in County Durham with two rows of dwellings facing across a rectangular or linear green with long narrow plots of intensively cultivated land behind (tofts).

Around most green villages were grouped the fields with their characteristic strips. Of these Hoskins writes:

> In its simplest form it probably consisted of two large fields – one on each side of the village, and often called the East Field and the West Field, or the North Field and the South Field. Each field covered perhaps a few score

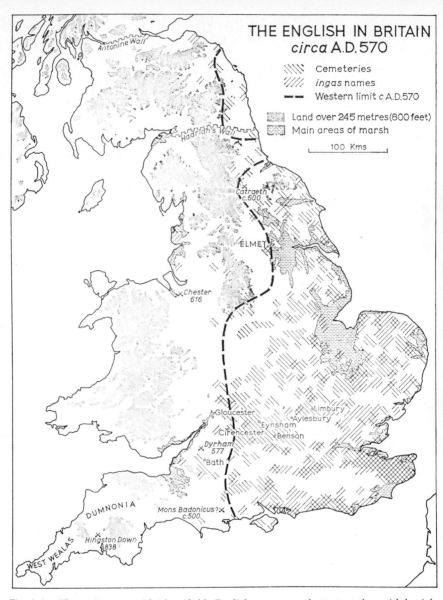

THE ENGLISH IN BRITAIN
circa A.D.570

⟍⟍⟍ Cemeteries
⟋⟋⟋ *ingas* names
— — Western limit *c* A.D.570

Land over 245 metres (800 feet)
Main areas of marsh

100 Kms

Antonine Wall

Hadrian's Wall

×*Catraeth*
c.600

ELMET

×*Chester*
616

×*Gloucester*

•*Limbury*
•*Aylesbury*
•*Eynsham*
Cirencester •*Benson*

×*Dyrham*
577

•*Bath*

DUMNONIA

Mons Badonicus?×
c.500

×*Hingston Down*
838

WEST WEALAS

Fig. 2.6   The main areas with identifiable English names are shown together with burial
sites. The gradual extension west and north into Celtic areas can be discerned, but as yet
there has been no threat from the Continent, so that eastern areas are the most popular,
being warmer and more easily farmed. (Source: H. C. Darby, *A New Historical Geography of
England*, CUP, 1973)

acres to begin with, but every decade and generation added to their area by
clearing the woodland and other wild ground around their circumference.[8]

Three- or four-field rotations were later developments. In contrast, the linear *street
villages* are somewhat later – some having been developed along busy main roads in
medieval times. Others are older, one was described in a life of St. Cuthbert in the

Plate 2.7   Finchingfield, Essex. One of the most famous 'green villages' with the buildings grouped around the green which is also the area of the pond. The pond is artificially formed in the gully of a tributary of the River Pant, and on the far side of the gully the Norman church can be seen on slightly higher ground. *(Aerofilms)*

seventh century, and several pre-date the Norman invasion. In less densely settled areas it may have been easier to expand along the line of the clearing rather than to hack out new areas in the forest behind the habitations. Both green and street villages presupposed the 'hierarchical democracy' of Saxon local government, where elders determined farming policy at village *moots* and elected leaders to represent them at Shire moots and *wittans*. The movement of people this involved helped to produce a new network of routes across the landscape. Where leaders were not found, or if individual squatting took place, fragmented (loose) villages of no discernible pattern tended to grow up, e.g. Middle Barton, Oxfordshire.

4. Scandinavian settlement

From the ninth century onwards the loose federations that formed the Saxon kingdoms were increasingly threatened by Danish raiders, and from the tenth century by the Norwegians. Penetration up river valleys was swift but eventual partition of the country led to a relatively stable distribution of English and Scandinavians

Table 2.3. Anglo-Saxon place-name endings (mid-fifth to eleventh century A.D.). (Source: A. Guest, *Man and Landscape*, Heinemann, 1974.)

Primary settlement invasion phase		Secondary settlement expansion phase		
Sequence 1	2	3	4	5
Homestead or Farmstead names		'Daughter' settlements	Wood clearance	Drainage settlements
ing	-ham -ton -tun	cot; -cote (outlying hut or cottage)	den; -dene (swine pasture)	delph; -dic (dyke or stream)
	-ingham -ington	croft (small enclosure)	hurst; -hirst (coppice on a hill)	eg; -ey; ea; -eig (island)
		field (open field)	fall (place where trees have been felled)	fen (fen)
		stead (place)	holt (wood)	lake mere
		stoke ('daughter' settlement)	leaze; -lee; lea; -ley; leah; -leigh (clearing in a forest or wood)	moss (swamp)
		stow (holy place)	riding; -rod (cleared land)	
		wike; -wick; wich; wic (outlying, inhabited place, usually a dairy or cattle farm)	weald; -wold (high woodland or wasteland)	
			wood	
			worthy (enclosed land)	

under the reigns of Alfred and Cnut in the tenth century. Most Danish place names are confined to the north east of Watling Street and the Lea Valley – roughly the line of the present A5 and A6 roads (see Fig. 2.7). Often these 'burghs' were merely forts, although in the Midlands they sometimes became the nuclei of the new administrative shires, growing to become sizeable towns. Surviving central settlements of this type include Derby, Leicester, Lincoln, Nottingham, and on a smaller scale, Stamford.[9]

It is likely, however, that although the local density of invaders might be high, as revealed by personal names in contemporary documents (totalling between 10 per cent of the population in Norfolk and 50 per cent in the northern part of the Danelaw) the total number of invaders was not great and their influence not long lasting. P. H. Sawyer believes that 'they settled where they could, most often on land left by the English or not yet occupied.'[10]

Although the Danes entered Yorkshire in A.D. 876 and the East Midlands or Mercia

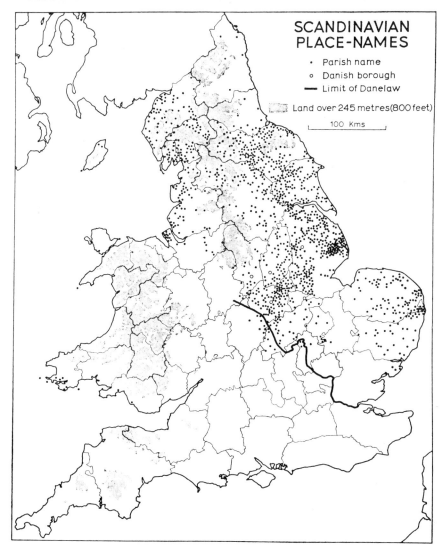

SCANDINAVIAN PLACE-NAMES

· Parish name
○ Danish borough
— Limit of Danelaw

▨ Land over 245 metres (800 feet)

100 Kms

Fig. 2.7   Scandinavian settlement pattern. Three main zones of penetration can be seen; the upper valleys of the Pennines, East Anglia and the southern and eastern parts of the Midlands. The conflict with Saxon kingdoms, especially Mercia and Wessex, was resolved by the establishment of a Danelaw boundary which ran from the Thames northwestward up the Lea Valley to the present site of Luton (Bedfordshire) and then roughly parallel with the routeway which forms the present A5 road. To the west of this border the Saxons occupied the country as far as the Offa's Dyke, which ran as a border with the Welsh along the Severn Valley and northwards towards Cheshire. (Source: see caption to Fig. 2.6)

in the next year, their hold was shortlived and they were driven out in A.D. 919, so that their settlements can be dated easily. Often the invaders took over existing villages and renamed them, so that it cannot be assumed that all settlements with place names of Danish extraction were Danish in origin. The attention of the Norwegians was limited to the north west and the Lake District, where they left evidence in the distinctive *thwaite* (meaning 'clearing') suffix of many sites. Despite

31

Table 2.4. Scandinavian (Norse, Danish and Jutish) place-name endings. (Source: A. Guest, *Man and Landscape*, Heinemann, 1974.)

Place-name ending	Meaning	Place-name ending	Meaning
beck	stream	kirk	church
booth	summer pasture or centre	laithe	barn
by	village	lund	grove
fell; -how	hill or mound	slack	stream in a valley
gate	road	tarn	lake
garth	enclosure	thorp	daughter settlement
gill	ravine or valley	toft	homestead
holm	an island in a fen	thwaite	forest clearing or meadow
wray	remote place	wath	ford
ings	marsh; meadow		

their incursion there is little evidence that the existing farming techniques or patterns were much disrupted; indeed it seems likely that those who stayed on adopted Saxon methods, which they found superior to the primitive shifting cultivation of their homeland. Later, more peaceable settlement, with English and Scandinavian living side by side, seems likely during the reigns of Alfred and Cnut. The early boroughs became prosperous because of the establishment of mints and markets. As Table 2.5 shows there were several 'moneyers', or coin makers in English cities by 1066.

Table 2.5. Moneyers in English cities, 1042–1066 (Source: J. C. Russell, *Medieval Regions and their Cities*, David & Charles, 1972.)

London	20
York	10
Lincoln	9
Winchester	9
Chester	8
Canterbury	7
Oxford	7
Thetford	6
Gloucester	6
Worcester	6

This relative peace was disrupted by the invasion of William of Normandy in 1066, followed by the establishment of a system of military government covering the whole country.

5. Norman and early medieval settlement (1066–1348)

By the time that the Normans had established sufficient control to organize the Domesday survey of 1086, it is likely that almost all the villages of the pre-industrial

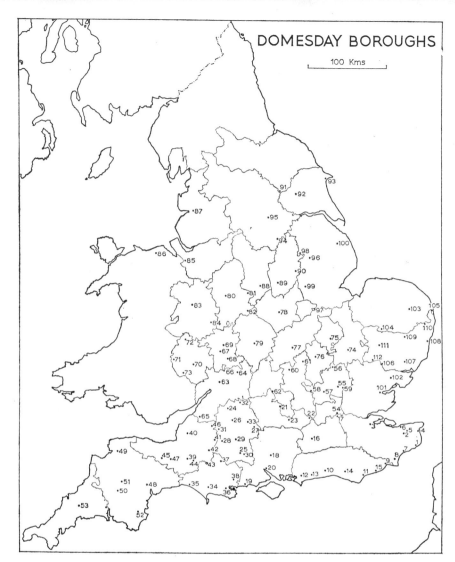

Fig. 2.8   English boroughs in 1086. Over a hundred boroughs were recorded in the Domesday book and their locations are shown on this map. Some declined because the estuaries upon which they were sited silted up (Rye) and others declined because of plague (Ashwell) or because of reduction in trade (Ewias Harold). Some, however, formed the nuclei for later expansion at the centre of medieval shires (Shrewsbury). (Source: see caption to Fig. 2.6)

period (many of which were later to disappear) had been established (see Fig. 2.8). England had a population of some 1.25 million. Settlement density varied widely, from four per square mile in the north to over eighty near Yarmouth and Norwich in East Anglia. As population grew, despite high death rates and short life expectation for the average peasant, it became necessary to cultivate more and more land and to establish more settlements. Penelope Lively has described the resultant landscape:

. . . A peasant was entitled to a 'stint' – a ration or allowance – of grazing

33

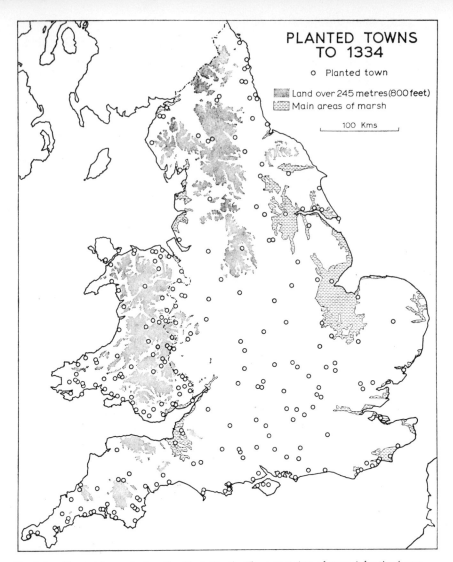

Fig. 2.9   Planted towns before the Black Death. The expansion of town 'planting' was chiefly in the more peripheral areas in an attempt to establish control over the marchlands. Often a town wall was built, and a castle to garrison troops within it. The main street of the town grew up along the route from the gate to the castle, as at Monmouth and Caernarfon. The inland planted towns were often attempts at encouraging new market centres in agricultural areas. (Source: see caption to Fig. 2.6)

rights according to his general status and the size of his land-holding, a stint being composed of so many oxen or sheep, and as time goes on we see the number of animals allowed being more sternly rationed. Obviously there was less waste available for them to graze on: pressure of population had forced the village to clear and cultivate it for growing crops. Ground cleared in this way is called an 'assart' and once again the process is reflected in the names of places.[11]

During the period before the Black Death of 1348 the population trebled and its expansion was visible in the establishment of new towns under the Angevin Kings, especially Edward I (see pages 49 to 52). These included new ports at Portsmouth (1194) and Liverpool (1207), and after Edward's Welsh conquest in 1282, the 'chequerboard' designs of Flint, Caernarfon and Abergavenny, among others. Simultaneously villages expanded as their cultivated areas grew, and were promoted to borough status (e.g. Devizes). Old established towns also prospered, especially when markets and fairs were allocated to them by the King.

The strength of the monarchy and growing prosperity of the regions might have little signficance for the peasant, but the effect on trade and building was remarkable. Between the Conquest and 1344 some 150 new boroughs were created (see Fig. 2.9); almost half of them by the impoverished King John (1199–1216). The advantage to a settlement of achieving borough status was that the burgesses had freehold of their lands and the right to hold fairs and markets and to collect tolls. For these privileges they paid the monarch, so granting a charter was a speedy way for the King to obtain some ready money. The 'planted towns', mostly located as new service centres in areas of rural expansion, numbered some 160 in England and 80 in Wales by the mid fourteenth century. Many decayed after the Black Death and the decline in population. Thus of twenty-three new towns in Lancashire only four, Lancaster, Liverpool, Preston and Wigan, achieved real size.

The rapid growth in population before 1338 meant that there were now few areas where cultivation was not attempted, especially at the expense of forest land. New villages were founded in the twelfth and thirteenth centuries (e.g. Woodhouse Eaves, Leicestershire) as more and more land was parcelled out to barons. At the same time Royal Forests and Game Preserves were created, limiting further expansion in the south and east. In Henry II's reign, almost one third of England was under Forest Law. Feudal affluence resulted in the annexation of land for parks (e.g. at Knowsley, 1299), although much unfarmed land was reclaimed as population grew. Parts of the Fens and Somerset Levels were drained and the huge sheep granges of the Cistercian monasteries began to tame the Cotswolds, Downs and Wolds. With increased forest clearance and marshland drainage the margin or profitable limit of arable land was rapidly being reached. This rising tide of population was stopped suddenly in the summer of 1348 by the introduction into Britain of bubonic plague. In the ensuing thirty years the population declined by 1.5 million people – between one third and one half of the total. The effect upon the rural landscape is shown in Fig. 2.10.

At this turning point in population and settlement growth, it is helpful to take stock and see how the pattern of landscape occupance in the British countryside had changed.

One generalization that can be made about the landscape by the medieval period is that, as in Roman times, a hierarchy of settlements and their regions had become re-established, now on a trading basis rather than a defensive one. The local village or town might be all that most people ever dreamed of visiting but there was already evidence of movement among the upper levels of society to and from the major centres, especially to the pre-eminent centre of government – London. Growing agricultural prosperity and civil peace permitted a largely rural population to exist securely and to produce the surplus necessary to maintain about 4.5 per cent of the population in towns where manufacturing and service activities were located. London was paramount in the hierarchy and this was reflected in government.

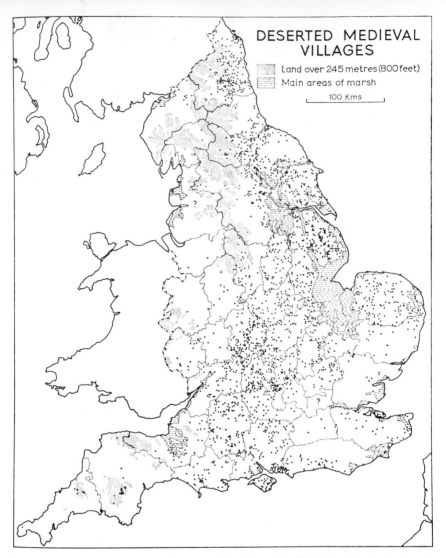

Land over 245 metres (800 feet)

Main areas of marsh

100 Kms

Fig. 2.10   Deserted medieval settlements. The effect of the Black Death in decimating the
population of villages and small towns is evident, although in some cases, even though the
site was abandoned, the survivors relocated nearby and re-established their village.
Isolated churches which continued in use after the mid fourteenth century often bear
witness to a relocated village population who could not afford to rebuild. (Source: see
caption to Fig. 2.6)

Power descended through the county towns and their barons, whilst wealth in
taxation and trade flowed upwards from the rural areas to support these urban
centres. As Russell has commented,

> . . . The region of London in the thirteenth century enjoyed singular
> prosperity which was only slightly reduced by the worsening climate and
> the relative density of population at the end of the thirteenth century. The
> region was fortunate in that period to have suffered only one civil war of
> relatively small impact and, in the last half century, border warfare along
> the northern frontier.[12]

6. Late medieval times (1348–1550)

The decimation of the population as a result of the plagues meant that the expansion of agriculture and with it of settlement ceased. The marginal lands were abandoned first, and it is reckoned that over 2000 villages became deserted, either through depopulation or relocation for health reasons. Allied to this, landlords enclosed unprofitable arable fields and turned them over to pasture, thus causing more tenants to be displaced. The effects of this abandonment were several. In some cases abandoned lands were turned over to deer parks, in others the cultivated areas shrank as the market for food declined and thus pastoralism with its smaller labour force took over. There was no incentive to revert to corn production until the late eighteenth century and by then improved technology made it possible to release even more people from the land. By 1500 there were eight million sheep in the country, but only three million people. Extensive farming seemed the only way for land owners to avoid bankruptcy and drastic enclosing of open fields took place. During this period many boroughs perished or dwindled to become 'rotten' (i.e. they continued to send MPs to Parliament, despite a greatly reduced population). Although new churches and bridges were constructed few new settlements were built, unless for particular commercial purposes (e.g. Queensborough for wartime victualling, Staithes for fishing). The impetus for expansion would next come not from the agricultural sector but from the industrial, with the post-Reformation extension of trade in the wake of Elizabethan overseas discovery.

7. The rural landscape since 1550

The development of the leather and cloth trade, especially with the Low Countries, increased demand for agricultural products. The yeoman farmer could be prosperous again, and there was a great upsurge in building in contrast to the depopulation and destruction of the previous century. As capital was required to participate in the new industries of the towns, which were in turn the source of increased income, land became concentrated in fewer hands and more enclosures took place. The English village of today, and indeed the English market town (if it has been bypassed by the railway as was Stamford [Plate 2.8]) is largely a product of this

Plate 2.8   Stamford, Lincolnshire. Sited on the north side of the River Welland, the town was an important centre of learning in the late middle ages, but it stagnated after the eighteenth century when no industry or railway came there because of restrictions imposed by the Burghley family who owned the manor. (*Author's photograph*)

period, when growing prosperity often found expression in the great 'wool churches' which were built by wealthy guilds or individuals. Again it was London which led the way in urban expansion, particularly in the late seventeenth and eighteenth centuries when the commercial success of England's colonies was providing a bonus to seaports and financial interests. This increasing prosperity eventually meant more jobs for everyone, and the power of attraction of the city grew. E. A. Wrigley points out that London increased in size by some 275 000 in the century between 1650 and 1750, despite the fact that the death rate in the city was higher than the birth rate, thus indicating substantial migration into the urban area.[13]

If the city was increasing in size despite its unhealthy conditions, migration must have constituted most of that increase. Wrigley goes on to point out that in order to sustain its growth rate, London must have been consuming half the national increase of the whole country each year. The pressure of population on resources in rural areas was alleviated by migration to London, other provincial cities and from the late eighteenth century onwards, overseas.

For a long time the Settlement Laws prohibited the free movement of labour in order to stop vagrancy and to prevent parishes from abandoning their own poor in the hope that they would go away. Here again we must bear in mind the influence of local conditions, and especially the enclosure of common lands. Darby indicates the variety of rural settlement:

> In old-enclosed country north of the Thames in Middlesex, in the Chilterns, in Essex, and in parts of East Anglia, farms were dispersed and hamlets, loosely ranged around spacious commons, at the edges of heaths or along roads, bore such names as '-end' and '-green'. . . .
>
> In many parts of England, particularly in the Midlands, new farms were arising among old villages. In distant Northumberland, where neither villages nor isolated houses had stood before, large farms were laid out with huts in rows to accommodate labourers. . . .
>
> Hamlets and isolated farms were characteristic not only of the uplands but also of formerly wooded districts in the English lowlands. Hamlets predominated in Cannock Chase, in Charnwood, in the Arden district of Warwickshire, in the Forest of Dean and in the well-wooded areas of southern and eastern England.[14]

By the mid nineteenth century, however, the obvious desire to migrate and the need of the new towns for labour had led to the repeal of the Settlement Laws with the result that new industrial towns, fed by immigrant population, were being built. The rise of the industrial town is a separate issue and will be dealt with in the next chapter. In the meantime it is worth noticing that the systems of land tenure in rural areas had, by this time, led to the establishment of very different types of village structure, which can be identified in the landscape today.

ASSIGNMENT
Settlements can best be studied in the field. The previous exercises in this chapter should have given you some ideas about the way in which villages have developed, and it will be useful to see how the pattern of settlement has evolved in your local area. Very often students' attempts at village studies produce a great mass of data which is interesting but which is difficult to sort into a meaningful pattern. It may be helpful if you try to organize your information under headings for different periods, for example:

(a)   *Blogborough at Domesday*
(b)   *Medieval Blogborough,*
(c)   *The effect of the Industrial Revolution,*
rather than under topics such as buildings and industry. In addition to an investigation of those features of the local village which have survived from the past, documentary evidence is also valuable. One useful exercise is to identify buildings which remain from different periods to see how rebuilding and expansion have taken place. The Handbook of Vernacular Architecture *is a valuable guide, and the British Council for Archaeology produce standard forms for logging industrial premises such as weavers' cottages, forges, corn mills, so that there is a permanent record of the fast disappearing features of the pre nineteenth-century landscape. (There is a list of sources of information on villages at the end of the chapter.)*

C. Village Society

So far we have attempted to classify villages and other rural settlements on the basis of their *origins*, and of their *physical form*. A third method of identifying the characteristics of particular settlements is in terms of the *social form* of the settlement. Confining ourselves to the situation during the eighteenth and early nineteenth centuries in Britain we can distinguish a variety of different groups of people occupying these villages (see Table 2.6). This we refer to as the rural class structure.

Table 2.6   Rural class structure. (Source: D. Mills, 'Has Historical Geography Changed?'; in *New Trends in Geography*, Open University Press, 1972.)

Class	Description
(a) The gentry	The landed family, members of the squirearchy or the aristocracy
(b) Upper middle class	Professional men, e.g. clergy, doctors, bailiff Gentlemen farmers Large tenant farmers
(c) Lower or rural middle class	Yeoman farmers, i.e. small owner-occupiers Tradesmen and craftsmen (masters) Smaller tenant farmers
(d) Artisan class	(a) Estate workers, e.g. carpenter, game-keeper, butler (b) Journeymen craftsmen (c) Miscellaneous such as postmen, railway workers, police
(e) Labourers	e.g. farm labourers, gardeners, housemaids

Whilst all these groups would probably have been present in a large village, the proportion of different classes and activities would have varied. Work done by an historical geographer, Dennis Mills,[15] suggests that one of the basic factors which

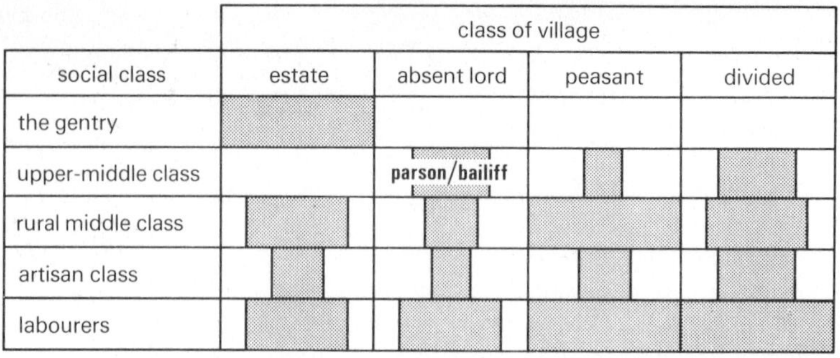

social class	class of village			
	estate	absent lord	peasant	divided
the gentry				
upper-middle class		parson/bailiff		
rural middle class				
artisan class				
labourers				

Fig. 2.11   The pattern of class groups within different types of villages. (Source: D. Mills, 'Has historical geography changed?', *New Trends in Geography*, Open University Press, 1972, D281, Block IV, Unit 14)

accounted for village social differences was the system of land ownership. He distinguishes those settlements that were dominated by a single landlord, either living in the village or operating as an absentee landlord on the one hand, and the settlements where no such control existed, on the other. The former category he refers to as 'closed villages' and the latter, which had no single important landowner, he terms 'open'. The pattern of class groups within these types of village he describes in terms of the relative numbers and proportional importance to the life of the community (Fig. 2.11). You will notice that Mills divides the open and closed village categories into those which are occupied by peasant owners of small plots, those where the residents are tenants (of one of several landlords), those where a major landlord is resident on the estate and those where one is an absentee.

1. Village classification based on land ownership

(a) Closed village
  (i) *Estate village* (resident landlord) – All aspects of village life dominated by the landowner/squire. Estate divided into a few large farms each with a tenant farmer employing a considerable force of labourers and having high socio-economic standing (see Plate 2.9).
  (ii) *Closed village with absentee landlord* – Landowner/Squire exerted a less forceful impact.

(b) Open peasant village
Characterized by fragmented land ownership and therefore a significant number of owner-occupiers each with the socio-economic standing of minor landlords. Average size of land holdings necessarily restricted and therefore little opportunity for expansion of farming activities. This encouraged commercial/industrial enterprise and many landowners developed side-lines (i.e. dual occupations commonplace). The small landowner had the advantage of being able to mortgage the property if necessary to raise capital for non-agricultural activities.

(c) Divided village
Inhabited by a number of relatively small owner-occupiers but may also have contained the seat of a minor landed family. Divided villages were unlikely to have incorporated such a wide range of shops, workshops, Non-Conformist chapels and community organizations as the larger peasant villages.

Plate 2.9   Castle Ashby, Northamptonshire. An estate village built close to, but screened from, the great house. The church is actually within the park of the castle, which dominated the village economically and socially. The farms are large and prosperous but few in number, and building has been strictly controlled. (*Aerofilms*)

2. Socio-economic relationships within villages

There would also be significant differences in the socio-economic relationships within the villages – greater security in the closed system and greater freedom in the open.

(a) Closed villages

In the closed village everyone knew his or her 'place'. The village worked as a closed economic, political and social system in which all parts were interdependent. The over-riding factor was the dependence of all the lower social strata on the resident family. Every aspect of life – economic, social, political, judicial, religious, educational – came under the scrutiny of the squire. In the open system, however, the interlocking network of economic, tenurial and social relationships was open to entry at many points and villagers could move about the network playing many different roles. A man might have dual occupations; could be both tenant and landlord; could be non-conformist and radical in his politics. He often paid for his 'privileges', however, by living in less attractive and less healthy housing.

41

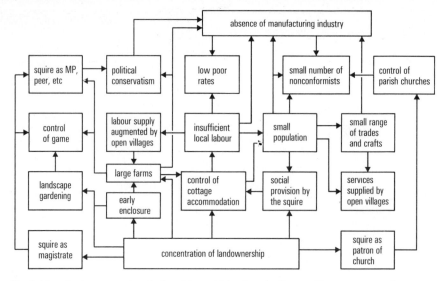

Fig. 2.12   Socio-economic relationships within closed villages. (Source: see caption to Fig. 2.11)

We may express these complex interrelationships in diagrammatic form (see Fig. 2.12). The concentration of landownership is a pervasive influence, bringing with it control of church, social services and livestock. One result is the restriction imposed upon industry by the 'squirearchy' which feeds back into the system, reducing the range of opportunities and earning power available to the residents.

Landowners used their control of cottage accommodation to restrict the size of the labouring population. In this way the tenant farmers were protected from having to pay high Poor Rates, thus making it possible for them to pay higher than average rents to the landowner. The tenants were also subject to the close social control of the squire, parson and farmer and only respectable workmen were allowed to remain in the closed community. For these reasons the population density of closed villages was relatively low. Few services developed in closed villages because of the reluctance of the large landowners to let properties to tradesmen. The class structure usually contained nothing to promote industry; the large tenant farmer was expected to employ all his capital on his farm, while the labourer had neither the time nor the money to begin serious side-lines.

(b) Open villages

In contrast we may consider the characteristics of open villages (see Fig. 2.13) where dispersal of land ownership was the key to a freedom to experiment in new techniques and enterprises.

Social control was relatively lax and the population density of the open peasant villages was often high. Some labourers who lived in open villages found employment in nearby closed villages, walking kilometres daily to their places of work.

The open villages were often more densely populated than the closed villages and therefore provided shops and related services with a bigger potential market. This attracted services to the open villages. Even so many individuals needed to be involved in two or more services in order to make a reasonable living and this is reflected in nineteenth-century directories of the open villages which indicate many dual occupations (farmer/butcher; publican/grazier; miller/baker etc.) The tendency

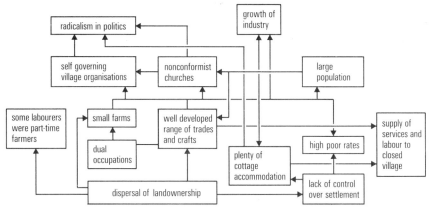

Fig. 2.13   Socio-economic relationships within open villages. (Source: see caption to Fig. 2.11)

for services to be concentrated into open villages may account for their growth in importance at the expense of the closed villages. It has been suggested that open villages are more likely to be situated along routeways of some significance and were thus more accessible and receptive to new ideas and external influences.

ASSIGNMENT
Having read of the characteristics of open and closed villages, you may wish to test whether there are examples of such settlements in your own area. From the previous exercise you will have built up a clear idea of the history of local settlements, including their pattern of land ownership. The local record office should be able to assist you in this enquiry.

In some areas there is clear visual evidence in local housing – initials stamped on plaques, almshouses, and uniform colour of paintwork are still found in some closed estate villages. Such evidence can be mapped or photographed. A list of the common characteristics for closed villages is given below.

Using this as a guide, map the distribution of housing and facilities for one or more villages in your own area, paying particular attention to property built at the same time or over a period by an individual landlord. (Reference to your County or Borough Record Office should produce maps of the village over a period of several hundred years.) Distinguish how the village has grown and which landscape features survive from earlier estates and enclosure maps, and which have disappeared. Often roads will follow stream or field boundaries and names of fields will give a clue to former usage. The age of hedges in fields may be roughly determined by counting the number of species: as a guide the hedge will be a century old for every species found in a thirty yard stretch. Using these methods you should be able to produce a map of the parish's development over time, and gain an idea of the history of its land ownership.

3. Residual characteristics of village organization

Closed estate village
Mansion with stables and other outbuildings
Estate lodges
Landscaped parkland
Model cottages built in a distinctive estate style

Many of the buildings of a similar age
Layout of village often carefully planned
Influential Anglican church
Church containing family memorials, mausoleums, tombs etc
Village school may be Voluntary Aided (i.e. Church foundation)
Evidence of the squire as a social patron – almshouses, reading room, cricket pitch, charities etc
Buildings purpose-built – little evidence of building conversion
Possibly a single public house
Few other services – perhaps one general store
No evidence of former cottage industry/crafts
Probably no Non-Conformist chapels
Arms of the manorial lord may be in evidence
Land of parish divided into a few large farms
Planned landscape, e.g. large, regular-shaped fields with uniform field boundaries
Coverts; woodland in regular stands to act as game preserve
Little twentieth-century development

Open villages
Possibly several medium sized manor farmhouses
Wide variety of building ages and styles, including modern property
Several shops, often in converted residences
Small workshops
Irregular field boundaries and sizes
Evidence of encroachment on to greens and commons
Non-Conformist chapels
Little evidence of planning, shape not clear, often much infilling
Several smallholdings..

D. Conclusion

Two related ideas may help us to explain the landscape in the light of the succession of settlers who came into Britain and either displaced earlier inhabitants or were assimilated by them. The first is the concept of *sequent occupance* – that gradually old centres were invaded by new inhabitants who added their own character. The second is that the landscape may be regarded as a *palimpsest*, that is composed of successive layers of new features superimposed upon the survivals of preceding generations. Deciphering the different levels is always complex and their persistence renders theoretical explanations of urban landscapes difficult. Only by archaeological survey is it possible to reveal all the levels of an area's development. The student must bear in mind the existence and persistence of earlier settlement features and land use decisions, as he or she seeks to explain a particular stage in the sequence of settlement.

Key Ideas

A. Geographical concepts of settlement location and morphology
1.   Relations between the physical and human environments at particular periods

(e.g. availability of raw materials, grazing land, the level of technology) can be exemplified by the choice and development of settlement sites.

2. Too precise a construction should not be placed upon individual place-name elements. Linguistic differences and the substitution of later names often complicate the picture of settlement thus gained.

3. Settlement nucleation or dispersal are often functions of the scale at which the settlement pattern is perceived, but certain general principles do govern their relative distribution of types.

4. Nucleated settlements are commonly associated with late enclosure of common land, a shortage of suitable sites and a need for defence.

5. Dispersed settlements are associated with early enclosure, agricultural specialization and the break-up of large estates.

6. Enclosure is an important factor in landscape evolution, having social as well as economic consequences.

B. *Settlement evolution in England and Wales*

1. Each sequential wave of settlers has left behind landscape evidence which provides a cumulative picture (or palimpsest) of settlement history.

2. Celtic settlements are characterized by isolated clusters of housing, often remote and on easily defended sites, now abandoned chiefly in northern and western Britain.

3. Roman remains are widespread, especially over southern England, where major villa colonies were established, many of which are preserved.

4. True Saxon settlement is largely located in south central England, many sites persisting as the nuclei of present day villages, of distinct circular or linear shape.

5. In the east and north east, place-name evidence acts as a good guide to the settlement location of invading Scandinavian settlers who occupied the Danelaw in the period up to the Norman Conquest.

6. In the early medieval period the market town grew to pre-eminence in Britain. Planted new towns acted as focal points for expansion as population grew.

7. After the Black Death, large numbers of settlements were abandoned, and can now be identified only by air photography or archaeological evidence.

8. Agricultural improvement and drainage led to the enclosure of large areas of common lands, especially in areas where monastic lands were broken up. This gave rise to a field pattern still extant today, with dispersed hamlets and farmsteads.

C. *Village society*

1. The arrangement of property and variety of functions within villages was largely controlled by landlords until the nineteenth century.

2. It is possible to construct models of traditional open and closed villages and to use these to test the experience of real settlements.

3. The web of social relationships within the village can also be measured by the use of models.

D. Conclusion

1. Sequent occupance implies that each successive wave of new settlers invaded old centres and added its own character.
2. Alternatively the landscape may be regarded as a palimpsest composed of successive layers of new features superimposed upon the survivals of preceding generations.

Appendix: Village Studies: Sources of Information

1. Topographical maps

The first and subsequent editions of Ordnance Survey maps at a scale of 1:2500 (approximately 25 inches to 1 mile) provide an excellent starting point for any detailed village study. The first edition will have been published between the 1850s and 1890. It is possible to use the sequence of editions to monitor changes in the morphology of the village which have occurred during the past century.

The first and subsequent editions of O.S. maps of a scale of 1:10560 (6 inches to 1 mile) which start in 1840, provide accurate information about changes which may have occurred in the field pattern of a parish.

Earlier topographical maps were usually drawn at smaller scales and therefore do not provide much detail about individual parishes or villages. First edition 1:63360 maps of the Ordnance Survey were published between 1801 and 1873.

2. Estate maps

The earliest estate maps date from the last quarter of the sixteenth century. They provide details about field patterns and other topographical information. Some counties are much richer in these records than others. It is clear that where large landowners existed, the chances of finding early maps are greatly increased. The estate maps may have been deposited in the local County Record Office or they may still be held by the large landowners themselves, e.g. Oxford and Cambridge Colleges.

3. Enclosure awards and maps

The enclosure of the common agricultural land was often a slow and gradual process beginning in medieval times. The enclosure awards and maps record only the late eighteenth- and early nineteenth-century Parliamentary Enclosure, which completed the pattern of the enclosed countryside. Enclosure was effected by a local committee of prominent men, authorized by Act of Parliament, who employed surveyors to divide and re-allocate the commons and heath-land remaining in the parish and, where these still survived, the open arable fields of the medieval three-field system. Parishes which had been more gradually enclosed have no awards.

The awards provide information about field names and boundaries, land-use, extent of glebe (i.e. Church) lands, roads and foot paths, and details of the farm units of individual families.

4. Tithe maps and awards

These generally date from the late 1830s or early 1840s, following the Tithe Commutation Acts from 1836. These Acts substituted a money rent, based on average corn prices for the past seven years, to be paid by landowners in commutation of tithes (From A.D. 787 compulsory tithes, one-tenth of all produce, had been exacted from the laity by the Church).

The large-scale maps show the fields of the parish, numbered for easy reference to a companion Schedule and Index. The Index is usually ruled in columns which specify for each numbered field its owners, occupier, field-name and description (whether arable, meadow, wood, pasture or premises), its date of cultivation and its acreage. A preliminary Schedule gives the area of the parish and the total subject to tithes, divided into total areas of arable, meadow, wood, pasture or premises.

Not all parishes have tithe maps and awards. Those parishes which were enclosed by Parliamentary Act took the opportunity of extinguishing their tithes at the same time, and so no tithe award was called for after 1836. Thus many parishes will have *either* a tithe map and award *or* an enclosure award. The availability of tithe maps and awards varies regionally. The coverage in Cornwall and Devon is nearly 100 per cent while in Northamptonshire only 23 per cent of all parishes have a tithe map and award.

5. Parish registers

These record the births, marriages and deaths which have occurred in the parish. In some parishes there are continuous registers dating back for centuries. These can be analysed to trace demographic change. Some parish registers also give details of the occupations of those listed. An analysis of the occupations of those who died in the parish will provide some idea of the changing nature of the employment structure of a village community.

6. Census schedules

These are the Census Enumerator's books in which he compiled detailed information about each household in his district. They are released only after 100 years have elapsed so that, to date, census schedules are available for 1841, 1851, 1861 and 1871. They provide a wealth of information and, for each household, give details of the head of household, the members of the family, servants and any lodgers or visitors who were resident in the house on census night. Details relating to age, sex, occupation and birth-place are given for each person recorded. Census schedules may be used to summarize the employment structure of a village and to trace patterns of population movement. They are stored on micro-film and may be referred to in a County Record Office.

7. Commercial directories

The county directories, which may date back to the eighteenth century, provide useful contemporary descriptions of settlements and often give details about the population, local fairs and markets, industries, buildings of historic interest, transport services and so on.

8. Useful secondary sources

(a) Local histories. They should be used with caution as, in many instances, the local historian was more concerned with describing a few public buildings of historical interest and with the family trees of the landed gentry than describing the living conditions and occupations of ordinary people.

(b) Victoria County History. This provides a reliable source of information and should certainly be referred to.

(c) Contemporary descriptions by travellers who visited the settlement in the past. For example, Daniel Defoe's *Tour through England and Wales* (1720) contains many references to the settlements of the time.

(d) The appropriate county volume in *The Buildings of England* series edited by Nikolaus Pevsner.

9. Parish land use

Agricultural statistics at parish level may be obtained from:
Ministry of Agriculture, Fisheries & Food,
Government Buildings,
Epsom Road,
Guildford, Surrey. GU1 2LD
Statistics relating to years from 1866 to 1963 are held at the Public Record Office, Chancery Lane, London WC2A 1LB.

Reading

A.   EVERSON, J. A. and FITZGERALD, B.P., *Settlement Patterns*, Longman, 1969, Chapters 1, 2, 3 and 4.

B.   HOSKINS, W. G., *The Making of the English Landscape*, Hodder, 1977.
HOSKINS, W. G., *Fieldwork in Local History*, Faber, 1967.
Also your regional volume in the *Making of the English Landscape* series, edited by Hoskins and now available for many English counties.
EKWALL, E., *Concise Oxford Dictionary of English Place Names*, Oxford University Press, 1977.

C.   MILLS, D., 'Has historical geography changed?', *New Trends in Geography: Political, Historical and Regional Geography*, Open University Press, 1972, D281, Block IV, Unit 14, pp. 56–75.

3 Urban growth

A. Pre-Industrial Towns
1. Medieval towns

The Norman Conquest brought stability and a strong, centralized government to Britain and these facilitated the establishment of a new social and economic order (see pages 32 to 36). Trade expanded and a greater emphasis was placed on the specialization of labour. The growth of towns was a key factor in the fundamental changes which occurred. Many of the towns which flourished during the middle ages grew organically from an already established base, gradually and naturally as the need arose. These towns developed within walls which could be extended relatively easily to contain additional growth. The layout was amorphous and unplanned and the buildings were linked and separated by a network of narrow, winding streets. Behind many of the town houses were long, narrow plots which were intensively cultivated so that, although the streets were often narrow and the houses packed closely together, much open space was included within the town walls. Population densities were, consequently, seldom high.[1]

Bruges, in Belgium, provides a good example of the organic growth of a medieval town, as the contemporary map illustrates (see Fig. 3.1). The growth of Bruges was closely associated with the development of the weaving industry in Flanders in the twelfth century. The town prospered after a freak tidal wave created a substantial harbour in what previously had been a narrow, silted channel connecting Bruges to the sea.[2] Even today the medieval core of Bruges remains largely intact although the network of canals which was formerly used for commerce is now neglected and used only by pleasure boats.

Not all medieval towns, however, grew from an already well established base. Some were planned or planted and built to a development plan in virtually a single operation. Such towns, known collectively as 'bastides' from the French *bâtir*, to build, were established by the monarch in newly conquered territories. For example, King Edward I established a number of new towns in Wales in the late thirteenth century after he conquered the country. Conwy provides a particularly fine example of such a town (see Plate 3.1). It was founded in 1284 to act as the regional focus for the Conwy Valley and the North Wales coast from Bangor to the south of the Clwyd.[3] The town was dominated by the castle from which extended the walls laid out in triangular form. The town walls were penetrated by only three gates. The new town site had previously been occupied by the Cistercian abbey of Aberconwy and, although Edward I had caused the abbey to be moved to a new site

Plate 3.1 Conwy, North Wales, is a fine example of a planned medieval town. The town is still dominated by the castle from which extend the walls laid out in triangular form. One of the three gates which penetrated the walls, Porth Ulchaf, can be seen in the bottom right-hand corner of the photograph. The abbey church of St. Mary still stands at the centre of the town and the medieval street pattern has been largely preserved. (*Aerofilms*)

higher up the valley, its church remained to serve the new borough. The medieval street pattern was arranged within the town walls and around the former abbey church. A sizeable market square was laid out and the remainder of the twenty-one acres divided into rectangular burgages.

During the middle ages scores of new towns were founded in Britain but not all of these prospered. For example, on the southern side of Poole Bay, Dorset, directly opposite the port of Poole, a site was chosen for the new town of Nova Villa.[4] A charter was granted by King Edward I in 1286, two town planners were appointed and the town was marked out on the ground. The new town failed to develop, however, and it has left no mark on the landscape. Other planted medieval towns

◀ Fig. 3.1   A part of the unplanned medieval town of Bruges from Marcus Gerard's map of 1562. A section of the town walls is shown in the top right-hand corner of the photograph. Note the network of narrow, winding lanes which separated the irregularly shaped plots, many of which were intensively developed with closely packed houses. The network of canals and many of the fine medieval buildings have been preserved and form important features in contemporary Bruges. (Source: part of Marcus Gerard's 1562 plan of Bruges)

grew and flourished for a time but then stagnated. Such was the case with Longtown in Herefordshire. A very small population was recorded in Domesday Book of 1086, but by the thirteenth century a border castle had been established and a simple network of streets laid out just outside the earthworks of the castle.[5] By 1310, one hundred burgages were recorded in Longtown but since then the borough has declined and a network of overgrown lanes and a few buildings are all that survive (see Plate 3.2).

Plate 3.2   Former High Street, Longtown, Herefordshire, now overgrown and neglected. A network of lanes still diverge from this 'street' which formerly was fronted by the Parish Church and a number of inns. *(Author's photograph)*

2. Renaissance towns

The Renaissance brought realization of the intellectual limitations of the medieval world with the rebirth of a spirit of enquiry and a resurgence of individual creativity. This new mood affected architecture and town planning. The theory and form of Classical architecture were rediscovered (initially by Italians) in the latter part of the fifteenth century, and architects strove to impose order and symmetry on town planning and development. Neo-Classical buildings had to be placed in an ordered context and town extensions incorporated formal squares linked by broad tree-lined boulevards. Thus there developed a close relationship between landscape planning and town planning. Grandiose, geometric plans for entire towns were devised such as that of Palma Nuova in Italy which was started in 1593 (see Fig. 3.2). Existing towns and cities were improved and adapted, sometimes, as with Rome in the fifteenth, sixteenth and seventeenth centuries, comprehensively and to spectacular effect. It is little wonder that the Renaissance has been described as the golden age of town planning and development.

The Renaissance in architecture and town planning was slow to be adopted in Britain, where many towns, such as London, retained an essentially medieval appearance and layout right up to the early seventeenth century. Even during the

Fig. 3.2   A simplified plan of Palma Nuova; founded in 1593. (Source: redrawn from an engraving in Braun and Hogenberg, *Civitates orbis terrarum* (1599))

seventeenth and eighteenth centuries few new towns were established in Britain and few large scale extensions made to existing towns. Most of the neo-Classical developments in British towns were small, piecemeal additions or arose from the redevelopment of slums and obsolete districts. There were exceptions, however, particularly where fire destroyed an existing city or town and a comprehensive programme of rebuilding had to be undertaken. Blandford Forum, in Dorset, provides such an example. It was virtually completely destroyed by fire in 1731 and rebuilt to a plan. The City of London is another, more obvious, example. The Great Fire of 1666 devastated the City; 13 200 dwellings, 89 churches and 400 streets were destroyed. Such a scale of destruction meant that a unique opportunity was presented for the remodelling of the City. Although Christopher Wren's plan for rebuilding the City (see Fig. 3.3) was rejected, specific requirements were stipulated which went some way towards controlling the nature of the redevelopment. Building materials were regulated and the opportunity taken to widen and straighten many of the narrow, medieval streets. Even an element of functional zoning was introduced (see page 84) as efforts were made to concentrate obnoxious, smoke-creating industries and to prohibit them from other parts of the City.[6]

Bath provides the pinnacle of the achievements in neo-Classical architecture and town planning in Britain. It was transformed from a small, medieval walled town into an elegant and prosperous spa. John Wood was the surveyor, architect and builder who master-minded the development although he was aided by his son and numerous successors including Robert Adam, Thomas Baldwin and John Palmer.

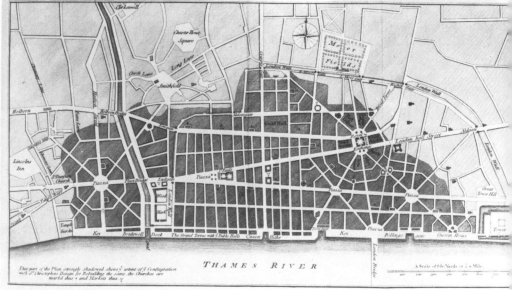

Fig. 3.3   Wren's plan for rebuilding the City of London, after the Great Fire of 1666. (*The Greater London History Library*)

Plate 3.3   Lansdown Crescent, Bath, an architectural masterpiece designed by John Palmer and built between 1789 and 1793. (*Author's photograph*)

Together they created a unique townscape of elegant neo-Classical facades; avenues, crescents (see Plate 3.3) and squares; lawns, trees and greenery; and impressive public buildings including the Pump Rooms, Assembly Rooms, theatres and churches.

Many of the ideas adopted by John Palmer and his associates in Bath were later incorporated into other ambitious schemes for town improvement such as the spa towns of Cheltenham, Buxton and Leamington and the development of Edinburgh's 'New Town' from James Craig's plan, accepted by the City Council in 1767.

Unfortunately, urban development in Britain in the seventeenth and eighteenth centuries was not always aesthetically pleasing. Such developments were the preserve of the privileged rich who increasingly isolated themselves from the urban poor. Working-class housing was often very poor, particularly where the unenclosed town fields prevented an extension of the built-up area. In parts of the English Midlands, in particular, the Lammas pasture rights, whereby burgesses had the right to graze their cattle and sheep over the open fields after the crops had been harvested, presented a disincentive to the enclosure of the open fields. In Nottingham,[7] for example, the burgesses were particularly opposed to the reallocation of the strips of the surrounding town fields into large compact blocks of land. The

Fig. 3.4   An eighteenth-century close in Nottingham. (*Nottinghamshire Local Studies Library*)

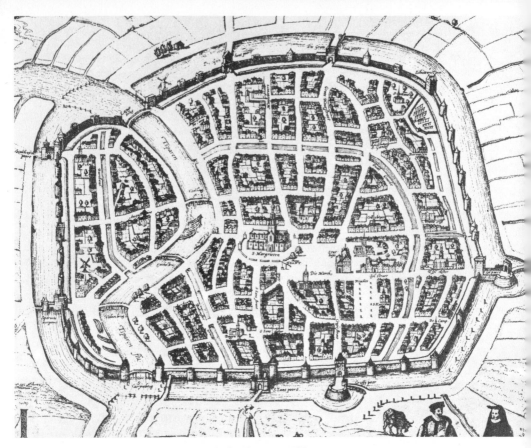

Fig. 3.5   Plan of Haarlem, Netherlands, circa 1585.

enclosure of the open fields and the attendant changes in land tenure were, however, prerequisites for the extension of the built-up area of the town. While the open fields survived, the town could not expand outwards. Instead, any increase in population had to be contained within the existing built-up area. As a result, within the space of three generations Nottingham degenerated from one of the finest towns in Britain to a town which contained some of the country's most squalid slums (see Fig 3.4). Every bit of available open space was developed and densities were excessively high. Only after the open fields were enclosed in 1845 could Nottingham expand once more but by then it was largely too late; housing and public health conditions were among the worst in the country. Not infrequently, the slums and squalid housing conditions which became such a feature of urban growth in the nineteenth century had their origins in the eighteenth century.

Nevertheless, for the most part, the pre-industrial city remained relatively small and compact. The built-up area was confined and links with the surrounding countryside persisted. Although there were great variations in the quality of housing, there was little social segregation and families of different classes often lived close together.

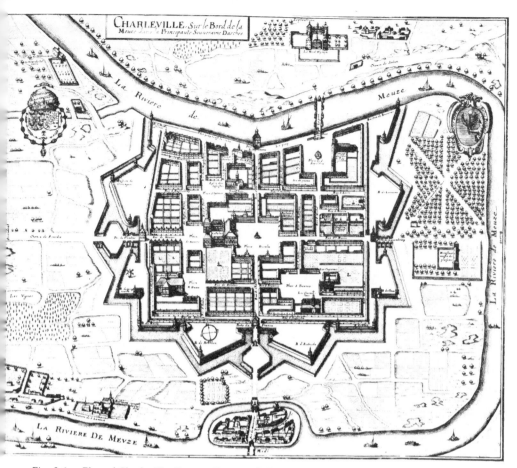

Fig. 3.6   Plan of Charleville, France. (Source: G. Burke, *Towns in the Making*, Edward Arnold, 1975)

ASSIGNMENT

Examine the plans of Haarlem (Netherlands) and Charleville (France) (see Figs. 3.5 and 3.6). Each represents a good example of one of the following: adapted or organic medieval; planned or planted medieval; Renaissance. Decide which category best fits each map. Compare the street layout and morphology and justify your choice.

B. The Consequences of Rapid Nineteenth-Century Urban Growth

Although pre-nineteenth-century urban growth in Britain was significant, by the onset of the nineteenth century most of the population were still rural dwellers. In 1801 the population of England and Wales was less than nine million and of these approximately 17 per cent lived in the fifteen towns of over 20 000 inhabitants (see Fig. 3.7). Only London, with 865 000, had a population in excess of 100 000. During the nineteenth century, however, urban growth was extremely rapid, particularly in the period from about 1840 to 1880. By 1891 the population had grown to over 29 million and nearly half lived in the 185 towns with populations in excess of 20 000. London's population had increased to a staggering 6.5 million, while the popula-

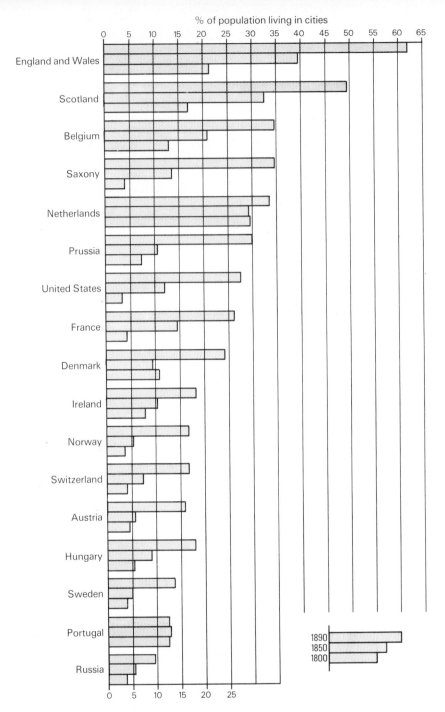

Fig. 3.7   The proportion of urban dwellers in selected countries living in towns of at least 20 000 in 1800, 1850 and 1890, or nearest census years. (Source: A. F. Weber, *The Growth of Cities in the Nineteenth Century*, Cornell Univ. Press, 1899, reprinted 1963, p.151)

tions of such industrial giants as Birmingham and Manchester increased ten-fold during the nineteenth century to 760 000 and 645 000 respectively by 1901. The growth rates in some northern industrial towns were even more dramatic. For example, Middlesbrough, a hamlet of only forty inhabitants in 1829, had a population in excess of 100 000 by the turn of the century.

Such rapid urbanization was the result of a combination of natural increase – high death rates were exceeded by even higher birth rates – and rural-urban migration. Migration was encouraged by both 'push' and 'pull' factors. Changes in land tenure and agricultural improvements, including the development of farm machinery, helped to create a landless peasantry which, in turn, was attracted by the job prospects in the rapidly developing industries in the towns.

1. Planned growth

Birkenhead, situated on the Wirral peninsula on the south bank of the Mersey Estuary, provides a further good example of a town which grew rapidly from a very small base during the middle decades of the nineteenth century. In 1821 the township was a relatively remote hamlet of about 200 inhabitants and 60 dwellings (see Fig. 3.8). About this time, however, a regular and reliable steam-powered ferry service was established which linked the settlement with Liverpool, and William Laird established a ship-building and repair industry in the adjoining Wallasey

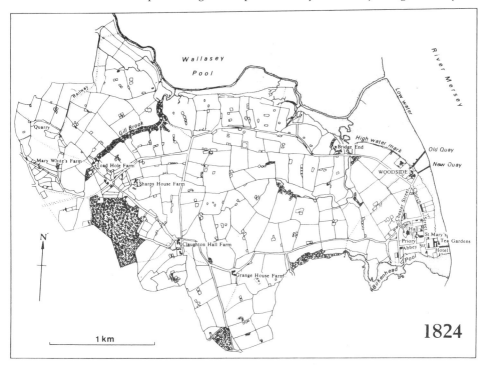

Fig. 3.8   Birkenhead, 1824. (Source: J. A. Patmore & A. G. Hodgkiss, *Merseyside in Maps*, Longman, 1970)

59

Pool. These events provided the impetus for urban growth and this was facilitated when William Laird purchased a considerable acreage of land in the centre of the township in 1824 and commissioned Gillespie Graham of Edinburgh fame to plan a new town. The streets were laid out in a grid pattern extending outwards from the elegant Hamilton Square. At first progress was relatively slow and the settlement grew to 2569 in 1831. The 1830s and 1840s, however, were two decades of particularly rapid urban growth (see Fig. 3.9) and by 1851 the population exceeded 24 000.

Chambers' *Edinburgh Journal* of 17 May 1845 provides a graphic contemporary description of the building of Victorian Birkenhead.

> When we had passed a mere frontier of streets overlooking the river we were at once launched into a mile's breadth of street building where unfinished houses, unmade roadways, brickfields, scaffolding, heaps of mortar, loaded wains and troops of busy workmen meet the eye in every direction. . . . Land which a few years ago hardly possessed a value is now selling £6 a square yard, and by good speculation in that line, large fortunes have been acquired.

Birkenhead continued to grow rapidly and absorb neighbouring townships as it

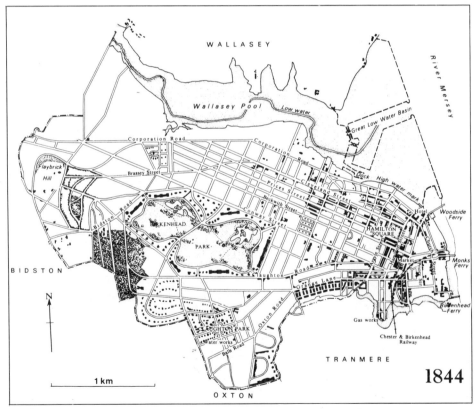

Fig. 3.9   Birkenhead, 1844. Note the planned layout designed by Gillespie Graham. (Source: see caption for Fig. 3.8)

sprawled outwards from its planned nucleus, but the grand design of Gillespie Graham was never realized, as Sulley's description of 1888 makes clear.

> Birkenhead possesses fine and broad streets, some of which merit the epithet of noble, and are unsurpassed in the United Kingdom; but the effect of these is marred and ruined by the paltry character of the greater part of the buildings which line them, by the undue proportion of cottage property, and by the unsightly gaps and vacant spaces which occur in nearly every thoroughfare throughout the town. Laid out on a magnificent plan, on an extensive scale, the place has not grown to the anticipated extent.[8]

2. Unplanned growth

The rapid rate of urbanization in England and Wales during the nineteenth century meant that approximately 200 000 people had to be rehoused each year.[9] There was no municipal housing, at least until the latter part of the century, and this considerable additional housing stock had to be provided almost exclusively by speculative builders. Housing conditions, particularly for the unskilled worker, were all too frequently appallingly bad. Housing densities were high and overcrowding commonplace. In the worst housing districts of many of the industrial towns such as London, Leeds, Nottingham and Liverpool, houses were built back-to-back and arranged around enclosed, unpaved courts. The only entrances to many of these courts were by narrow tunnels which penetrated the rows of terraced houses which lined the streets (look back at Fig. 3.4).

There was no sewerage provision and at the end of the courts were open earth middens. Refuse was not collected and no piped water was available. The houses themselves were extremely simple and provided only the most rudimentary accommodation. In Liverpool a common regional house type was a dwelling three storeys high, each floor consisting of a single room approximately twelve feet square, and a cellar. It was not uncommon for families to occupy single rooms or even the cellars which were pervaded by damp, polluted air.

It is hardly surprising that in these conditions diseases such as typhoid fever and tuberculosis were rife and frequent epidemics took a heavy toll. For example the cholera epidemic in London in 1849 was responsible for 14 000 deaths.[10] Life expectancy was extremely low and infant mortality rates tragically high. In Liverpool during the period 1839 to 1844 the average age at death was only seventeen years and more than half the children born failed to reach five years of age.[11]

In his novel *A Child of the Jago*, Arthur Morrison vividly describes the notorious Jago district of court houses in Shoreditch in the East End of London. Although the novel was first published in 1897, it could equally well refer to the poorest housing conditions that existed earlier in the nineteenth century.

> It was past the mid of a summer night in the Old Jago. . . . Below, the hot, heavy air lay, a rank oppression on the contorted forms of those who made for sleep on the pavement: and in it, and through it all, there rose from the foul earth and the grimed walls a close, mingled stink – the odour of the Jago. . . .
> . . . A square of two hundred and fifty yards or less – that was all there was of the Jago. But in that square the human population swarmed in

thousands. . . . On the pavement some writhed wearily, longing for sleep; others, despairing of it, sat and lolled, and a few talked. They were not there for lack of shelter, but because in this weather repose was less unlikely in the street than within doors; and the lodgings of the few who nevertheless abode at home were marked here and there by the lights visible from the windows. For in this place none ever slept without a light, because of three kinds of vermin that light in some sort keeps at bay. . . .[12]

3. Municipal involvement

It was only after a close correlation had been demonstrated between sub-standard housing, polluted water supply and the spread of disease that legislation was enacted in an attempt to improve working-class housing conditions. Liverpool, which had the unenviable reputation of being the unhealthiest town in Britain, pioneered the way with its 1842 Act to Improve the Health of the Inhabitants of Liverpool.[13] This stipulated a minimum width for streets and courts and minimum dimensions for house buildings. Under the Act courts had to be open at one end, their surfaces flagged and kept clean and privies had to be provided and maintained. Cellars in court houses were no longer to be used as separate dwellings. The 1844 Public Health Act, championed by Edwin Chadwick, aimed to secure the provision of adequate water supply, drainage and sewerage to combat waterborne diseases although, in the event, the Act proved largely ineffective because the local authorities were not obliged to adopt it. There followed a spate of health and

Plate 3.4   High density nineteenth-century terraced housing in Preston constructed on a grid-iron plan. Note how the houses are interspersed with industry thereby minimizing journeys to work. (*Aerofilms*)

housing legislation in the latter half of the nineteenth century which aimed at the provision of improved sanitary conditions, established minimum standards for house building and empowered local authorities to make by-laws governing town growth. The local authorities responded by making it illegal to build courts and back-to-back houses (in Liverpool under a by-law of 1864), and rows of improved terraces, *by-law housing*, became the universal house type for working-class families throughout England and Wales. These were usually arranged in a grid pattern of streets as this was the most convenient way of subdividing land for sale prior to building (see Plate 3.4).

The introduction of building restrictions and minimum standards, however, had unfortunate consequences for many of the poorest families. For, as building specifications improved and building costs rose, so rents also increased. The poorest families thus found themselves evicted from their condemned cellar dwellings or the victims of slum clearance programmes, but unable to afford the higher rents of the newly built and improved by-law housing. In addition much of the working-class housing was financed by small-scale speculators, often drawn from the ranks of the skilled artisans and the lower middle classes. The term 'the shopocracy' has been coined to describe them. For example, in Liverpool in the 1840s the average holding of working-class property exceeded eight houses per landlord in only three wards.[14] Such small-scale speculators were frequently unable to afford the much greater outlay necessary to meet the increased building specifications and investment in working-class housing became a less attractive proposition. Thus the improvement Acts interfered with market forces but at the same time provided no alternative form of housing for the least advantaged families. It was against such a background that certain local authorities somewhat reluctantly became involved in direct provision of housing.

The way in which local authorities almost stumbled into municipal housing involvement is well illustrated by the case of Liverpool, where the first council house dwellings in Britain were built in 1867.[15] By the 1860s the City Council was beginning to realize that without some positive measures to ensure provision of new and improved housing, other parts of its housing policy, such as the demolition of the courts and the eviction of families from cellar dwellings, were not likely to be successful. A sub-committee was thus set up to look into the provision of working-class dwellings. The committee suggested that a plot of land should be leased out of the Corporation Estate for the development of labourers' dwellings approved by the health committee. Members of the council subsequently advertised for a developer but received no offer and decided to go ahead themselves. As a result St. Martin's Cottages, which still stand beside the Vauxhall Road in Liverpool, were completed in 1869 (see Plate 3.5). The development, which comprised 124 dwellings was, by contemporary standards, built to a high specification, so much so that they eventually came to be occupied by persons of a higher income level than those for whom they were intended. St. Martin's Cottages were built essentially as an example to private developers and were not intended as the first instalment of a municipal building programme. In fact no further council dwellings were erected in Liverpool until 1885 and it was only from about 1895 onwards that municipal housing started to play a significant role in the rehousing of Liverpool's most disadvantaged families. This was in part a result of the Housing of the Working Classes Act of 1890 which extended the Corporation's powers to provide housing. Between 1895 and

Plate 3.5   St. Martin's Cottages, Liverpool. Completed in 1869, these were the first council houses to be built in England. *(Author's photograph)*

1914, 2392 corporation dwellings were built in Liverpool without any government subsidy.[16] Moreover they were mostly occupied by the families for whom they were intended, that is the most disadvantaged. This meant that the Corporation could not charge economic rents. In fact the rents charged were hardly sufficient to cover maintenance charges and the Corporation had a substantial housing deficit annually. Thus by 1914 the Corporation had accepted the principle of a housing subsidy, that is charging uneconomic rents to house some of the poorest families in the city. Nevertheless, by 1914 only 1.31 per cent of Liverpool's total population rented their houses from the local authority and, although this was a higher proportion than any other city in Britain (Swansea was second with 0.93 per cent), it was not until the housing legislation of the inter-war period had been passed that a nation-wide boom in local authority house building took place.[17]

ASSIGNMENTS

1.   *Look carefully at Figs 3.8 and 3.9 and describe the changes that occurred in Birkenhead between 1824 and 1844. Describe the form of the new and rapidly growing town and consider how the town plan was influenced by natural features such as lines of drainage, the coast and tidal creeks.*

2.   *Fig. 3.10 is an O.S. 1:2500 plan extract of a part of the 1908 edition of Scotland Ward, Liverpool. A section of the Leeds-Liverpool Canal, with its associated industry, is shown on the western edge of the map which is also close to the Liverpool dock system.*

   (a) With the aid of sketches, describe the layout of housing shown on the map.

   (b) Work out the housing density for 1 hectare for the southern part of the map.

   (c) St. Martin's Cottages are situated at the junction of Vauxhall Road and Silvester Street. Describe the relative advantages of their site and neighbourhood.

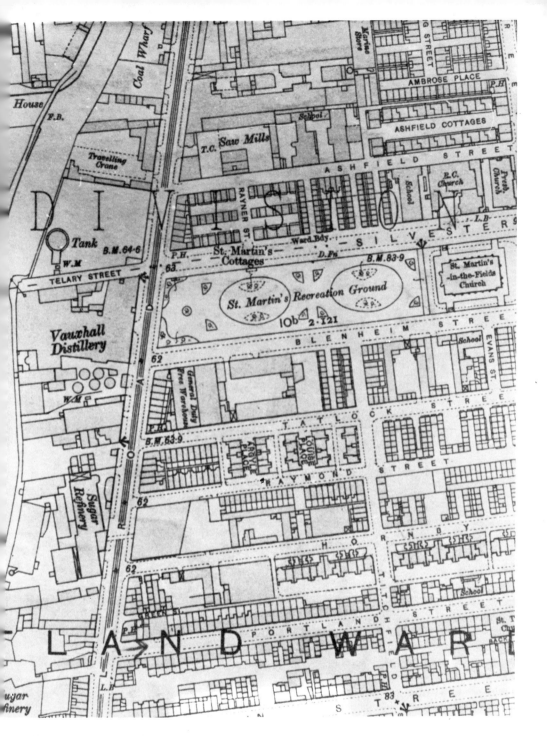

Fig. 3.10 An extract from the 1908 edition of a 1:25000 O.S. map showing part of Scotland Ward, Liverpool.

3. Try to find out how the local authority of your town or district first became involved in providing houses for working-class families. When were the first council houses built?

4. Compare the descriptions of nineteenth-century Birkenhead and the Old Jago. In what respects may both be regarded as failures?

C. Residential Segregation

The middle-class response to the squalor and unhealthiness of the exploding nineteenth-century towns was to take refuge in the emerging suburbs which developed rapidly from about the 1840s on the edge of the built-up areas. Increasingly, members of the middle class were no longer content to live in a socially heterogeneous community in the heart of the town where the poor were unobtrusively screened off in nearby courts. They were all too conscious of the risks of disease and periodic epidemics and wished to seek out a healthier environment on the edge of the town. The suburb thus evolved as a highly efficient means of permitting both functional and social segregation; functional in that it enabled homelife and work to be carried out in two discrete and often relatively distant places, and social in that it provided the means whereby middle-class families could live in physically separate, socially homogeneous and exclusive neighbourhoods. Furthermore, as had been observed by Engels during his stay in Manchester in the 1840s, the towns were constructed in such a way that the middle classes remained oblivious to working-class housing conditions on their journeys to work. In his *The Condition of the Working Class in England* he describes a main thoroughfare linking central Manchester with middle-class suburbs.

> So Market Street running south-east from the Exchange; at first brilliant shops of the best sort, with counting houses and warehouses above; in the continuation, Piccadilly, immense hotels and warehouses; in the further continuation, London Road, in the neighbourhood of the Medlock, factories, beerhouses, shops for the humbler bourgeoisie and the working population; and from this point onward, large gardens and villas of the wealthier merchants and manufacturers . . . one is seldom in a position to catch from the street a glimpse of the real labouring districts.[18]

So began the accentuation of segregation between classes in the growing Victorian towns of Britain, and the erosion of a sense of community. Suburban development was characterized by detached and semi-detached villas each constructed on relatively spacious plots. The low density development was possible because of the availability and relatively low cost of suburban land. Most of the occupiers could not afford to live in architect-designed houses and so the estates acquired a degree of uniformity, although variations on the basic house designs were achieved by projecting bays, gable ends, ornamental brickwork and other devices.

1. Transport developments

Suburban development was made possible through the availability of capital for house purchasing and by transport innovation which enabled people to travel farther to work. Capital was made available by the Freehold Land Societies and

Building Societies which had been started in the last quarter of the eighteenth century. These societies were to be found in almost every town in the country by the mid-nineteenth century.[19] The first important intra-urban innovation in public transport was the horse-drawn omnibus, a Parisian development imported by George Shillibeer in 1829[20], which provided a genteel alternative to the private carriage and which enabled the gentleman with limited means to live beyond walking distance from his place of work. Regular omnibus services were established to the growing London suburbs from about the mid 1830s and provided the only means of public transport to the City for some time. The success of suburban development often depended on easy access to an omnibus route. For example, in the south London suburb of Camberwell from 1835 to 1862 the omnibus was the only form of public passenger transport available.[21] Although omnibus fares were gradually reduced, they remained relatively high, beyond the reach of all but the better off. The omnibus became predominantly a one-class vehicle conveying the middle classes to their places of work.[22]

By the mid-1860s the construction of suburban railways had become an economical proposition. A railway mania followed whereby numerous suburban lines were built (see Fig. 3.11). The first underground railway in the world, the Metropolitan Line, was opened in the early 1860s to link Paddington with Farringdon Street and Moorgate.[23] The railways reduced travelling time and enabled people to live farther away from their places of work than the omnibus had. They pushed out the suburban frontier and enabled towns to sprawl deeper into the surrounding countryside. At first, however, like the omnibuses, fares were expensive and put the railways, as a means of daily travel, well beyond the means of all but the well-paid. There is some dispute over the relative importance of the suburban railway as an instigator of suburban development. It is of course unwise to generalize from specific case studies as each town had its own peculiar problems and responded to these differently, but it has been demonstrated that, at least for certain London suburbs, railway extensions usually *followed* rather than preceded suburban development. At best they served to reinforce population movements already in progress.[24]

In the latter part of the nineteenth century attempts were made to reduce the cost of commuting, so that more people could live beyond walking distance from their work places. The horse-drawn tramways introduced in the late 1860s went some way towards achieving this. In Camberwell, for instance, a network of routes was operational by 1872 and the fares were only a fraction of the cost of comparable rail fares.[25] The inner suburbs became even more accessible to workers with the passing of the Cheap Trains Act in 1882, which compelled all railway companies to introduce workers' fares as and when required by the Board of Trade. This was seen as a means of alleviating the housing problem which persisted in the heart of the cities. It certainly encouraged the filling up of the inner suburbs, which underwent a process of invasion-succession or filtering. Houses formerly occupied by middle-class families were subdivided into multi-occupation tenements for working people (see page 88). The process is aptly described by a contemporary writer, Charles Booth, who wrote, 'North of Peckham Road [Camberwell] is a large district becoming steadily poorer as the fairly comfortable move south and immigrants from Walworth

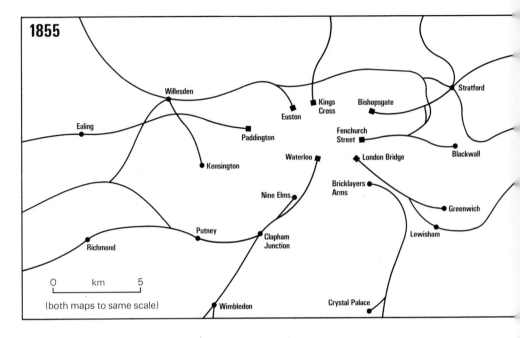

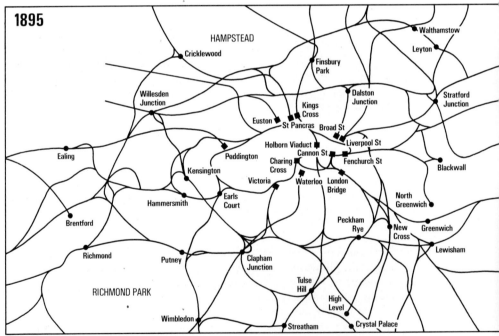

Fig. 3.11   London railways, 1855 and 1895. (Source: D. J. Olsen, *Growth of Victorian London*, Batsford, 1976)

arrive'.[26] We shall see in the next chapter that this process of invasion-succession was later to be recognized as the fundamental means by which towns grow, exerting a considerable influence on the structure of towns (see page 91).

2. Land ownership as a constraint on development

The Victorian suburbs were not subject to positive planning constraints. The layout and morphology of an individual estate was influenced by a combination of factors such as its relative proximity and accessibility to the city centre, the characteristics of the site and its ownership prior to development. In general the more distant suburbs (which incurred higher commuting costs) attracted only the better off. Likewise an elevated, well-drained site with pleasant views could command high land prices and this also influenced the way in which it was developed (see page 91). Land which had formed part of an extensive estate before its development was often developed quite differently from land where ownership had been fragmented. Where land had been in multi-ownership, development was likely to be more haphazard and of higher density, whereas when land which had formed part of a large estate was released for building the ensuing development was often carefully controlled. Covenants and stipulations in the leases on such lands were imposed to control housing densities and influence building standards. This is well illustrated in the case of Oxton, a suburb of Birkenhead within easy commuting distance of central Liverpool, which was developed particularly rapidly in the 1840s. The land had previously formed part of the estate of the Earl of Shrewsbury, who controlled the character of its development in the manner described by a contemporary writer. 'Although the land has been greatly divided among small holders on building leases, the principal portion yet remains subject to restrictions on the style and character of the houses whereby a pleasing appearance will be preserved, and a guarantee offered for the future well condition of the township.'[27] And so it proved to be.

ASSIGNMENTS
Fig. 3.12 is a section of Toxteth, Liverpool, as shown on the 1908 edition of the O.S. 1:2500 map.
(a) *Describe the style and layout of the houses.*
(b) *Measure the density of housing per hectare and compare it with the housing density in Scotland Ward, Liverpool (Fig. 3.10).*

D. Suburban Sprawl and the Beginnings of Town Planning

House building all but ceased during the First World War and consequently the housing problem was exacerbated. After 1918 the demand for houses with gardens in suburban locations continued to increase as average wages rose and changes in family structure occurred.[28] (In general, there were more smaller families and therefore more housing units were required). The introduction of more flexible forms of public transport such as electric trams from about 1900 and motorbus services from about 1918 made it increasingly possible for families to move to the suburbs on the edge of the towns.

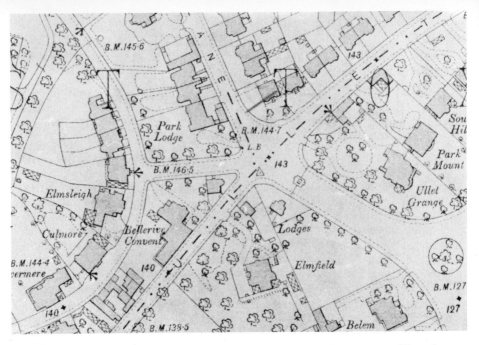

Fig. 3.12   An extract from the 1908 edition of a 1:2500 O.S. map showing part of Toxteth, Liverpool.

1. Inter-war council estates

With the exception of the occupiers of certain working-class suburbs such as West Ham in London, which had been developed in the nineteenth century, only the better paid could afford a house in the suburbs. It was, however, becoming increasingly recognized that working-class families had housing aspirations similar to those of their middle-class counterparts and that the housing problems of the congested town centres could be solved successfully only if more of the working-class families moved to suburban estates. This was made possible by the Housing and Town Planning Act of 1919 which made provision for a state subsidy to be paid to local authorities towards the cost of slum clearance and municipal housing development.[29] Up to that time all council house developments had been financed entirely by the local authorities themselves. The Act provided the necessary incentive for local authorities to become more involved. The Report of the Tudor Walters Committee on the Housing of the Working Classes, published in 1918, had advocated housing densities of only twelve houses per net acre,[30] thus it was inevitable that much of the municipal housing development of the inter-war period would be in the form of low density suburban estates (Fig. 3.13). The development of council estates in the inter-war period added a new dimension to suburban growth and helped to continue and accentuate the Victorian trend of keeping social groups apart.

The inter-war council estates were not without their problems. The sheer speed of development created its own problems. Thus the vast Norris Green Estate in Liverpool, housing over 25 000 people, was built up in four years.[31] The lack of constructive planning meant that the estates were often developed without adequate provision of shops, schools, clinics and other essential services. The houses

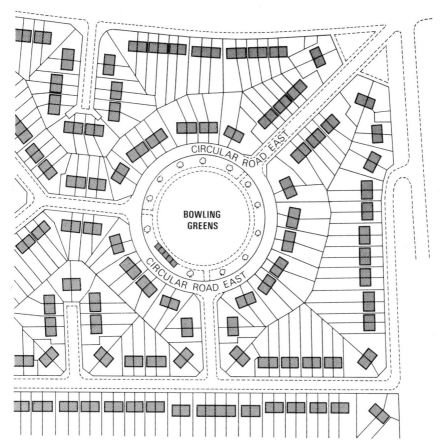

Fig. 3.13   Part of Norris Green, Liverpool, a low density suburban council estate built between the Wars.

themselves tended to be a standard, three-bedroom type, which created particular difficulties as young families grew up and other changes occurred within the family cycle. When the houses became too small or too large for family requirements, there was no suitable alternative accommodation in the area. The position was improved very little by the Housing Act of 1936 which stipulated the number of houses of different sizes which were to be incorporated in the new estates, for 82 per cent were still to be three-bedroom houses.[32] The lack of local employment opportunities and increased length of journey to work also created problems for many of the families and probably contributed to the above average rates of unemployment on many of the estates during the Great Depression. Nevertheless, the spaciously laid out inter-war council estates did provide an environment vastly superior to much of the inner city. Many of the estates developed at that time remain some of the most successful attempts at large scale public housing provision.

2. The need for planning

The inter-war period was a phase of unprecedented urban growth. Much private building, in particular, sprawled along main roads leading from the towns in the form of ribbon development, putting the agricultural land between the roads under considerable pressure. The urban frontier penetrated deeper and deeper into the surrounding countryside and it became increasingly recognized that it was necessary to introduce planning controls to contain urban growth. The 1930 Housing Act aimed at limiting suburban growth by attempting to encourage the more intensive development of the inner areas of cities while a Ministry Circular of 1933 required all local authorities to submit programmes of slum clearance. Much of the inter-war redevelopment was, however, unimaginative. Massive four and five-storey blocks of flats were often built with little awareness of their environments. Nevertheless even the most intensive redevelopment schemes left a surplus of population to be rehoused in the suburbs. Planning legislation was necessary if town growth was to be contained. There had been certain early legislation such as the Housing, Town Planning, etc. Act of 1909 which tried to regularize suburban development, but it was during the inter-war period that the foundations for later comprehensive planning legislation were laid. The 1932 Town and Country Planning Act proved largely ineffectual because local authorities were put under no obligation to prepare town planning schemes. A similar fate befell the Restriction of Ribbon Development Act of 1935 which attempted to restrict urban sprawl along main routes, and the Green Belt (London and Home Counties) Act of 1938 which tried to curtail London's growth. Nevertheless an attempt to control development within the urban system had been made, if somewhat belatedly. The extremely low density inter-war suburban development which consumed so much space was, at least in part, responsible for some of the less desirable later developments.

ASSIGNMENTS
1. *Compare the map extract of part of the Norris Green estate (see Fig. 3.13) with that of Scotland Ward (Fig. 3.10), Liverpool, in 1908. Describe differences in house types and layouts; the pattern of streets; landscape planning and housing densities.*
2. *Outline the advantages and disadvantages of suburban estate development compared with inner city redevelopment.*
3. *Why was it necessary to introduce planning legislation in the 1930s? How effective was it?*

E. Post-War Urban and Ex-Urban Growth

1. Post-war legislation

Inter-war planning legislation was largely ineffectual because it tried to grapple with particular problems that arose within the urban system rather than to treat the system as a whole. The first comprehensive piece of planning legislation was the Town and Country Planning Act of 1947 which put all local authorities in England and Wales under a statutory obligation to prepare Development Plans and submit these to the appropriate Minister for approval or amendment.[33] The Development Plans were to state the general use to which each plot of land and building was to be put. The Act aimed at controlling future development by requiring each potential developer to submit detailed plans of his proposals for consideration by a Planning Committee. Local authorities could thus refuse applications for what were considered to be undesirable proposals. Previously they could do this only by purchasing the land on which the development was planned. The 1947 Act also designated a Green Belt around London. The legislation provided a framework for controlling urban growth. The housing problem remained, however, exacerbated by the destruction and damage to property during the Second World War. For example, in 1951 Manchester had 67 000 unfit dwellings while the situation in other cities such as Glasgow, Liverpool and certain of the London boroughs was even worse. The post-war dilemma was how to solve the housing problem while at the same time containing the spread of cities and conurbations.

2. The Public Sector: slum clearance and overspill

The 1950s saw the instigation of vast slum clearance programmes in most of Britain's large cities. The majority of the families affected were rehoused in the extensive post-war estates which developed on the edge of the built-up area or on redeveloped sites in the inner city, but there was a surplus which could not be rehoused within the city limits. Many of these overspill families either moved to New Towns designated under the New Towns Act of 1946 (see pp. 247) or to 'expanded towns' which were designated under the Town Development Act of 1952. The expanded towns provided houses and jobs for the overspill families and in return received financial help from central government and a housing subsidy paid over a number of years by the city from which the family had moved.[34] (See Fig. 9.3, page 251.)

Even with the introduction of overspill policies the housing problem remained as slums were created as quickly as they were cleared. Thus surveys conducted in the mid 1960s into housing conditions in Liverpool and Manchester revealed that approximately 40 per cent of the total housing stock in each city was unfit for habitation.[35, 36] It was information such as this that encouraged the local authorities to make even more stringent efforts to get to grips with their housing problems. Slum clearance programmes were stepped up so that in the late 1960s many thousands of houses were being demolished each year in Britian's industrial cities.

The Housing Act of 1969 changed the emphasis in housing policy and, through the provision of increased grants, encouraged the rehabilitation rather than the demolition of older property. In Development Areas grants paid to house owners for improvements to their properties increased to 75 per cent of the total costs incurred and at the same time the scope of the grants was increased to cover inter-war property. In addition local authorities were empowered to create General Improvement Areas (GIAs) in districts of older property and within these house owners were obliged to make improvements to their property, while the local authority undertook to enhance the urban environment by measures such as landscaping and pedestrianization. As a result of the 1969 Act local authorities reappraised their housing stocks and many houses which previously had been designated for demolition under slum clearance programmes were reprieved and rehabilitated instead. This radical change in policy which occurred in the late 1960s was brought about by a number of interdependent factors which included:

(a)   A realization of the effects of overspill policies on the cities themselves. In the period 1961-71 the populations of nearly all Britain's largest cities declined substantially. For example Greater London's population fell from 7 997 234 to 7 452 346; Liverpool's from 745 750 to 610 113 and Manchester's from 662 030 to

543 868. In addition, many jobs in manufacturing industry were also lost as the manufacturers followed, or even preceded, the overspill families to the New and expanded towns. Thus the overspill policies were a major contributory factor to the malaise of the inner city.

(b) Demographic changes which have meant that, after a period of continuous post-war growth, the population has stabilized in the mid seventies to reach a situation of zero growth in 1976 (Fig. 3.14). Thus it can now be seen that many overspill schemes and New Town Development projects which had been designed in the 1950s or early 1960s to take into account projected continuing increases in Britain's population were based on false assumptions.

(c) An increase in home ownership so that by 1974, 52 per cent of all dwellings in Britain were owner-occupied. This trend threatens to create a potential surplus of council property in many of Britain's towns (Fig. 3.15).

(d) A growing awareness of the need to sustain existing communities and the difficulty of creating a comparable sense of community in new housing areas.

The emphasis on rehabilitation of older property was continued under the 1974 Housing Act which allows local authorities to designate Housing Action Areas (HAAs). These are districts of around 300 to 400 houses which are to be totally rehabilitated in five to seven years. Half the cost of environmental improvements and 75 per cent of the cost of house improvements are funded by central government. In addition, there has been a growing awareness of the plight of many of the inner city areas and an urban aid programme has been initiated which, amongst other measures, allows for the establishment of Comprehensive Community Programmes (CCPs) which aim to identify the whole range of social, economic and environmental problems in areas and devise proposals to deal with these within a restricted time-scale.

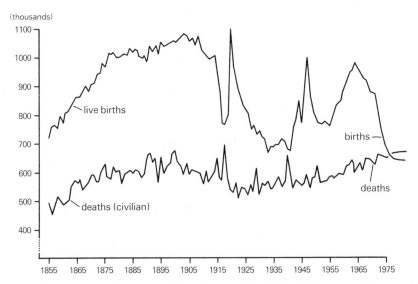

Fig. 3.14   Demographic change in England and Wales 1855–1975. (Source: *Demographic Review*, Reproduced with the permission of the Controller of HMSO, 1977)

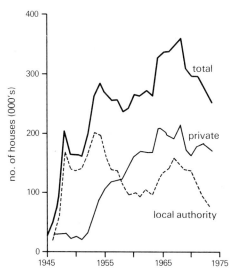

Fig. 3.15   Changes in the proportion of housing tenure in England and Wales since 1945.
(Source: Mitchell, *Annual Abstract of Statistics – Housing and Construction Statistics*, CUP,
1962)

3. The Private Sector

No resumé of post-war urban growth would be complete without some reference to
the private housing sector, for it is here that much of the growth has been concentrated. This has been in the form of vast estates of detached or semi-detached
properties which have extended the urban frontier rapidly outwards (Plate 3.6). In
addition much infilling has taken place where low density Victorian suburban
houses have been demolished and replaced by high-rise flats or small estates.
Alternatively the houses may have remained, often converted into flats, while the
extensive gardens have been divided into additional building lots.

A further characteristic feature of post-war growth has been the development and
modification of surrounding villages through ex-urban growth.[37] This is not a new
phenomenon, for the modification of villages close to towns invariably precedes
suburbanization. But in the post-war period, a rapid increase in car ownership has
provided many families with a flexible means of travelling to work and thereby
enabled a more complete physical separation of home and work place. Thus ex-
urban growth has proceeded at an unprecedented pace and the 'dormitory village'
has become commonplace. Ex-urban growth has been controlled partially by planning policies implemented by local authorities. These have often distinguished
'conservation villages' in which growth is restricted or prohibited entirely from
villages where substantial development has been permitted. Even in the conservation village, however, it is not possible to prevent substantial changes occurring in
the population structure, as old villagers die or move away and their houses are
occupied by commuters or retired couples who move out from the accessible towns.
The growth and ensuing change in character of the villages often creates friction
through the development of two distinct social groups which often co-exist rather
than integrate. This in turn has led to the demise of a single social hierarchy in the
village (see pages 39 to 44 and Chapter 9).

ASSIGNMENTS

1.   Assess the strengths and weaknesses of an overspill policy as opposed to a policy that emphasizes rehabilitation of older property in terms of: (a) the environment/townscape; (b) the establishment or maintenance of a sense of community; (c) the provision of and access to essential services; (d) industrial development. Consider both the short and long term implications of pursuing either policy.

2.   Refer to Fig 3.15. Describe and account for fluctuations in house building and the proportion of private and local authority housing development between 1920 and 1973.

Plate 3.6   Suburban development, Edinburgh. Note the low density private housing estate in the foreground. Such suburban development has resulted in a rapid extension of the urban frontier in the inter-war and post-war periods. (*The City of Edinburgh District Council*)

F. The Supply of Housing and the Decision-taking Filter

With the exception of New Towns which are planned as complete systems, urban growth arises from a mixture of many fragmented developments. These may range from extensive council and private housing estates to small-scale infilling.

Each development is affected by decisions taken by many individuals and groups including landowners, builders and developers, politicians and planners. Decisions are arrived at after a consideration of a wide range of interdependent factors such as innovations in building and transport technology; availabiliy of capital for house building and purchase; government policy and legislation; planning constraints; demographic and social trends, and so on. These influences act at different levels. Some, such as government legislation and the general state of the economy, act at a national level and affect development throughout the country. Others, such as the employment structure within a region, regional unemployment rates and the ability of a region to attract new jobs, operate at a regional level. Others, such as the properties of individual development sites, the attitudes of local elected representatives to council and private development, operate at a local level. Dr. M. C. Carr in a study of suburban development in Bexley, Kent, suggested that it is helpful to arrange these influences into what he described as a 'decision-taking filter'.[38] This recognizes that changes operating at a national level will only have an impact on individual developments after they have filtered down through more local and specific influences. Table 3.1 is an attempt to present these influences in a more ordered framework.

Collectively, decisions taken within this framework affect both the morphology and speed of development. Urban growth in Britain has tended to occur in cycles (see Fig 3.16) which are influenced, in particular, by national economic factors such as mortgage interest rates, the Bank rate and the general state of the economy (1a). The nature of specific housing developments, such as the layout of roads, building densities and the type of ownership of houses constructed, is influenced by a

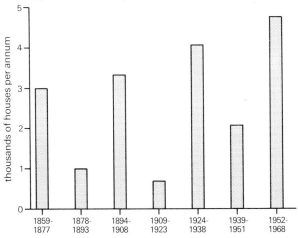

Fig. 3.16   Fluctuation in the number of houses (thousands per annum) authorized by the Dean of Guild Court to be built in Glasgow between 1859–1968. (Source: J. H. Johnson, *The Geographical Process at the Edge of the Western City*, Wiley, 1974, p.76)

Table 3.1 The Decision-taking Filter which affects Housing Supply. (After M. C. Carr.)

Factors affecting Decisions

SCALE	a. ECONOMIC	b. SOCIAL	c. DEMOGRAPHIC	d. POLITICAL	e. TECHNICAL	f. PHYSICAL
1. NATIONAL	The general state of the economy. Mortgage interest rates. Availability of money for house purchase. Employment levels.	Changes in tenure (council/private).	Population growth rates. Population migration. Changes in population structure (e.g. average family size.)	Housing and other legislation affecting town growth. Planning legislation. Attitude to public/private housing.	Transport innovation affecting private sector (e.g. increase in car ownership). Innovation in construction industry (e.g. tower crane, reinforced concrete, prefabricated construction methods etc.).	
2. REGIONAL	Employment structure. Ability of region to attract new jobs. Rates of unemployment. General well-being of the region.	Demographic and social characteristics of the region.		Regional planning policies.		
3. LOCAL	Availability of land for development. Land ownership (whether part of a substantial estate or in fragmented ownership). The way in which adjoining land is used.	The perceived characteristics of the neighbourhood.	The age-sex structure of residents of neighbouring housing districts.	Planning constraints. Local government policy.		Nature of the individual sites e.g. elevation, aspect, drainage. Accessibility of the site to public transport and main road networks.

combination of decisions taken at all levels (1b, 1d, 1e; 2b; 3a, 3b, 3c, 3d, 3f). For example, high-rise development was incorporated into many council estates and redeveloped areas from about 1955 to 1970 because it speeded up the process of slum clearance. It also left more land available for recreational and other purposes. At the same time population densities increased, which helped to alleviate the acute shortage of land (1c). High-rise development was made possible by innovations in the construction industry such as the tower crane and new forms of poured concrete (1e). It was actively encouraged by the 1956 Housing Subsidies Act which amended housing subsidies and granted local authorities a bigger subsidy per dwelling the higher the development (1d). The extent to which an individual authority built high-rise flats depended on decisions taken at a local level by Planning Committees. Such decisions were based on the recommendations of planners, architects, civil engineers and other local government officials (3d). After about 1970, high-rise development became less popular. The social disadvantages of high-rise living had become apparent and safety reassessments were made after the Ronan Point disaster, whereby a multi-storey block, which had been constructed in prefabricated sections, collapsed after a gas explosion. Multi-storey blocks had by that time exerted a strong influence on the morphology of much post-war urban development.

The decision-taking filter emphasizes the complexity of influences on urban growth and change. Increasingly it was recognized that, despite its subsequent amendments, the Town and Country Planning Act of 1947 could not cope with constantly changing conditions. Its emphasis on the Town Development Plan with its mass of precise detail was too inflexible. It has been superseded, therefore, by the Town and Country Planning Act of 1968 which requires local authorities to submit Structure Plans to the Minister for approval. These are essentially strategy statements which set out a number of alternatives. The interdependence of all facets of development is recognized (see p. 41).

ASSIGNMENTS
1. *Find out about any alternative strategies for urban development in your county. Discuss the strengths and weaknesses of each of the proposals.*
2. *Try to apply the ideas contained in the decision-taking filter to demonstrate how a large housing estate with which you are familiar (private or council) has been affected by decisions taken at different levels (national, regional and local).*

G. Conclusion

This chapter has examined how the processes of urban growth have affected the patterns of development. It has been concerned in particular with those factors which have influenced town growth in Britain, where central government and local authority controls interact with market forces. Similar influences operate in all Western democracies although the precise balance between central control and free market forces differs substantially. In the United States, for example, the role of central government is weaker and market forces exert a greater influence in determining the nature and speed of urban growth. One outcome of this is the much smaller proportion of the housing stock which is in public ownership, only 3 per cent compared with 32 per cent in Great Britain in 1977. In contrast, in Communist countries greater state control means that urban growth is less spontaneous. It is important to have some understanding of the processes of urbanization before going on to examine the structure of towns, for it is in these processes that we begin to see explanations emerging.

Key Ideas

A. *Pre-Industrial towns*
1. The establishment of a new social and economic order in medieval times encouraged the growth of towns.
2. It is possible to distinguish unplanned or organic medieval towns from those which were planned or planted.
3. Not all of the planted medieval towns flourished. Some failed to grow at all, while others prospered for a time and then declined.
4. The Renaissance was characterized by attempts to impose order and symmetry on town planning and development and a close relationship developed between landscape planning and town planning.
5. The Renaissance probably marks the pinnacle of achievement in town planning in Western Europe, as exemplified at Rome, London and Bath.
6. Most of the neo-Classical developments in British towns took the form of piecemeal extensions to existing towns.
7. Restrictions in land ownership sometimes resulted in developments of excessively high densities and contrasts in the quality of housing were accentuated.

B. *The consequences of rapid nineteenth-century urban growth*
1. The historical phenomenon of rapid urban growth has never been more dramatically represented than in nineteenth-century Britain.
2. Urbanization changed fundamentally the pre-existing patterns of settlement. It was concentrated in particular areas in response to chance locations and the exploitation of resources and the development of industry and trade.
3. Urbanization was partly a consequence of migration into the towns, a process which had appalling consequences for the migrants in terms of squalid housing conditions, gross overcrowding and a debilitating environment.
4. Measures to improve the quality of working-class housing were introduced only after a clear correlation had been demonstrated between bad housing conditions and the spread of disease. This encouraged the involvement of central government and legislation in the areas of housing, public health and education.
5. Improved housing standards and pressures on space led, however, to rising rents and evictions, making worse the problems of poorer sections of the community.
6. It rapidly became clear that housing subsidies were essential if local authorities were to provide housing for the most disadvantaged families.

C. *Residential segregation*
1. In early nineteenth-century Britain, the different social classes of the towns, though identifiable as separate groups, tended to live in relatively close proximity.

2. As urban transport facilities developed, the more well-to-do groups increasingly moved outwards (centrifugally), while incoming poorer social groups colonized the property which had been left (a centripetal movement).
3. Thus exclusive, socially homogeneous neighbourhoods developed, where levels of rent and costs of commuting provided selecting mechanisms.
4. Factors influencing 'exclusiveness' included social distance (as well as distance on the ground) and physical aspects of site (well-drained, commanding situation, etc.)
5. Land ownership prior to development frequently exerted a significant influence on the type of development which occurred i.e. the density and quality of housing.

D. *Suburban sprawl and the beginnings of town planning*
1. In this century, demands for suburban living space have increased the pressure on rural areas around the towns.
2. Cheaper fares from the late nineteenth century have made it increasingly possible for less affluent people to commute, again increasing demands on suburban space.
3. Additional pressure has come from twentieth-century slum clearance programmes, moving less well-to-do groups out to suburban council estates.
4. Building of estates has not generally been accompanied by adequate planning for employment and social facilities.
5. Inter-war suburban development took place with a minimum of planning constraints and this resulted in much private development sprawling along roads out of the city centre, as ribbon development.
6. The consequences of these pressures have been an alarming increase in urban sprawl, towns becoming conurbations, and conurbations joining to form a megalopolis.
7. From 1930 legislation has been introduced to limit suburban growth, leading to the establishment of green belts.

E. *Post-war urban and ex-urban growth*
1. Increasingly, post-war planning strategies have regarded the town as an open system which is part of a broader regional and national framework. The interdependence of all facets of development is recognized.
2. For over two decades, overspill schemes were regarded as integral to housing solutions but since the Housing Act of 1969, increasing emphasis has been placed on rehabilitating older property and improving the environmental quality of inner urban areas.
3. This change in policy emphasis has arisen from a realization of the harmful effects of overspill schemes on inner city areas in particular. The number of people living in such areas has fallen dramatically; fundamental changes have occurred in the population structure and there has been a loss of jobs, notably in manufacturing industry, and a deterioration in social and other services.
4. An increase in car ownership has provided many families with a flexible means of travelling to work and enabled a more complete physical separation of home and work place. This has encouraged ex-urban growth and the development of the dormitory village.

82

F. Supply of housing and the decision-taking filter

1. Urban growth arises from decisions taken by many individuals and groups after a consideration of a wide range of interdependent factors. These factors act at different scales; local, regional and national.
2. The decisions affect both the morphology and rate of urban development.
3. The need for flexibility in town planning is recognized by the Town and Country Planning Act of 1968, which requires counties to devise Structure Plans which establish broad strategies for all aspects of development.

Additional Activities

1. Refer to the mosaic of photographs of the Woodchurch and Ford Estates, Birkenhead, Merseyside (Plate 3.7). This area has been developed from the 1930s through to the present day. Consider the type of buildings, their style and layout and try to date each phase of development. Justify your conclusions.
2. Examine the role of central and local government in affecting the supply of housing in Britain in the last hundred years.
3. Discuss the assertion that: 'Britain has always lacked a coherent housing policy; decisions about housing have always been taken for reasons of short-term expediency.'
4. Debate the motion that 'Planners have failed in their attempts to find solutions to Britain's post-war housing problem'.

Reading

A. BURKE, G., *Towns in the Making*, Arnold, 1975, Chapters 4, 5, 6, 7 and 8.
B. HOSKINS, W. G., *The Making of the English Landscape*, Penguin Books, 1970.
C. JOHNSON, J. H., *Urban Geography, An Introductory Analysis*, Pergamon, 1972 ed., Chapters 1 and 2.
D. JOHNSON, J. H., *Suburban Growth*, Wiley, 1974, Chapter 4.
E. ROBSON, B. T., *Urban Social Areas*, Oxford University Press, 1975.

◀ Plate 3.7   Housing development in the Woodchurch and Ford estates, Birkenhead, Merseyside. These large council housing estates have been developed from the 1930s through to the present day. *(Author's photographs)*

4 Urban morphology

A. Functional Zones

We have seen in the previous chapter that until the nineteenth century urban growth in Britain was a relatively slow and gradual process. We have also observed that during the nineteenth century urbanization rates increased dramatically. This rapid urban growth often coincided with the development in towns of factory industry which required a considerable workforce living near the factories. Transport innovations encouraged the expansion of towns. It became easier for people to move within towns, and for many to live farther from their places of work and from certain essential services which were available only in the town centre.

The pattern of urban growth was frequently influenced and sometimes constrained by natural barriers and both existing and new lines of communication. For example, land which was liable to flooding could not be built on and was, therefore, often preserved as open space. Similarly a very sharp break of slope may have restricted development, while land of contrasting physical qualities may have attracted different types of urban development. The expensive, low density residential area may require free-draining sites commanding attractive views, while heavy industry may favour extensive areas of flat land offering scope for future expansion. Canals and railway lines frequently exerted considerable influence on town growth, acting as barriers to movement so that different functions often developed on either side of them. More recently, the development of dual carriageways, inner ring roads and even urban motorways have all provided further constraints on town growth.

As a town grows, there is a tendency for different functions to occupy different areas within the town so that housing, industry or commercial activities become the dominant functions in different parts of the town. These broadly dissimilar *functional areas* or *zones* are readily recognizable. Residential areas can be distinguished from the town centre where commercial activities dominate, and from extensive industrial estates (see Fig. 4.1). Sometimes, the barriers to development described in the previous paragraph also act as boundaries to the functional zones, in which case the zones may be quite discrete and easily distinguished. This is by no means always the case, however, and careful mapping of building function may have to precede any attempt to distinguish functional zones within a town. Even then it might be discovered that in part of the town the types of building are inextricably mixed, and it will not then be easy to designate such areas with a single descriptive name.

Fieldwork and map work will also reveal that frequently within zones of broadly

84

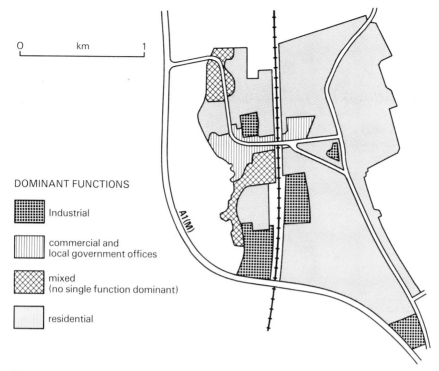

DOMINANT FUNCTIONS

▓ Industrial

▐ commercial and
local government offices

▨ mixed
(no single function dominant)

░ residential

Fig. 4.1   Functional zones in Biggleswade, Beds.

similar function more subtle spatial contrasts can be discerned. For example, an extensive residential area may contain a number of contrasting districts based on ownership and housing age and quality. Thus council housing estates are often physically separate from private housing estates, and districts of high density, nineteenth-century terraces are readily distinguishable from those of low density, expensive modern housing. Similarly, within a large town centre, where commercial activities dominate, it may be possible to distinguish different sub-areas. Different specialist functions, such as department and specialist stores, banks and insurance offices, and places of entertainment, are dominant here. These functional contrasts are often reflected in the arrangement and layout of the buildings and in the street patterns. The large scale Ordnance Survey map extracts which you used in the previous chapter (see Figs. 3.10, 3.12) clearly illustrate contrasts in the patterns of high density nineteenth-century, as against low density villa and inter-war, council residential areas.

The arrangement and layout of the buildings and the function or use of land and buildings in a town are collectively described as the town's *morphology*. The search for pattern and order in a town inevitably involves an attempt to distinguish clearly identifiable *morphological zones*. In order to gain some understanding of the spatial relationships that exist within the complexities of a town, we must use some form of simplification. The distinguishing of morphological or, at a simpler level, functional zones provides a useful starting point in this respect. Furthermore, the development of such zones results from a variety of processes and, if we are to understand how these processes operate we must study their effects.

85

B. Models of Urban Growth

The study of *urban structure* attempts to emphasize significant spatial relationships between the broad land use zones in a town. A number of descriptive models have been developed which summarize these. They seek to identify certain spatial characteristics which are common to all towns and provide some understanding of the processes which bring these about.

E. W. Burgess's Concentric Zone Model is one of the earliest attempts to provide some insight into urban structure and this will be considered first. (See Fig. 4.2.)

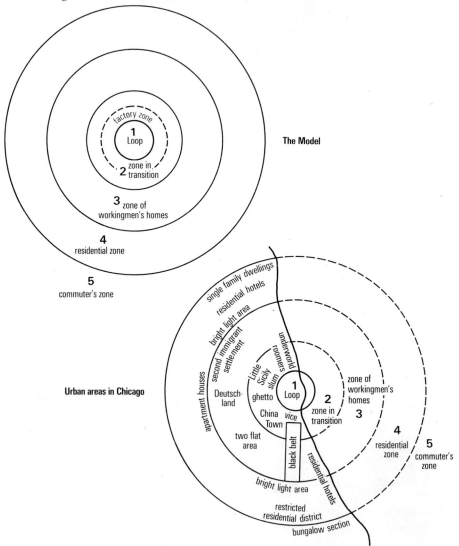

Fig. 4.2   Burgess's concentric model of urban structure. (Source: original appeared in R. E. Park, E. W. Burgess & McKenzie (eds.), *The City*, University of Chicago Press, 1925)

1. The concentric zone model

(a) The model described

The concentric nature of the rapidly growing nineteenth-century industrial towns was apparent to the keen observer even in the relatively early stages of their development. For example, Frederick Engels included the following description of Manchester in the 1840s in his *The Condition of the Working Class in England.*

> Manchester contains, at its heart, a rather extended commercial district, perhaps half a mile long and about as broad consisting almost wholly of offices and warehouses. . . . The district is cut through by certain main thoroughfares . . . lined with brilliant shops . . . unmixed working people's quarters stretch like a girdle, averaging a mile and a half in breadth, around the commercial district. Outside, beyond this girdle, lives the upper and middle bourgeoisie, the middle bourgeoisie in regularly laid out streets in the vicinity of the working quarters . . . , the upper bourgeoisie in remoter villas with gardens . . .[1]

It was, however, left to E. W. Burgess and his associates, who made comparable observations almost a century later (in the 1920s), to develop the concentric zone model. The model was based on empirical research in a number of American cities, particularly Chicago, and it described the concentric arrangement of functional zones within a city. Burgess claimed that although no one city that he studied perfectly exemplified the concentric zone model, all 'approximate in greater or lesser degree to this ideal construction'.[2] He acknowledged, however, that the model would probably not hold for all cities throughout the world.

In his search for a greater understanding of a complex urban system, Burgess adopted some of the fundamental concepts used by the plant ecologists (the ideas of competition, dominance, invasion, succession) in their study of plant associations. He envisaged that, within the city, people *competed* for limited space. Those who were best able to pay for them achieved the most desirable locations for their homes, and businesses. Those individuals and functions with the lowest level of economic competence had the least choice and were, therefore, left with the poorest locations. Burgess suggested that this process led to *functional zoning* and *residential segregation* within cities. In other words, within different areas of the city different single functions formed the *dominant* element. (These concepts are returned to in Chapter 5, pages 131 to 137).

Burgess observed that the zones are arranged concentrically around the city centre, and that each is distinctive in age and character.

(i) Central Business District (CBD)

At the heart of the city is the Central Business District (CBD) which forms the commercial, social and cultural hub (see Chapter 6). The CBD is the most accessible part of the city, being at the focus of the urban transport network. Here are situated mainly offices, large departmental stores, specialist and variety goods shops as well as the main theatres, cinemas and best hotels. These activities can best afford to pay the high rates and rents required for such advantageous sites. (See Plate 4.1.)

(ii) Zone in transition

Surrounding the CBD there is a zone in transition or deterioration, where the land

Plate 4.1   The Central Business District, Sheffield. The commercial core is the most intensively developed part of the urban system and contains many multi-storey buildings. (*Aerofilms*).

use is very mixed and is constantly changing. It is too inaccessible to be sought after by prosperous commercial enterprises, such as department and variety goods stores and large office blocks, but too near to the noise and grime of the city to provide sites for anything but the poorest residential buildings where the most deprived social groups live. It is an unwanted zone, often characterized by blight (i.e. decay) and abandonment, and probably contains retail services such as poor quality cafés, vacant and derelict buildings and barren spaces where slums have recently been demolished. In addition, being a zone of change, it will probably include many large and formerly fine houses, often Georgian or Victorian, which are now used for other purposes. Some may have been renovated and divided into offices, others may now be occupied by light industries, while those which still serve as dwellings are likely to have degenerated into overcrowded slums. (See Plate 4.2.)

(iii)   Working-class zones

The zone in transition is surrounded by a zone of working-class houses. This zone contains some of the older residential buildings in the city and in particular, rows of Victorian terraced houses. (See Plate 4.3.) These originally housed families who

Plate 4.2 The zone in transition is characterized by blight and neglect. Formerly prosperous residences have been subdivided to form small workshops and these are intermixed with warehouses, vacant and derelict sites and poor quality housing. (*Author's photograph*)

Plate 4.3 High density nineteenth-century housing in Burgess's zone of working men's houses. Note the juxtaposition of houses and heavy industry. (*Author's photograph*)

moved from poorer quality property in the zone in transition, but who were still compelled by travelling costs and rents to live near to their places of work.

(iv) Middle-class zone
Adjacent to this zone of working-class houses is what Burgess described as a zone of better residences, where the terrace has been replaced by semi-detached and detached houses of the middle class (see Plate 4.4). Some light industry will also

89

Plate 4.4   Middle-class housing. The Burgess model envisages this sort of low density housing development occurring in the outer suburbs. *(Author's photograph)*

Plate 4.5   The commuters' zone or rural-urban fringe on the edge of Glasgow. Note how low density housing development is interspersed with playing fields, a golf course and farmland. *(Aerofilms)*

probably be situated here, perhaps in industrial estates which have developed near the edge of the built-up area (although this was not integral to the original model).

(v) Commuters' zone

The Burgess model also recognizes a rural-urban fringe zone, the commuters' zone, beyond the continuous built-up area. Dormitory suburbs have developed there and certain space-consuming, but, nonetheless, essential urban functions are also situated there. These include public utilities, such as sewage disposal plants and refuse tips, and recreational facilities, such as golf courses. These urban functions will probably be interspersed with non-urban land use such as agricultural land and woodland. (See Plate 4.5 and pages 233 to 237.)

To summarize, Burgess envisaged that the lower status groups are to be found near the city centre and the high status groups at its periphery.

Burgess also acknowledged the likely occurrence within the broader zones of what his co-worker R. E. Park had described as *natural areas*. These are districts which are culturally distinct and are occupied by people of similar race, language and socio-economic status. For example, in his original model of the structure of Chicago, Burgess indicates a 'black belt', wedging out from the zone in transition (Fig. 4.2). These 'natural areas' might be bounded by physical constraints such as topographical features or main lines of communication.

Burgess noted that his idealized concentric zones would be modified by *opposing factors*. These included such features as high ground, which might offer good views and provide a slightly more favourable micro-climate (including less winter fog), which would lead to the persistence of a high-class residential area within the inner zone. He also acknowledged that the distribution of heavy industry might act as a distorting factor on zoning. It is more likely to be concentrated in areas of poor quality, cheap land, such as on river floodplains or, as with portside industry, at points of break of bulk, rather than to be distributed in a concentric arrangement.

The Burgess model 'was also intended to serve as a mechanistic framework for urban growth and change.'[3] Burgess saw the mechanism of urban growth as similar to the ecological process of invasion and succession, by which population groups gradually filtered outwards from the centre as their status and level of assimilation improved. By this means, higher status residential areas came to be occupied by lower income groups and ethnic areas of one type were overtaken by people of a different ethnic stock. This invasion/succession process was also the mechanism by which residential areas were taken over by commercial and business undertakings, a process which can still be identified in contemporary British cities (see Fig. 4.3).

(b) Criticisms of the concentric zone model

Since E. W. Burgess first outlined his concentric zone model in the 1920s a number of criticisms have been levelled at it. These include the following:
  (i) The model considers ground floor functions only, and little attention is paid to the height of buildings and variations of function on different floors.
  (ii) The model emphasizes clear cut boundaries between the concentric zones. These cannot, however, be justified by gradient studies which suggest no abrupt division between zones but rather that they merge gradually from one to another (see page 109). But if the gradients are as continuous as some research has demonstrated, this implies that zonal lines can be drawn at random at any radius from the centre.

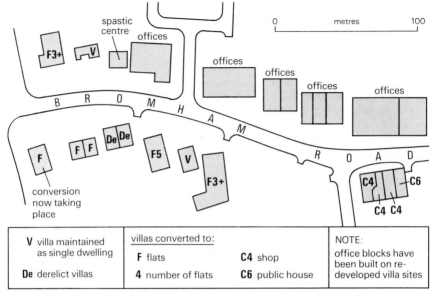

Fig. 4.3 Villa conversion and replacement, Bromham Road, Bedford. The process of invasion and succession envisaged by Burgess is in evidence on the edge of the CBD. Commercial functions are penetrating a district which until relatively recently was a residential one. (Source: based on an O.S. map. Crown Copyright Reserved)

(iii) The concentric zones are displayed as distinctive ecological areas but field studies confirm that, where the zones can be identified, they lack homogeneity. In fact they display a significant degree of internal heterogeneity.

(iv) The model pays scant attention to the distribution of industry. Burgess merely regards heavy industry as a distorting factor. It could be argued that in any model of urban structure, greater consideration should be given to the location of industry within the urban system.

(v) In suggesting invasion/succession as the dominant process by which towns grow, Burgess was insufficiently aware of the *forces of inertia* that exist within a city. Some buildings simply do not lend themselves to conversion as readily as others. It is perhaps no accident that the process is often best observed in districts of decaying Georgian terraces or Victorian villas.

(vi) Above all else, the model has been criticized because it is rooted in a specific historical and cultural context (i.e. the USA of the 1920s). It is limited 'to a particular situation, at a particular time in a particular country'[4], and this inevitably limits its universality. It can, therefore, be argued that it is most applicable to cities of the developed Western world but certain trends operating since the 1920s make the model less appropriate. These include:

  (a) the decline of the CBD, and the emergence of suburban business centres, a process most in evidence in North America;

  (b) transport innovations, in particular wide-spread car ownership which has increased the mobility of a growing proportion of the urban population; and

  (c) the increasing level of public intervention, e.g. development control, and the provision of public sector housing in the UK, and the Zoning Laws of the USA which regulate 'types of use, density of use and height of buildings.'[5]

Hardly surprisingly, the model has been demonstrated to be of little value in attempting to interpret the internal structure of the pre-industrial city, either past or present. G. Sjoberg[6] (1965) has demonstrated that within the feudal city there was no clear cut functional differentiation of land use. For example, merchants and craftsmen often lived at their place of work. Where a zonal pattern of land use could be identified, however, it was in many respects the inverse of that identified by Burgess in North American cities in the 1920s. The market place and certain status functions were situated at the centre of the feudal city and the surrounding residential areas declined in terms of residential prestige towards the periphery, the poorest families living outside the city walls (see Fig. 4.4).

One of the main reasons why the concentric zone model has been so criticized is that Burgess failed to state the pre-conditions which must exist if the model is to be applicable without modification. It was left to J. A. Quinn (1950)[7] and L. F. Schnøre

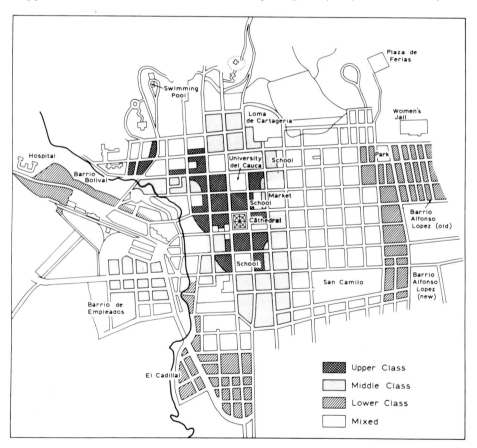

Fig. 4.4 The distribution of social classes in Popáyan, Columbia. (Source: H. Carter, *The Study of Urban Geography*, Edward Arnold p. 169; after A. H. Whiteford, *Two Cities of Latin America*, New York)

(1965)[8] to describe these later. They suggested that the following conditions must apply if the concentric zones envisaged by Burgess are to develop:

(i) A uniform land surface, i.e. no differences in the physical qualities of land in different parts of the city.

(ii) The city has a mixed industrial-commercial base.

(iii) The city has a single commercial focus situated at its most accessible part, the centre. There is much competition for central area sites because space at the centre of the city is restricted. Thus central area sites are highly valued.

(iv) Property is privately owned. There is economic competition and an efficient transport system which is equally easy, cheap and rapid in every direction within the city (i.e. the conditions which appertained in the USA in the 1920s).

(v) There is a heterogeneous population living in the city. There are contrasts in race, degree of cultural assimilation, social class and occupations. The standard of living and, by implication, volume of purchasing power, differ greatly.

(vi) The higher socio-economic groups have a greater degree of freedom of choice as against the very restricted choice of the poor.

In the absence of any of these conditions, the concentric zones will develop in, at best, a modified form.

Much of the criticism of the model perhaps misses the point of what the model is trying to achieve. It is not an attempt to provide a pattern which can be applied to all cities throughout the world in an unmodified form. Burgess recognized that in any town there will be a number of opposing factors which will prevent this from happening. The model is important rather because it represents a pioneer attempt to give some meaning to the complexities of morphological zones within an urban system and to suggest a process of urban growth which might give rise to these. It provides a refreshingly novel way of looking at cities and a yardstick with which the structure of any city can be compared.

ASSIGNMENTS

1. List the factors which Burgess considered might distort the development of concentric zones in a town. Summarize other 'opposing factors'.

2. Why does the concentric zone model lack 'universality' (i.e. it cannot be applied to any city throughout the world)?

3. How far does the distribution of council estates in Sunderland (see Fig. 4.5) comply with the key concepts of residential segregation envisaged in the Burgess model? Account for the discrepancy.

4. Devise a simple, generalized model to illustrate social structures within the town of Popayan, Columbia (Fig. 4.4). In what respects does your model differ from the Burgess model? Try to account for the differences.

5. (a) Why is it necessary to make the simplifying assumptions suggested by Quinn and Schnøre?

(b) Consider each of the simplifying assumptions in turn. Suggest how the model would need to be modified if it did not apply.

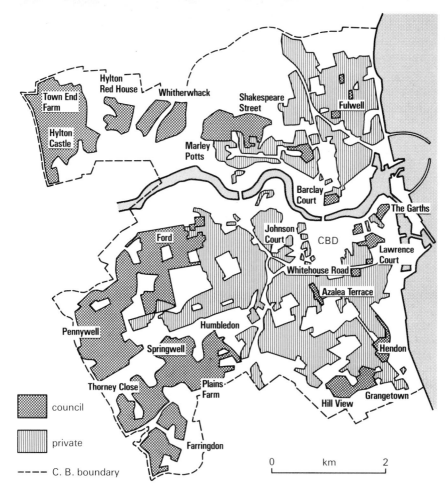

Fig. 4.5   The distribution of council estates in Sunderland. (Source: B. T. Robson, *Urban Analysis: a Study of City Structure with Special Reference to Sunderland*, CUP, 1975, p.97)

2. The sector model

The concentric zone model has proved to be remarkably persistent and has acted as a point of reference for much later research into urban structure, the most notable example being Homer Hoyt's sector model[9] (see Fig 4.6).

The sector model should be seen as an extension of the Burgess concentric zone model. It was developed from research conducted by Hoyt into residential rent patterns which were mapped by blocks in sixty-four widely distributed American cities. Hoyt's findings were first published in 1939 in a volume of the US Federal Housing Administration, *The structure and growth of residential neighbourhoods in American cities*.

Hoyt concluded that 'there is a general pattern of rent that applies to all cities . . . rent areas in American cities tend to conform to a pattern of sectors rather than of concentric circles'.[10] In other words, residential areas of a particular class develop outwards from the city centre in the form of wedges or sectors. Thus a residential

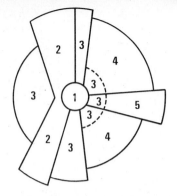

1 Central Business District

2 wholesale light manufacturing

3 low class residential

4 medium class residential

5 high class residential

Fig. 4.6   Hoyt's sector model of urban land use. (Source: after H. Hoyt, *The Structure and Growth of Residential Neighbourhoods in American Cities*, US Federal Housing Administration, Washington, 1939).

district of a particular class in one sector of the city would migrate outwards in that direction by new growth on its outer edge. He further suggested that because the high income groups could afford to pay for the most desirable sites the 'high-grade residential areas pre-empted the most desirable space and were powerful forces in the pattern of urban growth.'[11] Other grades of residential areas were arranged around the high-grade areas, the poorest occupying the least desirable land in the zone in transition or adjacent to manufacturing districts. (See Fig. 4.7.)

Hoyt suggested that sectors, rather than concentric zones, developed because of differences in accessibility from outlying districts to the city centre. The high-class housing estates were built in those sectors where transport links with the city were particularly good as, for example, along a suburban railway line. He contended that sectors were most likely to develop in towns which had a radial network of routes diverging from the city centre. Hoyt also found that sectors of high-class residential areas were particularly well pronounced towards: (a) high ground and open spaces; (b) existing outlying, smaller settlements; (c) the homes of influential leaders within the community.

The process of sector development is well exemplified by Pritchard's sequence of maps of the social geography of Leicester 1870–1958 which are reproduced in Fig. 4.8. They clearly demonstrate the development of a high-class residential district in the south east of the town which migrated outwards as the town grew. By 1911 it had reached the town boundary and could shift no farther. Thereafter, gradually, it was virtually surrounded by housing districts of only slightly lesser quality which acted as a buffer, shielding the exclusive residential district from the 'encroachment' of working-class property.

The sector model has been criticized on the grounds that it is constrained by its narrow focus on housing and rent. There have, however, been a number of attempts to extend the scope of the model. R. L. Morrill, for example, suggests that a variety of complementary uses occurs within each sector, with the intensity of land use decreasing with distance from the CBD.

> Thus, within the upper-class sector, for instance, the gradient will go from wealthy shops, to expensive high-rise apartments, to older upper-class apartments, through newer upper-class residential suburbs and industries that utilize professional skills, such as research laboratories.[12]

96

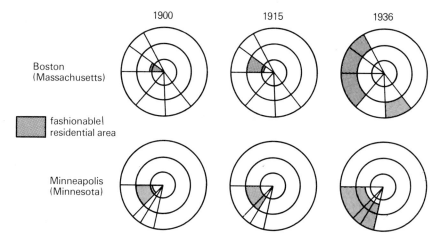

Fig. 4.7   A theoretical pattern of the migration of 'high rent' residential areas over time in two US cities. (Source: after *The Structure and Growth of Residential Neighbourhoods in American Cities*, Federal Housing Administration, 1939, p.115)

The sector model complements rather than contradicts the concentric zone model by adding a *directional element* while not discounting the distance variable. It pays more attention than the Burgess model to the importance of transport in the functioning of a city, and has proved to be a more useful tool in incorporating industrial districts into an analysis of urban structure.

It has been suggested that the two models are essentially complementary because each describes a different facet of urban social structure. Hoyt's research into rents and house values was essentially concerned with the distribution of the socio-economic variable, social status and class, within the city and this was found to be sectoral. In contrast, Burgess's research was based primarily on the density of settlement and the distribution of different house types. Both these elements are indicative of stages in the family life cycle, i.e. family size and composition, and this was found to be zonal.

ASSIGNMENTS

1.   How does the evidence presented in Fig. 4.8 support Hoyt's sector theory?
2.   Which factors did Hoyt suggest influenced the directional movement of the sectors of high class housing in a city?
3.   (a) In what ways does Morrill envisage a decrease in the intensity of land use the farther it is from the CBD?
      (b) How does Morrill's modified sector model differ from that devised by Hoyt?
4.   How far do the criticisms of the concentric zone model developed on pages 91 to 94 also apply to the sector model?

Fig. 4.8   The social geography of Leicester 1870–1938. (Source: R. M. Pritchard, *Housing and the Social Structure of the City*, CUP, 1976, pp.81, 83, 84, 87)

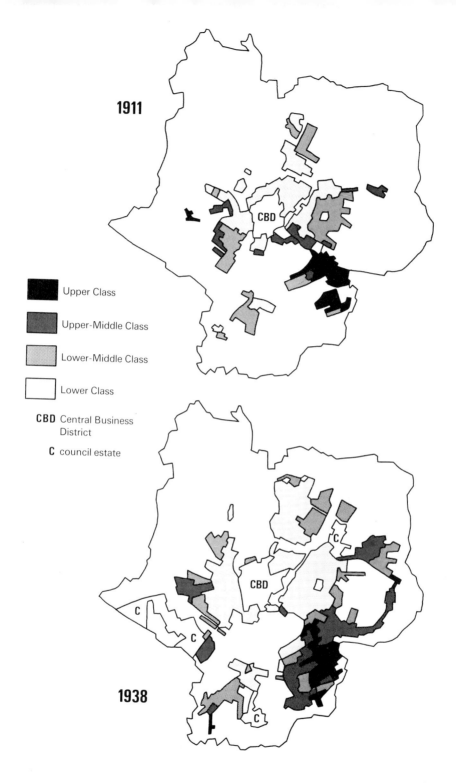

1911

Upper Class

Upper-Middle Class

Lower-Middle Class

Lower Class

CBD Central Business District

C council estate

CBD

1938

C

C

C

CBD

C

C

3. Composite models

(a) The multiple nuclei model

Both the concentric and sector models envisage zones developing outwards from a single centre. C. D. Harris and E. L. Ullman challenged this idea, abandoning the CBD as the sole focal point, and suggesting alternatively that the zones will develop around a number of quite separate discrete nuclei in addition to the CBD.[13] (See Fig. 4.9.) The number of nuclei will depend on the size of the city, and the larger the city

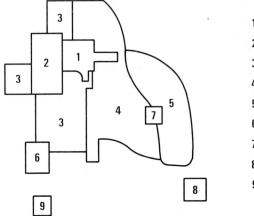

1 Central Business District

2 wholesale light manufacturing

3 low class residential

4 medium class residential

5 high class

6 heavy manufacturing

7 outlying business district

8 residential suburb

9 industrial suburb

Fig. 4.9   Harris and Ullman's multiple nuclei theory of urban structure. (Source: after C. D. Harris & E. L. Ullman, *The Nature of Cities*, Annals of the American Academy of Political and Social Science, 1945)

the more numerous and specialized are the nuclei. Some of the nuclei, such as some of the suburban shopping centres, could be quite recent developments, while others will have been former village and small town centres which have been enveloped by the city's growth. Harris and Ullman suggested that the reasons for the development of functional zones were combinations of:

(i) *Specialized requirements of certain activities.*   For example, shops need to be accessible to their customers; industry requires large blocks of relatively cheap land.

(ii) *Tendency for like activities to group together.*   With this arrangement shops benefit through an increase in the number of potential customers and the customers benefit because they can compare goods and prices in near-by shops before making a purchase.

(iii) *The repulsion of some activities by others.*   Certain unlike activities such as heavy industry and high-class housing are detrimental to each other and are, therefore, unlikely to be located close together.

(iv) *Differences in the ability of various activities to pay rents and rates.*   Only large prosperous commercial enterprises can afford to pay the high site values demanded in the city centre whereas warehousing, which requires much space, is commercially feasible only on cheaper sites.

The multiple nuclei model envisages that the city will neither develop along zonal nor sectoral lines but will take on a cellular structure in which distinctive forms of land use have developed around certain nuclei within the urban area. Thus heavy industry may be concentrated on the floor of a low-lying valley; zones of light industry may develop along the main road and rail routes and better residential areas may be concentrated on higher ground away from noxious industry.

(b)   The Mann model

Both the concentric zone and sector models were developed from research conducted in American cities. As a result of his empirical studies in Huddersfield, Nottingham and Sheffield, P. H. Mann[14] combined both models to produce a revised model which applies to a medium-sized British city which is not part of a conurbation but which is large enough to depict functional zones (see Fig. 4.10).

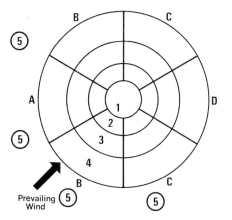

1 Central Business District

2 Transitional zone

3 Zone of small terrace houses in sectors C, D· larger by-law housing in sector B; large old houses in sector A.

4 Post 1918 residential areas, with post 1945 development mainly on the periphery.

5 Commuting distance 'dormitory' towns

A Middle class sector

B Lower middle class sector

C Working class sector (and main council estates)

D Industry and lowest working class sector

Fig. 4.10   Mann's model of the structure of a hypothetical British city. (Source: after P. Mann, *An Approach to Urban Sociology*, Routledge & Kegan Paul, 1965)

The model identifies a CBD surrounded by a zone in transition which, Mann contends, may be seen best on the sides of cities which lead to the more middle-class residential areas. Extending outwards from the CBD are sectors of different social status, where industry is associated with the 'lowest working-class sector'. The model assumes the prevailing wind is south-westerly and, therefore, the most expensive residential sectors are in the west and industrial sectors in the east. He suggested that the sectors of working-class houses are likely to be more extensive or more numerous than those of middle-class houses as the working-class population outnumbers that of the middle-class by three to one.

Mann saw the concentric element in his model as being largely a reflection of houses of a particular age rather than a particular type. Thus houses become progressively newer the farther they are from the CBD. In Zone 4, both council and private houses will probably occur but their distribution is likely to reinforce the class sectors which already existed.

The ideas encapsulated in Mann's model have been refined by B. T. Robson.[15] He envisaged that three factors, *socio-economic status*, *age structure* (including stages in the family life cycle) and *housing environment* (including house tenure) collectively exerted a considerable impact on the structure of British cities. He represented the

101

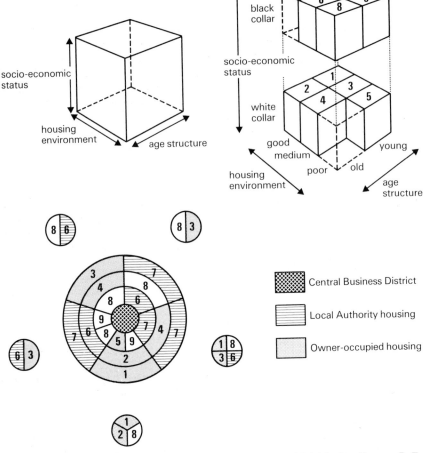

Fig. 4.11 Social, housing, and physical space in an idealized British city. (Source: B. T. Robson, *Urban Social Areas*, OUP, 1975, p.27)

inter-relationship of these in a three-dimensional diagram within which he envisaged the following sub-types (see Fig. 4.11):

Type 1 Inter-war owner-occupied
Type 2 High-status owner-occupied
Type 3 Post-war semi-detached owner-occupied
Type 4 Post-war detached owner-occupied
Type 5 Student bedsitters
Type 6 Inter-war council estates/inner-city council flats
Type 7 Post-war council estates/inner-city high-rise
Type 8 Privately rented low status
Type 9 Rooming

These sub-types are superimposed on the city structure diagram in Fig. 4.11. The model incorporates both sectoral and concentric elements. Socio-economic status can be seen as sectoral and stages in the family life cycle concentric, but superimposed on this pattern is house tenure which adds a further complication.

(c) The Rees model

Rees, basing his conclusions on detailed work conducted in Chicago which is developed further in the next chapter (see pages 127 to 131), adds another element, *ethnicity*, in the development of his composite model (see Fig. 4.12).[16] Socio-economic status again takes on a sectoral form (A) and stages in the family life-cycle a concentric form (B), being related to housing of different age and type. The ethnic areas form nuclei (C) which are superimposed on the simpler structure (D and E). The composite model (I) has been transformed to reflect the shape of the physical growth of Chicago (F) and to take account of the existence of industrial concentrations.

(d) The Lawton model

The Mann model is a useful descriptive tool but it throws little light on the processes of urban growth which interact to create the urban structure. In contrast, Professor R. Lawton's model (see Fig. 4.13), largely derived from research into social and demographic conditions in Liverpool, examines the processes of urban development in the nineteenth century. The model identifies a historic nucleus with 'successive belts of housing wrapped around the older city' and within these 'sectors of individuality, derived from the character of adjacent areas'.[17] The concentric development of the city (stages A, A1 and A2) reflects its cyclical growth – the city growing rapidly during phases of prosperity but consolidating or even stagnating during periods of recession. On Merseyside, for example, the pre-1914 building booms occurred in the 1840s (associated with Irish immigration), the early 1860s, the late 1870s and the 1900s. Within these successive belts of housing the morphological details of development were greatly influenced by topography and pre-existing patterns of land ownership. Villages, and even small towns, were overtaken by the outward growth of the city and became absorbed within the built-up area as inliers of older buildings with more varied functions.

These rapid phases of growth were made possible initially by in-migration from surrounding rural areas and neighbouring small towns. The intensity of migration into different sectors of the city was influenced by the competition from other centres of attraction which presented 'intervening opportunities' to the migrant. Many of the migrants at first moved to the poorest housing conditions in or close to the historic core of the city, while some moved straight away to the relatively cheap working-class houses which were being developed in new estates on the edge of the built-up area. There was also a much less intensive counter current of dissatisfied migrants, many of whom returned to their places of origin.

The model also considers the role of intra-urban movement in the development of the city. Some of the poorer working-class families eventually moved into better residential districts in a form of classic invasion-succession while the middle class developed, through contiguous outward growth, a distinct sector of more advantaged houses. Contemporary with this sector development, some of the more affluent and adventurous families established homes in peripheral villages which, consequently, took on a suburban role. Patterns of in-migration and intra-urban migration are well exemplified in Lawton and Pooley's schematic diagram of mid-Victorian Liverpool's urban structure (see Fig. 4.14).

Professor Lawton claims no universal applicability for his model. 'Yet, if we are to understand and *explain* the facts revealed by detailed studies, ideas of this kind are

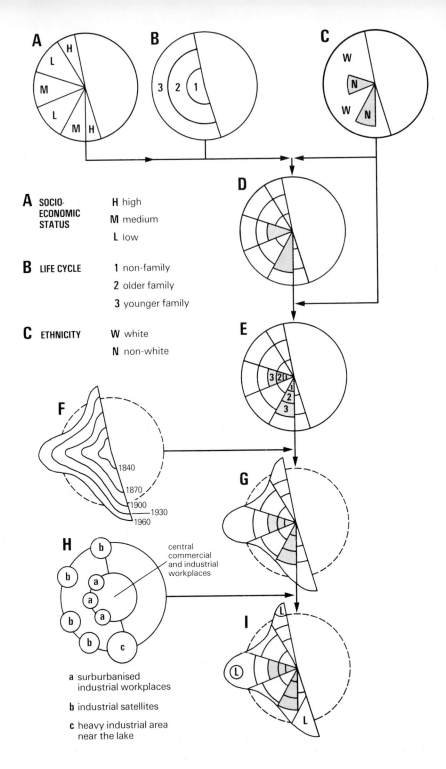

A SOCIO-
ECONOMIC
STATUS

H high
M medium
L low

B LIFE CYCLE

1 non-family
2 older family
3 younger family

C ETHNICITY

W white
N non-white

central
commercial
and industrial
workplaces

a surburbanised
industrial workplaces

b industrial satellites

c heavy industrial area
near the lake

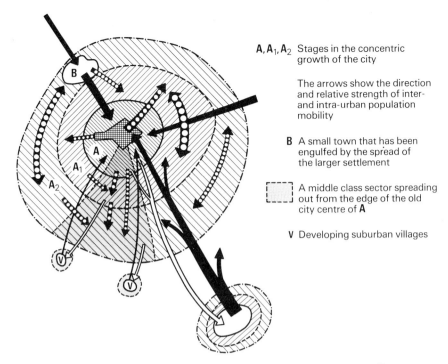

A,A₁,A₂ Stages in the concentric growth of the city

The arrows show the direction and relative strength of inter- and intra-urban population mobility

B A small town that has been engulfed by the spread of the larger settlement

A middle class sector spreading out from the edge of the old city centre of **A**

V Developing suburban villages

Fig. 4.13   Lawton's model of urban development in the nineteenth century. (Source: R. Lawton, 'An Age of Great Cities', *Town Planning Review*, 1973, Vol. 43)

useful as theories against which individual cases may be tested and from which lessons of practical relevance from other places and other times may be drawn.'[18]

ASSIGNMENTS

1. Describe the sequence of diagrams shown in Fig. 4.15. How far is it possible to regard the sector and multiple nuclei models as extensions of the concentric zone model in a way analogous to the development of Von Thünen's land use model?[19]

2. Do observations made in your nearest large town support Mann's contention that the zone in transition can be seen best in those sides of towns which lead to the more middle-class residential areas? Why is this likely to be the case?

3. What influence does the prevailing south-westerly wind exert in localizing certain functional zones within a city?

4. (a) Discuss the modifications which need to be made to Professor Lawton's model to take into account twentieth-century urban growth. Consider the development of municipal estates; New Town development; overspill into expanding towns; urban growth; urban renewal.

    (b) In what respects does Lawton and Pooley's model of mid-Victorian Liverpool's urban structure include both sectoral and concentric elements?

    (c) Give a reasoned explanation of the population movements which contributed to the city's structure.

◀ Fig. 4.12   An integrated model of the structure of Chicago. (Source: after P. H. Rees 'Concepts of Social Space; towards an Urban Social Geography' from B. J. L. Berry and F. E. Horton, *Geographic Perspectives on the Urban System*, Prentice Hall, 1970, p.310)

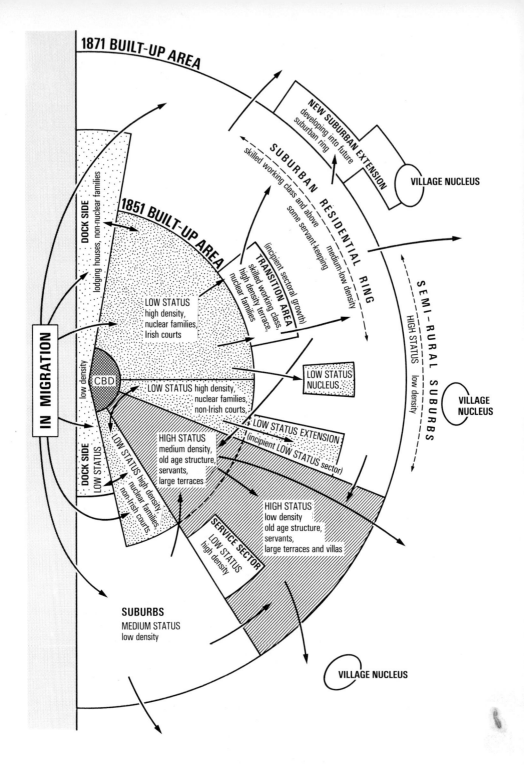

1871 BUILT-UP AREA

NEW SUBURBAN EXTENSION
developing into future
suburban ring

VILLAGE NUCLEUS

SUBURBAN RESIDENTIAL RING

Skilled working class and above
some servant-keeping
medium-low density

SEMI-RURAL SUBURBS
HIGH STATUS
low density

VILLAGE NUCLEUS

DOCK SIDE
lodging houses, non-nuclear families

1851 BUILT-UP AREA

TRANSITION AREA
(incipient sectoral growth)
skilled working class,
high density terrace,
nuclear families

LOW STATUS
high density,
nuclear families,
Irish courts

low density

CBD

LOW STATUS high density,
nuclear families,
non-Irish courts,

LOW STATUS
NUCLEUS

LOW STATUS EXTENSION
(incipient LOW STATUS sector)

IN MIGRATION

DOCK SIDE
LOW STATUS

LOW STATUS high density,
nuclear families,
non-Irish courts

HIGH STATUS
medium density,
old age structure,
servants,
large terraces

HIGH STATUS
low density
old age structure,
servants,
large terraces and villas

SERVICE SECTOR
LOW STATUS
high density

SUBURBS
MEDIUM STATUS
low density

VILLAGE NUCLEUS

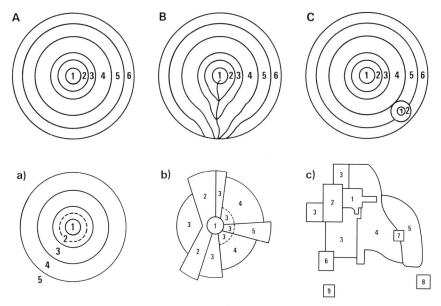

Fig. 4.15   Von Thünen's model (A) of rural land use and his two modifications (B and C) (for explanation of key see Fig. 8.6) compared with the concentric (a), sector (b), and multiple nuclei (c) urban models. (Source: D. T. Herbert, *Urban Geography: A Social Perspective,* David & Charles, 1972, p.73)

(e)   An empirical study of the structure of Sunderland
Fig. 4.16 illustrates B. T. Robson's idealized model of the patterns of residential segregation in Sunderland. It was obtained by superimposing rateable values of houses, which are based on the amenities of a property and its general location, and the degree of subdivided houses in the private sector. Robson describes his model as follows:

> The Central Business District lies to the south of the river with industrial areas following both banks of the river and extending south along the coast to the south of the river mouth. The residential pattern in the north has some elements of the sectoral developments suggested by Hoyt (in that the highest rated area forms a partial sector adjacent to the amenity area of the seaboard), but in the main the northern area is in the form of a series of concentric rings of the Burgess type, progressing outwards from a poor, subdivided zone adjacent to the industrial area flanking the river, through a medium-rated area extending to the east-west railway line, and to a higher rated zone north of this and running to the boundary of the town. To the south of the river, the residential areas have developed a pattern closely akin to the sectoral model of Hoyt with four principal sectors: a low-class sector in the east which is highly subdivided at its northern apex; a highly rated sector next to it which reaches out from the inner areas in an expanding area to the southern boundary; a middle-class sector running out to the west; and finally, a second low-rated sector flanking the industrial areas of the river. As Hoyt's model would suggest, a

◀ Fig. 4.14   A schematic diagram of mid-Victorian Liverpool's urban structure. (Source: after R. Lawton and C. Pooley, *The Social Geography of Nineteenth Century Liverpool*, Final report to S.S.R.C., University of Liverpool Geography Department)

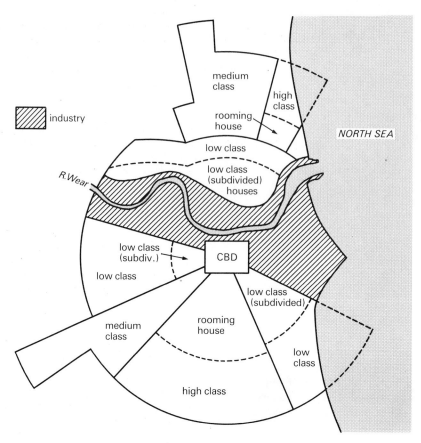

Fig. 4.16　A model of patterns of residential segregation in Sunderland, 1963. (Source: B. T. Robson, *Urban Social Areas*, OUP, 1975, p.12)

> rooming-house area has developed at the townward apexes of both of the highly rated sectors, one to the north of the river, the other, more extensive, to the south.'[20]

Robson refers to the juxtaposition of sectoral development in one part of the town with concentric ring development in another and suggests that neither the Burgess nor the Hoyt model can provide a total explanation of the patterns of residential segregation.

Robson contends that the location of the high-class residential areas exerts great influence in the total urban structure. He suggests that the two principal factors which determine their location are:

1. *Maximum accessibility* to the CBD while meeting certain other requirements such as a good site, nearness to amenity land and access to the sea front.
2. *Avoidance of industrial areas*, particularly, as in Sunderland, where much local manufacturing industry is heavy and noxious.

Collectively these two factors are primarily responsible for determining the residential pattern and help to explain the development of sectors and concentric zones on opposite sides of the river. To the south, direct access to the CBD could be achieved by residential sectors which were not in contact with the industrial belt fringing the river. This, however, was not possible to the north of the river where a concentric zone of lower-rated housing developed to act as a buffer between the industrial belt and the area of better quality housing.

ASSIGNMENT
Robson suggests that empirical research conducted in other river-based towns with industrial zones fringing the river and the CBD close to but not adjacent to the river indicates that a structure similar to that of Sunderland will develop, i.e. sectors and concentric zones will be juxtaposed. Refer to Lawton and Pooley's model (Fig. 4.14) and consider how far this is true of nineteenth-century Liverpool.

C. Gradient Studies

A great virtue of the Burgess and Hoyt models is their simplicity. They are generalized descriptive models which also suggest a mechanism for urban growth. They remain useful as a way of representing land use patterns within a city by identifying broad zones. However, since they are based on empirical research they are essentially *inductive* rather than *deductive*. Later attempts to present the models in the form of a deductive theory led inevitably into the field of gradient studies.

1. Land economics and urban land use: gradient theory

Within an urban system, land values are determined by location, an idea first put forward by R. M. Hurd in 1903.[21] As a city grows, so remoter and therefore inferior locations are brought into use. This has the effect of increasing the value of the more accessible, central sites as more potential users compete for a convenient site which can minimise transport costs or the costs of *friction of distance*. This competition for land finds expression in terms of economic rent – the price potential users are prepared to pay for accessibility. Thus patterns of land use within cities are arrived at through the competition of functions for favourable locations. 'The use that can extract the greatest return from a given site will be the successful bidder'.[22] This gives rise to the development of an orderly pattern of land use within an urban system, spatially organized so that the various functions which are integral to urban life can be carried out most efficiently.

Fig. 4.17 illustrates the rent-paying ability (i.e. 'bid rents') of each broad category of land user, against distance from a single, most accessible central core. Retail users will compete for the most accessible, central sites which will provide them with the greatest customer potential and thereby enable them to maximise profits. Offices also require accessibility and a central location in order to assemble their substantial work forces, but these can avoid the very high rents of the peak land value intersection (see page 162), and can afford to be located in a more marginal central location. Likewise, multi-storey flats will give larger returns per unit area of land than single houses for families and will, therefore, be able to compete for more accessible locations. They will not, however, be able to compete with the rent-paying ability of commercial enterprises. Agricultural uses are the least intensive and are, therefore, outbid by all urban uses. If the separate graphs are superimposed, some indication

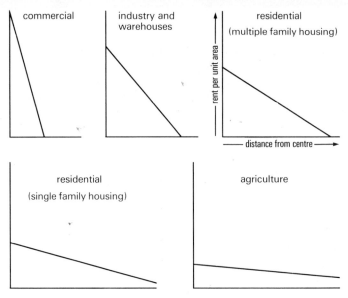

Fig. 4.17　Bid rents for different users of urban land in relation to distance from the city centre. (Source: after B. J. L. Berry, 'The spatial organization of business land uses' from W. L. Garrison et al, *Studies of Highway Development and Geographic Change*, Greenwood, 1959)

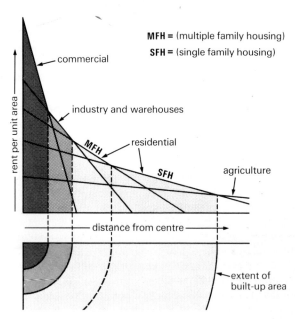

Fig. 4.18　Graphs to show the idealized relationship between bid rents and urban land use. (Source: G. J. Fielding, *Geography as Social Science*, Harper & Row, 1975, p.166)

of the dominant land use in relation to distance from the city centre can be obtained. (See Fig. 4.18.)

The urban land market can thus be visualized as a rent or land-value surface. The market centre will be the point of the highest site value. As rent declines with distance, value falls and land uses change. If sites of equal value are connected in the form of a series of contours, then a configuration of a cone-like structure emerges (see Fig. 4.19). Note the extremely high value attached to the city centre sites in

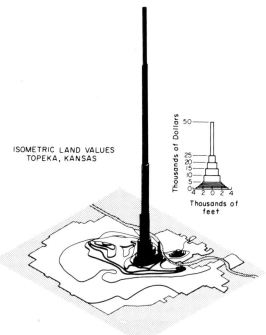

Fig. 4.19   The distribution of land values in Topeka, Kansas. (Source: after D. Knoss, *Distribution of Land Values in Topeka*, (Lawrence, Kansas) 1962)

Topeka and the very steep decline of these values with distance from the centre.

Similar research conducted in a number of cities has enabled a generalized picture of the average land-value surface to be obtained. The highest values occur in the city centre and decrease towards the periphery. The surface is modified, however, by two additional elements:

(a)   Main traffic arteries that have higher land values.
(b)   The intersections of main arteries where secondary commercial centres develop.

The development of additional nuclei causes the surface to be modified in a way illustrated in Fig. 4.20.

Distance from the market centre has been the only variable so far considered. W. Alonso[23] suggested that, in reality, the rent bid curve is derived from a whole series of factors. He highlights just two of these:

(a)   The quantity of land which each user wishes to acquire. For example, the house

(a) Small single centre town

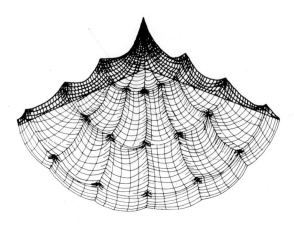

(b) Large city

Fig. 4.20   The pattern of land values in relation to main roads and secondary commercial centres. (Source: after J. Simmons, *The Changing Pattern of Retail Locations*, Research Paper No. 92, 1964)

purchaser or industrialist may prefer to purchase larger plots of land in less convenient locations.

(b) Individual tastes and preferences which determine how users spend their disposable income. In this case, the amount spent on land and travel costs as a proportion of that spent on all goods and services. Some will choose to devote a higher proportion of their disposable income to travel costs in order to secure the advantages of a suburban environment.

   Alonso suggests that it is through the complex interaction of each of these variables, as well as others not identified, that the individual arrives at an equilibrium solution to the problem of the optimum location of home or business. This will depend on how the user values convenience as opposed to amenity, the priorities by which he or she allocates any disposable income, and so on.

ASSIGNMENTS

1. *Look at Fig. 4.18 (page 110). How far do the zones projected from the idealized gradient of land rent as a function of distance from the CBD conform to those envisaged by Burgess in his concentric zone model?*

2. *How does the development of secondary commercial centres cause the idealized gradient of land rent to be modified?*

2. Urban density gradients

Since 1918 the built-up area of most British towns has increased greatly, very largely through the development of low density residential suburbs. The inter-war sub-urbs, in particular, often have spacious layouts and incorporate many of the 'garden city' concepts developed by such pioneers as Ebenezer Howard and Patrick Geddes. This rapid growth was made possible by the improvement of public transport services. Most of the low density development occurred on the edge of the built-up area so that C. Clark,[24] working in the early 1950s, was able to hypothesize that population densities decline according to their distance from the city centre. That is, the population densities decrease at a slower rate the farther the area is from the centre. Clark tested his hypothesis by the technique of *gradient analysis*. For thirty-six cities throughout the world and using population data from 1801 to 1950, he compiled scatter diagrams plotting the logarithms of population density (the dependent variable) on the y axis, and the distance from the city centre (the independent variable) on the x axis and confirmed that densities decline with distance from the city centre.

Work conducted in the early 1960s in a number of American cities by B. J. L. Berry, J. W. Simmons and R. J. Tennant[25] demonstrated, however, a weakening of this

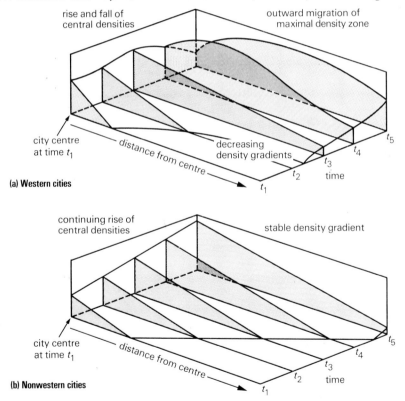

Fig. 4.21   Urban density gradients in western and non-western cities. (Source: after B. J. L. Berry et al, *Geographical Review* 1963, **53**, p.403)

relationship. They concluded that the gradient has tended to flatten out in post-war years as a result of:

(a) Urban renewal
Since 1945 slum clearance programmes have been accelerated and many former areas of nineteenth-century terraces have been comprehensively redeveloped. This has invariably resulted in a reduction in the population density. This is the case even where multi-storey blocks of flats have been constructed as much more open space is provided after redevelopment.

(b) Acute land shortages in the suburbs
An increased demand for lower density semi-detached and detached houses and planning policies which restrict the amount of land available for building, have caused land values to rise steeply. One response to this has been the construction of much higher density housing estates in the suburbs since about 1950.

ASSIGNMENTS
1. *Table 4.1 provides details of population densities of Liverpool wards for 1951, 1961, and 1971. (See Fig. 4.22.) Using semi-logarithmic graph paper, draw scatter diagrams which plot the population of each ward against mean distance from the CBD for each of the post-war decadal censuses. Regression analysis may be used to test the significance of the degree of relationship between the two variables. Alternatively, if the sets of data are ranked, Spearman's Rank Correlation could be employed (see pages 192 to 193).*

    Do the urban densities gradients for Liverpool tend to flatten out from 1951 to 1971? Why?
2. *Fig. 4.21 illustrates changes in the urban density gradients that have occurred in western and non-western cities. The non-western cities graph is based primarily on analyses of population data of Indian cities. In what key respects do the two graphs differ? Attempt to account for these differences. Consider also the contrasting impact of transport technology.*

Key Ideas

A. Functional zones
1. The pattern of urban growth is influenced and, at times, constrained by natural barriers and lines of communication.
2. There is a tendency for different functions to occupy different areas within the town.
3. Within the broad functional zones, more subtle spatial contrasts can often be identified, based on for example, building age, ownership, environmental quality or categories of function.
4. A town's morphology includes both the arrangement and lay-out of buildings and the function of land and buildings.
5. Urban structure describes the significant spatial relationships that exist between broad land use zones.

Name of ward	Mean distance from City Centre (km.)	Area (ha.)	1951 poptn.	1951 density per ha.	1961 poptn.	1961 density per ha.	1971 poptn.	1971 density per ha.
Abercromby	1.3	106	22 264	210	17 887	168.7	8 125	76.65
Aigburth	6.1	474	17 894	37.8	18 788	39.6	18 640	39.32
Allerton	7.1	650	12 164	18.7	14 019	21.6	14 288	21.98
Anfield	3.5	219	23 174	105.8	20 020	91.4	18 560	84.75
Arundel	3.8	204	19 176	94	18 541	90.9	18 653	91.44
Breckfield	2.5	70	19 137	273.4	16 613	237.3	11 629	166.13
Broadgreen	5.6	270	18 372	68	17 064	63.2	16 532	61.23
Central	0.7	248	15 816	63.8	12 571	50.7	7 321	29.52
Childwall	6.3	503	18 570	36.9	24 262	48.2	23 739	47.19
Church	4.8	324	19 790	61.1	18 632	57.5	18 549	57.25
Clubmoor	5.0	206	17 683	85.8	15 863	77	15 212	73.84
County	4.5	174	22 903	131.6	19 488	112	17 101	98.28
Croxteth	5.9	464	13 672	29.5	16 626	35.8	16 833	36.28
Dingle	3.4	143	25 175	176	19 721	137.9	13 006	90.95
Dovecot	7.1	385	24 825	64.5	23 096	60	24 392	63.36
Everton	1.6	87	22 493	258.5	17 195	197.6	4 429	50.91
Fairfield	3.1	244	22 546	92.4	20 832	85.4	14 866	60.93
Fazakerley	7.2	308	18 836	61.2	16 482	53.5	16 857	54.73
Gillmoss	7.7	738	19 955	27	27 293	37	29 135	39.48
Granby	2.1	77	19 625	254.9	18 239	236.9	12 237	158.92
Kensington	2.3	101	20 915	207.1	18 129	179.5	14 134	139.94
Low Hill	1.6	71	18 046	254.2	14 706	207.1	5 951	83.82
Melrose	3.4	75	16 891	225.2	14 135	188.5	10 499	139.99
Netherfield	1.8	54	17 488	323.9	13 853	256.5	5 886	109.00
Old Swan	4.5	215	24 924	115.9	21 679	100.8	18 774	87.32
Picton	3.5	152	23 211	152.7	20 639	135.8	17 238	113.41
Pirrie	6.3	508	26 812	52.8	24 603	48.4	22 598	44.48
Princes Park	2.6	118	21 700	183.9	20 272	171.8	11 760	99.66
St. Domingo	2.3	72	21 082	292.8	18 461	256.4	7 026	97.58
St. James	1.0	279	21 215	76	18 800	67.4	13 039	46.73
St. Mary's	8.5	492	18 259	37.1	17 495	35.6	14 277	29.02
St. Michael's	4.0	310	13 719	44.3	13 502	43.6	13 153	42.43
Sandhills	4.3	372	18 686	50.2	15 810	42.5	8 004	21.52
Smithdown	2.3	100	22 400	224	19 760	197.6	10 260	102.60
Speke	11.4	871	17 040	19.6	27 142	31.2	22 881	26.27
Tuebrook	4.0	175	21 073	120.4	18 622	106.4	16 068	91.82
Vauxhall	1.8	83	20 459	246.5	15 684	189	8 287	99.84
Warbreck	5.8	274	22 252	81.2	20 699	75.5	18 844	68.77
Westminster	2.9	57	13 808	242.2	11 867	208.2	8 509	149.28
Woolton	8.3	982	16 788	17.1	26 660	27.1	41 211	41.97

115

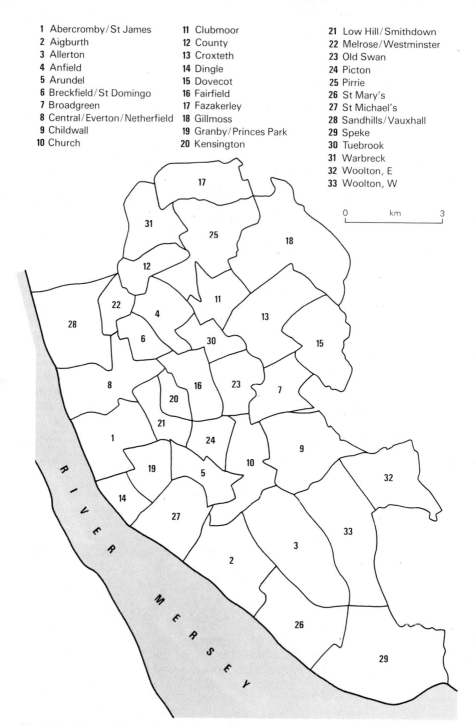

1 Abercromby/St James
2 Aigburth
3 Allerton
4 Anfield
5 Arundel
6 Breckfield/St Domingo
7 Broadgreen
8 Central/Everton/Netherfield
9 Childwall
10 Church

11 Clubmoor
12 County
13 Croxteth
14 Dingle
15 Dovecot
16 Fairfield
17 Fazakerley
18 Gillmoss
19 Granby/Princes Park
20 Kensington

21 Low Hill/Smithdown
22 Melrose/Westminster
23 Old Swan
24 Picton
25 Pirrie
26 St Mary's
27 St Michael's
28 Sandhills/Vauxhall
29 Speke
30 Tuebrook
31 Warbreck
32 Woolton, E
33 Woolton, W

Fig. 4.22   Electoral district wards, Liverpool 1974.

B. *Models of urban structure*

   B1   The concentric zone model (Burgess)

(a) The model described

1. Within the city different functions compete for limited space.
2. In certain areas of the city single functions dominate to form distinctive functional zones.
3. The functional zones are arranged concentrically around the city centre.
4. Lower status groups are to be found near the city centre and the high status groups at the periphery.
5. Both within and traversing the concentric zones are natural areas, that is districts which are culturally distinctive.
6. The idealized concentric zones will be modified by 'opposing factors'.
7. Towns grow by a process of invasion and succession whereby population groups gradually filter outwards as their status and level of assimilation improve.

(b) Criticisms of the concentric zone model

1. The model emphasizes clear cut boundaries between the concentric zones but gradient studies indicate no such abrupt divisions.
2. The model is rooted in a specific historical and cultural context and, therefore, lacks universality.
3. Since the 1930s, fundamental changes have occurred in Western cities and these make the model less appropriate.
4. In the pre-industrial city both past and present high status groups frequently live near the city centre and the poorest families on the edge of the built-up area.
5. Only if certain conditions are met will the idealized concentric zones develop in a town.

   B2 The sector model (Hoyt)

1. The sector model envisages that residential areas of a particular class develop outwards from the city centre in the form of wedges or sectors.
2. The model adds a directional element while not discounting the distance variable.
3. High-grade residential areas pre-empt the most desirable locations and are powerful forces in urban growth.
4. Differences in accessibility within a town influence the location of sectors of different status.
5. The Burgess and Hoyt models are complementary and describe different facets of urban social structure.

   B3 Composite models

1. *The multiple nuclei model (Harris and Ullman)*

   The multiple nuclei model envisages a city with a cellular structure with distinctive forms of land use developing around a number of discrete nuclei.

2. *The Mann model*

   The Mann model combines sectors and concentric zones to produce a model applicable to a medium-sized British town. Robson suggests that the structure of British cities is derived from the inter-relationship of socio-economic status, stages in the family life cycle and housing tenure. In broad terms, socio-economic status is arranged sectorally and stages in the family life cycle concentrically.

3. *The Rees model*

   Rees considers also the influence of ethnicity as a factor influencing urban structure.

4. *The Lawton model*

   (a) During the nineteenth century urban growth was cyclical, periods of rapid development alternating with periods of little growth. This accounts for the concentric element within the city.

   (b) A middle-class sector developed through contiguous outward growth and beyond this peripheral villages acquired a suburban role.

C. *Gradient studies*

   C1 *Land economics and urban land use*

1. In a town land users compete for a convenient site in order to minimize the costs of friction of distance.

2. Some activities are better able than others to bid for the most accessible central area sites and this gives rise to an orderly pattern of land use.

3. Site values decline according to distance from the market centre and land use becomes progressively less intensive.

4. The rent bid curve is derived from a range of factors additional to distance from the market centre.

   C2 *Urban density gradients*

1. Population densities decline in a negative exponential form with distance from the CBD.

2. Due to urban renewal and land shortages in the suburbs the urban density gradient has tended to flatten out in post-war years in Western cities.

3. In non-Western cities urban density gradients have remained constant as the cities have grown outwards.

Additional activities

1. Burgess envisaged that towns grow by a process of invasion and succession. The process can still be seen in operation in districts of substantial Victorian villas and Georgian terraces adjacent to town centres. If there is such a district in your town you will be able to attempt some of the following suggestions to test Burgess's invasion-succession concept.

   The original function. Use street directories to determine when the villas were built and the occupation of the first head of household. If the villas were erected before 1871, refer to the census schedules (see page 47) for additional details of the composition of the entire household. Use early editions of large scale O.S. maps and plans in conjunction with the contemporary directories to construct a sequence of maps to show the changing functions of the buildings.

The conversion and replacement of villas. Map the present day functions of the villas using the following key. Record the information on an O.S. 1:2500 plan.

Notation for conversion of villas.

Villas still maintained as a single dwelling		**V**
Villas converted to flats and maisonettes (the number refers to the number of dwellings)		**F3, M4**
Villas converted to:	hotel	**C1**
	hospital/nursing home	**C2**
	school	**C3**
	shop	**C4**
	medical surgeries	**C5**
	public house	**C6**
	(list other examples)	
Vacant villa		**Va**
Record also:	conversion of outbuildings (e.g. stables into a dwelling)	**S/H**
	conversion of gardens (e.g. to provide parking space)	**G/P**
Replacement and Infilling	derelict villas	**De**
	vacant building plots	**P**
	inter-war houses	**Ih**
	bungalows	**Ib**
	flats	**If**
	post-war houses	**Ph**
	bungalows	**Pb**
	flats	**Pf**

Notes for mapping. It is often difficult to establish in the field which villas have been converted into flats. An exterior staircase, additional front doors, door bells and letter boxes provide a useful guide, but, in some cases, multiple occupancy of a villa can only be definitely established if the most recent electoral register is referred to. This lists each house and occupiers over eighteen years of age.

Try to discover how well maintained are the rear gardens of the villas and record if they are obviously neglected. The rear gardens are often quite extensive and could provide suitable building sites. If neglected, there is a greater likelihood that the house-owner would be willing to sell a part of the garden as a building plot.

The results of your survey may be summarized on a bar graph showing the total original stock of villas and the proportion converted to different functions.

Implications of building conversion

(a) Rateable values are increased if villas are converted into separate self-contained flats. Recent changes in rateable values may be obtained from the rate books.

(b) The population of the district is likely to increase if many buildings have been converted. Electoral registers provide a useful indication of changes in population density. Select the registers for ten-year intervals and place an appropriate number of dots beside each building to represent the number of people residing there in each year. Remember, however, that you are only recording the adult population and that registers for 1970 and later include eighteen to twenty-one year olds.

(c) The population structure of the district is likely to change. More families with young children may move into the area. If this is the case, are facilities such as schools, clinics and playgrounds still adequate? Such social considerations are difficult to evaluate other than by the use of sample interviews. Devise a suitable questionnaire which may be used in an area of villas to assess the implications of change.

2. Discuss the motives of individuals who deliberately choose less convenient locations (i.e. in relation to the CBD) than they can afford to pay for.

3. How far does the concentric zone model provide some understanding of the contemporary Western city?

4. How does the concept of economic rent account for the distribution of functional zones within a city?

Reading

B. The Open University, 'Zoning within Cities', *Understanding Society*. Course Unit 21.

EVERSON, J. A. & FITZGERALD, B. P., *Inside the City*, Longman, 1972, pages 21–42 and 53–75.

CHORLEY, R. J. & HAGGETT, P., (eds.), *Socio-Economic Models in Geography*, Methuen, 1968, pages 335–345.

JOHNSON, J. H., *Urban Geography, An Introductory Analysis* (2nd edition), Pergamon, 1972, pages 170–195.

C. MORRILL, R. L., *The Spatial Organization of Society*, Duxbury Press, 1970, pages 163–174.

HOYT, H., 'Recent Distortions of the Classical Models of Urban Structure', *Land Economics*, XL, **2,** May 1964, pages 199–212, and reproduced in BOURNE, L. S., (ed.), *Internal Structure of the City*, OUP, pages 84–96.

5 Residential areas

Introduction

The discussion of the internal structure of towns in the previous chapter has indicated the social patterning which can be distinguished within them. One of the more evident patterns relates to variations in the degree of well-being within the city. Though a focus of particular recent interest among urban geographers, the recognition of social contrasts in the well-being of urban residents is nothing new. For example, Charles Booth in his *Life and Labour of the People in London* included a map of poverty in London in 1889–90 (see Fig. 5.1). Using information collected by the School Board Visitors, he calculated that at that time nearly one third of London's population lived below the poverty line. His maps revealed, however, that the poor were not evenly distributed. Districts of severe poverty almost encircled the City of London and extended along the banks of the River Thames as far as the Isle of Dogs and East Greenwich. There were, in addition, outlying areas of extreme poverty in parts of Pimlico, Notting Dale, Paddington, Barnsbury, Holloway and Peckham.[1]

Booth's work was a source of inspiration for the Chicago School of urban sociology of the inter-war period (see pages 87–91). But it is only relatively recently that the full implications of social patterning have been appreciated. This chapter attempts to summarize some of the interesting research work which has been undertaken to provide a greater understanding of the patterns and processes operating within residential areas of a town.

In the opening section, quantitative techniques which have been developed to identify social sub-areas are examined. This is followed by a discussion of the concept of social space and other related key ideas. Attention then focuses on a study of the neighbourhood, which combines both spatial and social attributes. The chapter goes on to examine some of the processes which help to create social patterns in a city. In this section the factors contributing to residential segregation and (at a rather different scale) residential mobility are considered, with particular reference to the process whereby families choose where to live.

A. Social Patterning: Quantitative Approaches

Within towns it is possible to distinguish 'comparatively homogeneous sub-divisions which are characterized by an internal consistency and by a personality which distinguishes them from other parts of the city.'[2] Together these make up a mosaic of separate but inter-related sub-areas. One important aspect of the work of

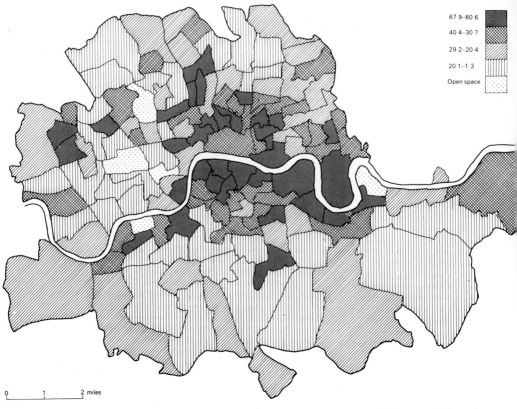

Legend:
67·9–60·6	(dark)
40·4–30·7	(medium)
29·2–20·4	(diagonal)
20·1–1·3	(vertical)
Open space	(dotted)

0   1   2 miles

Fig. 5.1   Degrees of poverty in London, 1889. (Source: after Shepherd, Westway & Lee, *A Social Atlas of London*, OUP, 1974, p.26)

urban social geographers has been to try to distinguish and delineate such sub-areas, and a number of techniques have been developed.

Some of the early attempts were based on a single criterion such as house types, the distribution of occupations, or variations in rateable value. For example, in his study of Newcastle-under-Lyme, D. T. Herbert hypothesized that spatial variations in rateable values, which are based on the amenities of a property and its general location, would provide a good indication of social difference in the town.[3] He mapped four categories of rateable value to define his sub-areas (see Fig. 5.2). Herbert tested the usefulness of rateable values as an index of social differences by mapping other, related criteria such as the distribution of house types and the homes of professional people and comparing these maps with his rateable values map. In his Sunderland study, however, B. T. Robson found that although there was a significant positive correlation between social class (as derived from the census socio-economic groups data) and rateable values for enumeration districts which included private and mixed housing estates, there was no such correlation for enumeration districts with 90 per cent and more council housing.[4] While social class varied quite markedly from one council estate to another, this was not reflected in comparable variations in rateable values. Robson concluded that rateable values are of limited value as a single measure in any attempt to distinguish social areas within a town where there are many council housing estates.

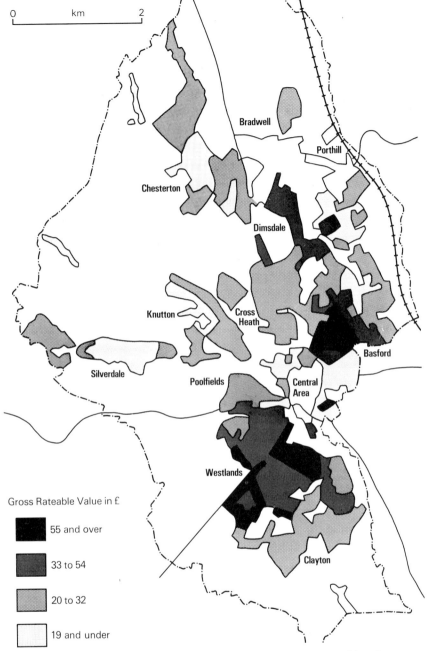

Gross Rateable Value in £

■	55 and over
▨	33 to 54
▧	20 to 32
□	19 and under

Fig. 5.2 Residential sub-areas in Newcastle-under-Lyme based on rateable values.
(Source: after D. T. Herbert, *Urban Geography; a Social Perspective*, David & Charles, 1972)

1. Social area analysis

The fundamental disadvantage of using a single criterion, such as rateable values, to define urban sub-areas is that no one criterion can take into account the great variation that exists within residential districts. Alternative techniques which incorporate a number of criteria or variables are, therefore, preferable. One such example is *social area analysis*, developed in the early 1950s by a group of American sociologists, E. Shevky, W. Bell and M. Williams.[5] They argued that the growth of towns is accompanied by fundamental social change as an urban-industrial society emerges. They evisaged the city as a product of all the complexities of modern society, and suggested that the broad changes that occur within society as a whole will be mirrored, on a much smaller scale, in the city's social organization. This in turn will be reflected in a mosaic of comparatively homogeneous sub-areas which can be delineated. The researchers' technique of analysis depended on the successful identification of these broad trends, and their measurements within the city through the use of appropriate census and other data. Table 5.1 summarizes their method.

Table 5.1. Social area analysis. (After Shevky, Bell and Williams.)

Broad societal trends	Expressed by the construct:	Measured by:
1. Changes in the distribution of skills	Economic status	Occupation: No. of skilled and unskilled manual workers, per 1000 employed persons. Education: No. of persons who had completed 8 years or less of schooling, per 1000 aged 25 years or over.
2. Changes in the structure of productive activity	Family status	Fertility: No. of children aged 0-4 years per 1000 women aged 15 to 44. Women at work: No. of females employed in relation to the total no. of females aged 15 years or over. Single-family detached dwelling units: single-family homes as a proportion of all dwellings.
3. Changes in the population composition	Ethnic status	Ethnic and minority groups in a given area in relation to their proportion in the urban areas as a whole.

This information was obtained for American cities from census tracts, small areal divisions each containing between about 3000 and 6000 persons. The scores for each variable were standardized (i.e. converted so that the spread is from 0 to 100) and the scores for the sets of variables were then combined to give average scores for the

124

constructs of economic status and family status. This information was then plotted on to a two-dimensional 'social space' diagram which had as its axes economic status and family status. Four broad categories were distinguished on each axis, giving a possible sixteen types of sub-areas arranged in a matrix (see Fig. 5.3). A further refinement was the indication of high and low ethnic status or segregation scores through the use of shaded and unshaded circles.

In D. T. Herbert's social space diagram for Winnipeg (Fig. 5.3), the shaded circles indicate those census tracts in which ethnic and minority groups are segregated.

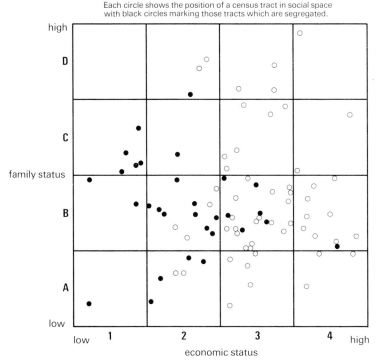

Each circle shows the position of a census tract in social space with black circles marking those tracts which are segregated.

Fig. 5.3   Social space diagram for Winnipeg. (Source: see caption for Fig. 5.2)

The social space diagram is then used as the basis for identifying and mapping social areas. Contiguous census tracts which occur within the same cells in the social space diagram are combined to form distinct social areas (see Fig. 5.4). Thus it is possible to distinguish parts of the city in which the scores for economic status and family status are both low or both high or where one is low and the other high and so on.

If social area analysis as a technique for delineating urban sub-areas is to have validity it must be clearly demonstrable that the three constructs, economic status, family status, and ethnic status are independent and that there is a high correlation between the variables in each of these constructs. Research work applying the method of analysis to cities outside North America has, however, failed to do this.

D. T. Herbert employed social area analysis in a study of Newcastle-under-Lyme in England which used enumeration districts as the areal basis for his study.[6] These

125

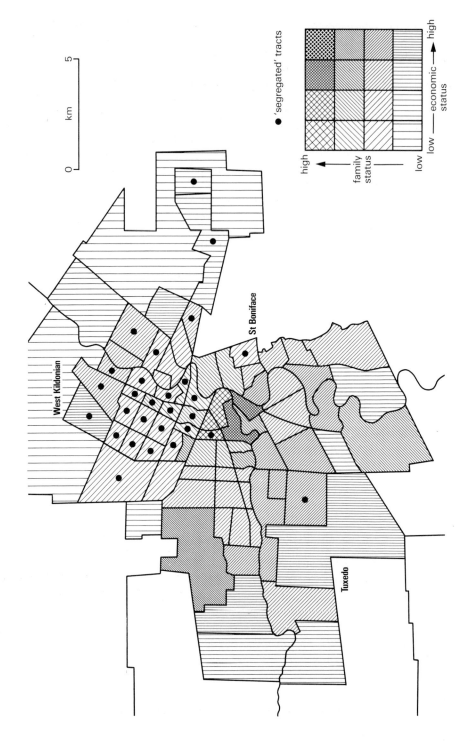

were considerably smaller than the equivalent American census tracts. Herbert used four of the variables suggested by Shevky and his associates: *occupation* and *education* as indices of the construct economic status, and *fertility* and the proportion of *women at work* as indices of the construct family status. His research revealed, however, that the indices chosen were unsuitable. Women at work and fertility, both chosen to express family status, bore no relationship at all to each other. There was, however, considerable relationship between levels of occupation and fertility, although occupation is regarded as an index of the construct economic status and fertility as an index of the construct family status. Herbert concluded that in his Newcastle-under-Lyme study, social area analysis was invalid as an analytical tool.[7]

Other European studies have also demonstrated that the constructs economic status and family status are not independent. D. C. McElrath's study of Rome showed fertility to be more highly correlated with economic status than with other measures of family status.[8]

Thus the theoretical underpinning of social area analysis has been challenged and its validity as an analytical tool brought into question. In retrospect the technique is important only in so far as it prepared the ground for the development of more sophisticated techniques such as multivariate analysis.

2. Multivariate analysis

Social area analysis as a technique is limited by the small range of variables that can be employed. The availability of high speed computational facilities made it possible for multivariate approaches to be adopted and for large amounts of data to be handled objectively. Such analysis is highly complicated and lies largely outside the scope of this book, but no discussion of city structure and the residential areas of the city would be complete without some reference being made to the evidence it has produced. Multivariate analysis uses *factor analysis* and the related techniques of *component analysis* to examine a large number of variables, which are in some way related to social characteristics within towns. These are then collapsed into a smaller range of significantly associated variables, which indicate underlying components of social characteristics.

Factor anlysis summarizes the inter-relationships among the input variables which are fed into the computer. If variables 'a' to 'm' are fed in, it may be shown that 'a', 'f', 'g' and 'l' are grouped and therefore explain 60 per cent of the phenomenon. For example, they might be indices of socio-economic status, such as the proportion of white-collar workers; the proportion continuing on to some form of higher education and the proportion of professional and managerial employees.

P. H. Rees used fifty-seven variables in his factor analysis of Chicago.[9] These were collapsed to ten factors which are shown, in decreasing order of significance, in Table 5.2.

◀ Fig. 5.4   Social areas in Winnipeg, 1961. (Source: see caption for Fig. 5.2)

Table 5.2 Factor analysis of Chicago. (Source P. H. Rees, Chapter 10 in B. J. L. Berry & F. E. Horton, (eds.), *Geographic Perspectives in Urban Systems*, Prentice Hall, 1970.)

Factor	Variance %	Cumulative %
1. Socio-economic status	17.8	17.8
2. Stage in life cycle	14.2	32.0
3. Race and resources	13.1	45.1
4. Immigrant/Catholic status	10.8	55.9
5. Population size and density	7.5	63.4
6. Jewish/Russian population	3.8	67.2
7. Housing built in 1940s; workers commute by car	3.0	70.2
8. Irish/Swedish population	2.6	72.8
9. Mobility	2.4	75.2
10. Other non-whites/Italians	2.1	77.3

The table shows the proportion of the total variance which can be accounted for by each factor. In Rees's study, therefore, the first four factors cumulatively account for 55.9 per cent of the total variance. Most studies employing factor analysis have produced similar results – the first two, three, or four factors generally account for between half and two-thirds of the total variance. This means that attention can be focused on those factors which are most important and (collectively) significantly influence social patterning within cities.

Variation in each factor can be mapped using census tracts or enumeration districts as the areal unit. P. H. Rees did this in his study of Chicago and in Fig. 5.5 spatial variations in the socio-economic status of the population (Factor I) are shown. The low status districts in the inner city and 'black belt' can be easily distinguished from the high status suburbs. The factor scores can also be plotted on to a two dimensional social space diagram. In Fig. 5.6 this has been done for Factor I. By this means the enumeration districts can be divided into four broad categories, those comprising (i) high status, older, small families; (ii) high status, younger, large families; (iii) low status, older small families, and (iv) low status, younger, large families. The information so derived has been used to construct a model of the social areas of the Chicago metropolis (Fig. 5.7) which includes both concentric and sectoral elements.

In both factor analysis and principal component analysis the selection of the input variables is of the utmost importance, as they will determine the results obtained. In his study of Sunderland, B. T. Robson[10] selected a total of thirty variables 'with an eye to their possible theoretical import,' the aim being to select a sufficient cross-section of variables so as not to give undue weight to any one aspect of urban social structure. Nevertheless the selection of the variables does introduce an element of subjectivity into the technique. A further problem is posed by the interpretation of the principal components, that is, giving meaning to what are really no more than mathematical artefacts.

It must be remembered that multivariate analysis is no more than an analytical technique which enables vast amounts of data to be handled for small areal units within towns and cities. Nevertheless, provided the input variables are selected

Fig. 5.5 The distribution of four socio-economic status groups in metropolitan Chicago, ▶ 1960. (Source: after P. H. Rees, *The Factorial Ecology of Metropolitan Chicago*, Masters thesis; University of Chicago, 1968)

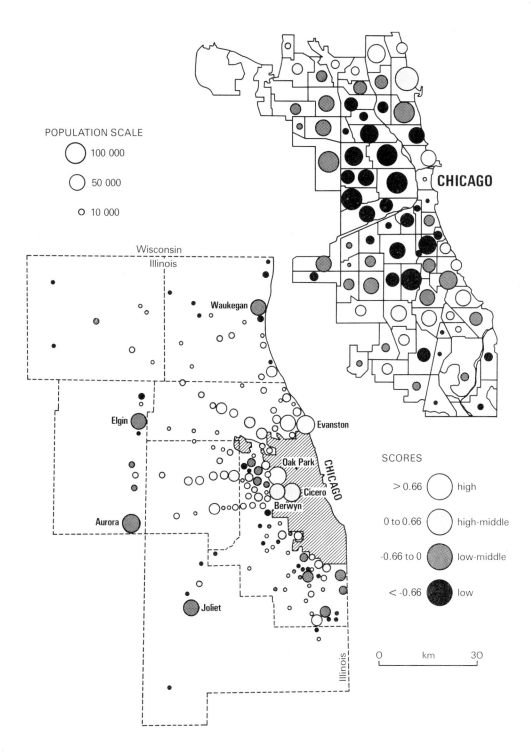

POPULATION SCALE

⬭ 100 000

⬭ 50 000

○ 10 000

Wisconsin
Illinois

Waukegan

Elgin

Evanston

Oak Park

Cicero

Berwyn

CHICAGO

Aurora

Joliet

Illinois

CHICAGO

SCORES

> 0.66 ○ high

0 to 0.66 ○ high-middle

-0.66 to 0 ◓ low-middle

< -0.66 ● low

0   km   30

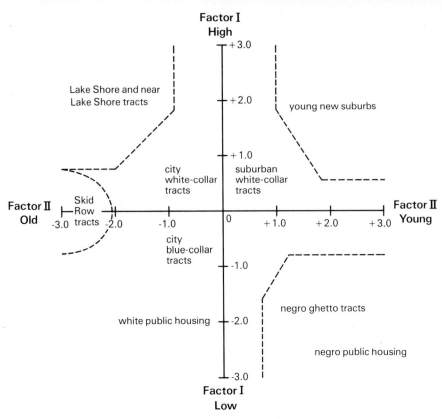

Fig. 5.6 Social space diagram for Chicago. Each census tract can be plotted on the diagram which has as its axes Factor I Socio-economic Status and Factor II Stage in the Life Cycle. (Source: see caption for Fig. 5.5)

Fig. 5.7 Social areas of Chicago. The groupings of census tracts obtained from Fig. 5.6 are used as the basis for Rees's model. (Source: see caption for Fig. 5.5)

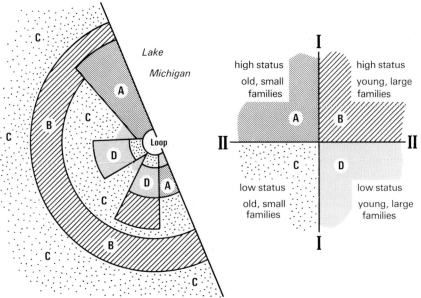

carefully and the results interpreted shrewdly it is a technique which does make it possible to distinguish social patterning within cities.

ASSIGNMENTS

Refer to the enumeration district (E.D.) data for Bedford (see Fig. 5.8, Table 5.3). The data has been standardized and is presented in the form of numbers per 1000 households for each E.D. so that it is possible to make direct comparisons between E.D.s in terms of amenities and degree of overcrowding.

1.   *Working in groups, draw choropleth maps to illustrate spatial variations for each factor. Collectively the maps will provide some indication of spatial variations in social well-being in the town. Before you can begin to compile your maps you will need to consider the following:*

   (a)   The number of categories to use: As a general rule these must not exceed five times the logarithm of the observations (in this case the number of E.D.s).

   (b)   The choice of limits of the categories: A variety of methods may be used to select these. For example:

      (i) Fixed intervals or classes of equal range in which case:
      $$\text{Class interval} = \frac{range}{number\ of\ classes}$$

      (ii) There may be an equal number of E.D.s. in each class. Rank the data, decide on the number of classes and divide the total number of E.D.s by the number of classes. This will tell you how many E.D.s should be included in each class.

      (iii) You may plot the E.D. data on a scattergram and have class limits where breaks occur on the scattergram.

   (c)   Method of mapping: Decide on a suitable scheme of density shading or colouring. The intensity of shading or colouring should reflect the intensity of the category it is meant to portray. With this series of choropleth maps E.D.s in which people are least well off should be shown by the densest shading.

2.   *Use a test of correlation, such as the Spearman Rank Correlation Coefficient, to discover the degree of correlation between each of the variables (see pages 192–193).*

B. Social Space: Behavioural Approaches

In Chapter 4 we saw how the Chicago-based urban ecologists, R. E. Park, E. W. Burgess and R. D. McKenzie, applied certain of the principles and processes of plant ecology in their study of city structure. They considered that analogies could be made between plant and human communities and that the concepts of plant ecology could be applied in a study of land use and people within cities.[11]

Competition was a fundamental principle. People competed for limited space and for access to the most desirable locations for their homes and commercial enter-prises. Some groups, however, had greater competitive power than others and this led to a position of *dominance* – the most economically powerful securing the most favourable locations for themselves. This process in turn led inevitably to the *segregation* of similar types of persons and activities. The most affluent chose to cluster together in isolated high class residential areas. Slums, on the other hand, represented areas of minimum choice, in which people with the least economic

Fig. 5.8   Enumeration districts, Bedford. (Source: Department of Census and Surveys, Titchfield, Hants)

Table 5.3. Data for Enumeration Districts, Bedford.

Ward	Enumeration District	No. of householders per 1000 with exclusive use of basic amenities (hot water, bath and inside W.C.)	No. of households per 1000 lacking an inside W.C.	Density of population. No. of households per 1000 with more than 1.5 persons per room	Total population of enumeration district	No. of people born in Indian sub continent	Percentage of E.D's population born in Indian sub continent
De Parys	A28	710	14	14	298	7	2.35%
	A29	796	6	19	428	28	6.54%
	A30	736	18	9	478	3	0.63%
	A31	878	5	0	543	12	2.21%
	A32	532	18	37	469	8	1.70%
	A33	656	26	84	470	7	1.49%
	A34	995	0	0	753	3	0.40%
	A35	1000	0	0	685	3	0.44%
	A36	988	0	0	580	0	—
	A37	995	0	0	693	5	0.72%
	A38	1000	0	0	692	2	0.29%
	A39	1000	9	0	385	4	1.04%
	A40	1000	0	6	641	3	0.46%
	A41	1000	0	110	725	4	0.55%
	A42	1000	0	5	621	1	0.16%
	A43	994	0	0	354	1	0.19%
	A44	1000	0	0	183	2	1.09%
	A45	982	0	0	752	4	0.53%
	A46	1000	0	0	767	3	0.39%
	A47	1000	0	0	677	7	1.03%
	A48	765	5	33	411	6	1.46%
	A49	952	0	0	398	4	1.00%
	A50	1000	0	0	497	4	0.80%
	A51	940	0	0	151	0	—
Goldington	A01	1000	0	0	684	2	0.29%
	A02	1000	0	0	493	3	0.61%
	A03	985	0	0	411	0	—
	A04	994	0	0	544	4	0.73%
	A05	1000	0	0	678	7	1.03%
	A06	976	0	0	547	6	1.10%
	A07	1000	0	0	500	5	1.00%
	A08	969	13	0	600	2	0.33%
	A09	993	0	22	462	3	0.65%
	A10	940	20	0	515	4	0.78%
	A11	1000	0	0	631	0	—
	A12	1000	0	28	624	2	0.32%
	A13	938	51	11	433	2	0.46%

Ward	Enumeration District	No. of householders per 1000 with exclusive use of basic amenities (hot water, bath and inside W.C.)	No. of households per 1000 lacking an inside W.C.	Density of population. No. of households per 1000 with more than 1.5 persons per room	Total population of enumeration district	No. of people born in Indian sub continent	Percentage of E.D's population born in Indian sub continent
	A14	987	0	9	891	2	0.11%
	A15	995	0	15	656	3	0.46%
	A16	1000	0	0	582	2	0.34%
	A17	985	0	0	448	2	0.45%
	A18	1000	0	0	572	4	0.70%
	A19	983	0	6	573	0	—
	A20	1000	0	10	363	0	—
	A21	984	4	4	838	0	—
Kingsbrook	A39	967	26	0	453	0	—
	A40	1000	0	0	517	2	0.77%
	A41	1000	0	26	728	0	—
	A42	938	52	5	557	1	0.18%
	A43	969	25	6	457	4	0.87%
	A44	1000	0	0	550	0	—
	A45	955	13	13	593	0	—
	A46	888	0	13	631	6	0.95%
	A47	957	0	11	504	7	1.39%
	A48	936	0	15	581	2	0.34%
	A49	904	51	0	478	15	3.14%
	A50	877	48	11	555	5	0.90%
	A51	911	22	22	638	1	0.16%
	A52	500	384	80	422	106	25.12%
	A53	761	71	19	344	0	—
Cauldwell	B01	898	57	16	708	6	0.85%
	B02	806	154	8	751	95	12.65%
	B03	975	0	20	712	2	0.28%
	B04	977	12	0	523	12	2.29%
	B05	990	0	5	526	2	0.38%
	B06	974	0	6	643	2	0.31%
	B07	984	0	22	514	0	—
	B08	943	14	5	645	10	1.55%
	B09	837	116	7	437	5	1.14%
	B10	772	214	28	536	104	19.40%
	B11	494	481	6	480	16	3.33%
	B12	671	226	68	513	84	16.37%
	B13	606	286	63	668	165	24.70%
	B14	546	271	104	858	182	21.21%
	B15	595	314	67	751		

A23	994	0	0	479	4	0.83%
A24	959	54	0	388	0	—
A25	990	0	0	586	2	0.34%
A26	980	24	4	835	8	0.96%
A27	813	68	6	469	3	0.64%
A28	698	210	31	482	19	3.94%
A29	672	274	0	522	15	2.87%
A30	633	38	52	494	15	3.04%
A31	620	45	9	466	7	1.50%
A32	759	84	16	445	32	7.19%
A33	730	94	0	398	8	2.01%
A34	714	130	15	492	8	1.63%
A35	825	58	10	549	20	3.64%
A36	891	44	0	515	4	0.78%
A37	902	82	5	487	10	2.05%
A38	972	11	0	443	2	0.45%
Queenspark						
B16	968	0	12	587	1	0.17%
B17	879	89	21	589	52	8.83%
B18	730	139	66	423	64	15.13%
B19	756	207	32	666	67	10.06%
B20	904	67	0	474	9	1.90%
B21	647	327	67	623	116	18.62%
B22	762	165	55	544	92	16.91%
B23	661	268	31	403	17	4.22%
B24	657	241	51	533	42	7.88%
B25	739	102	57	566	27	4.77%
B26	928	9	0	294	1	0.34%
B27	636	348	11	589	34	5.77%
B28	996	0	0	590	0	—
B29	1000	0	0	390	1	0.26%
B30	986	0	0	368	5	1.36%
Harpur						
A01	720	37	93	322	0	—
A02	840	25	25	239	3	1.25%
A03	579	21	116	278	13	4.68%
A04	651	33	46	350	7	2.00%
A05	880	7	28	312	4	1.28%
A06	567	0	153	307	3	0.98%
A07	577	89	24	243	10	4.11%
A08	749	6	34	414	4	0.97%

Ward	Enumeration District	No. of householders per 1000 with exclusive use of basic amenities (hot water, bath and inside W.C.)	No. of households per 1000 lacking an inside W.C.	Density of population. No. of households per 1000 with more than 1.5 persons per room	Total population of enumeration district	No. of people born in Indian sub continent	Percentage of E.D's population born in Indian sub continent
	A09	777	68	41	717	37	5.16%
	A10	1018	0	37	425	14	3.29%
	A11	1014	0	0	207	0	—
	A12	984	0	0	453	6	1.32%
	A13	685	118	34	593	44	7.42%
	A14	693	213	10	598	8	0.17%
	A15	585	301	41	588	32	5.44%
	A16	507	300	20	437	26	5.95%
	A17	254	699	23	404	0	—
	A18	236	630	31	320	8	2.5%
	A19	955	31	0	576	5	0.87%
	A20	573	121	75	446	48	10.76%
	A21	993	0	4	365	2	0.27%
	A22	608	34	108	401	16	3.99%
	A23	500	20	59	236	12	5.08%
	A24	726	91	91	586	48	8.19%
	A25	311	49	93	502	76	15.14%
	A26	477	367	55	454	32	7.05%
	A27	671	47	59	230	0	—
	A54	494	382	0	267	9	3.37%

power lived. In other words segregation was a result of the operation of the combination of the forces of *selection*.

The urban ecologists, and R. E. Park in particular, recognized that the analogy with the biological world was an imperfect one 'since man is subject to impulses other than the basic need for survival'[12] and human activity is not, therefore, based solely on the sub-social forces of competition. People are also influenced by their culture and traditional values, and these will affect their behaviour.

1. Places may acquire sentimental and symbolic connotation

Despite these qualifications, urban ecologists were criticized because they laid insufficient stress on the cultural processes which distinguish humans from other organisms. Later studies have attempted to redress this imbalance. For example W. Firey in his pioneering work in Boston analysed the environment in terms of its cultural as well as its purely physical characteristics.[13] In other words, he considered that space (i.e. parts of a town) might acquire certain sentimental and symbolic connotations and these associations could become of overriding importance, counteracting the forces of sheer competition. Firey identified certain cultural and non-rational values operating in Boston which had exerted a considerable influence on the morphology of the town. For example the district of Beacon Hill, situated close to the commercial core of Boston, should in theory have been invaded by commercial land uses, if ecological processes alone operated (see pages 87–91). Yet it had remained a high class residential district. Firey suggested that this was because the district had acquired certain sentimental and symbolic associations which were collectively recognized and these had preserved it from commercial encroachment. In a rather different vein, cultural associations influenced the social composition of the population residing in North End, an area of dilapidated slum dwellings which would have been regarded by the classical ecologists as representing an area of minimum choice. This district had acted as a reception area for immigrant Italian families and retained certain sentimental associations for such families even after they had improved their economic status and could have moved to better residential districts.

2. Images of the urban environment

It is from pioneering work such as that of W. Firey that the concept of *social space* has developed. Social space may be defined as a synthesis of objective, physical space and the perceived dimensions of space.[14] It embraces both *activity space* and *awareness or perceptual space*.

SOCIAL SPACE

ACTIVITY SPACE   AWARENESS SPACE

Activity space describes the distribution of people (where they live), and the movement of people – to work, to shop and for social events (how people live within a spatial context). Awareness space describes the way people perceive their environment. An individual looks at the urban environment selectively, mentally organizing what is seen and giving it meaning. Environmental images are influenced by personal values, aspirations and cultural traditions. These act as a kind of filter distorting what is seen and giving the objective dimensions of the environment subjective meaning. Images of the urban environment possessed by the individual thus form a link between reality and behaviour. J. Doherty's schematic representation of this link is shown below[15] (Fig. 5.9).

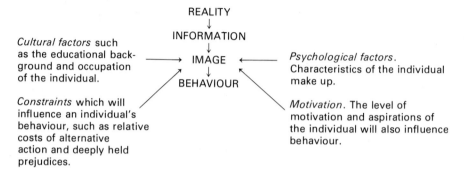

Fig. 5.9   Reality-behaviour links. (Source: based on D. T. Herbert, *Urban Geography; a Social Perspective*, David & Charles, 1972, p. 253)

Pocock and Hudson in their book *Images of the Urban Environment* include a series of mental maps of Durham, each compiled by different categories of people: the child, the student, working-class and middle-class residents and tourists.[16] (See Fig. 5.10.) None conforms more than approximately to reality. The child's view (a) is egocentric – school and nearby house loom large – while the student's map (b) over-emphasizes the district around the University with which he or she is most familiar. The mental map of the middle-class resident (d) is more accurate and detailed than that of the working-class resident (c). The tourists possess another distinctive viewpoint (e) (f). Their grasp of the structure of the town centre is limited and they concentrate on the aesthetic rather than the functional. The fact that we perceive places differently in turn influences the way we behave. The student, with a limited perception of Durham, is unlikely to use facilities in certain parts of the town which are unfamiliar, even if those facilities may be superior to the ones used frequently, and the tourists are unlikely to stray out of the city centre which they perceive to be surrounded by a somewhat hostile ring road.

Although each individual creates his or her own image there is a broad measure of image agreement amongst members of a social group, each member sharing common experiences and cultural traditions. A pilot study conducted by the Advance Planning Section of the Los Angeles City Planning Commission explored this concept, comparing the environmental imagery of five different samples. Each represented a distinctive social group drawn from contrasting locations in the city.[17] Figs. 5.11 and 5.12 are the composite mental maps of Los Angeles as envisaged by two of these groups, one from Avalon, near Watts, a predominantly black sample located in a south-eastern district of the city, another from Westwood, a non-ethnic upper-class district adjacent to the University of California campus. The composite

Fig. 5.10   People's perceptions of Durham. (Source: D. Pocock & R. Hudson, *Images of the* ▶ *Urban Environment*, Macmillan, (London and Basingstoke) 1978, p.64)

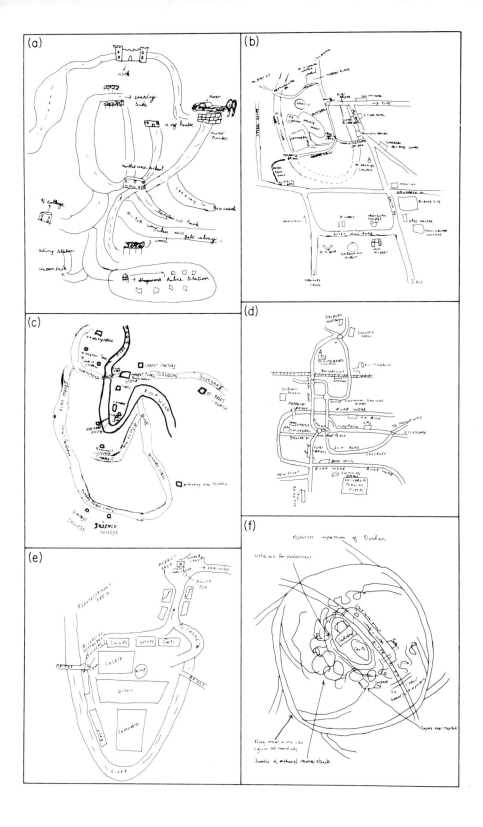

mental maps incorporated the following elements which had been identified previously by K. Lynch in his seminal work *The Image of the City*.[18]

(a) Paths – channels along which the observer moves.

(b) Edges – linear elements comprising boundaries between districts and/or barriers to movement.

(c) Districts – medium-to-large sections of the city perceived as having some common identity.

(d) Nodes or centres – strategic points such as route junctions and enclosed squares.

(c) Landmarks – distinctive features in the townscape.

These reveal that Avalon respondents had a rather restricted conception of the city. They primarily distinguished a number of parallel routes leading from Avalon to the city centre and several discrete and unconnected districts. In contrast, the

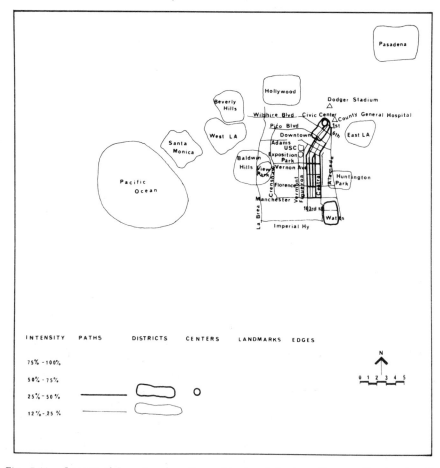

Fig. 5.11   Images of Los Angeles: the residents of Avalon. (Source: Reprinted with permission from R. M. Downs and D. Stead (eds.), *Image and Environment*, Aldine Publishing Co., (New York) 1973)

140

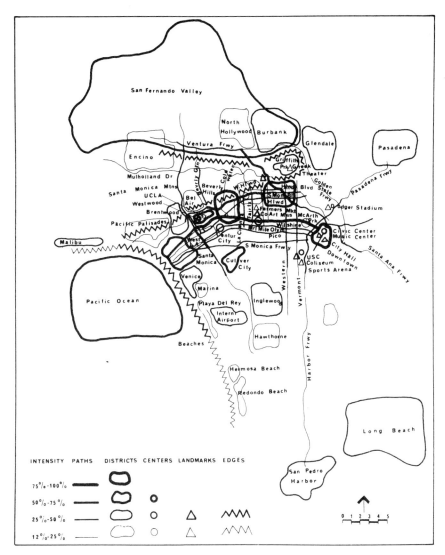

Fig. 5.12   Images of Los Angeles: the residents of Westwood. (Source: see caption for Fig. 5.11)

perceptions of the Westwood respondents were well formed and detailed and indicated a good general knowledge of the entire city and its environs.

These variations in the degrees of awareness as displayed by groups and individuals are fundamental to an understanding of the concept of social space. For, as we have seen, social space involves the inter-relationship of both *awareness space* (the perceived dimensions of space) and the more objective and easily identifiable *activity space*. It provides some insight into 'how individuals and groups pattern space by their perceptions and activities.'[19] The concept of social space may be better understood by a study of the neighbourhood, the local area with which we are most familiar and with which we can often most readily identify.

1. *We have seen that people's mental images of place do not necessarily conform very closely to reality. To test this draw as accurate a mental map as you can of a route from the main entrance of your school or college to a place nearby and ask one of your friends to follow it.*
2. *Select two landmarks/buildings in your town which are approximately equidistant from your school or college. One of these should be more frequently visited than the other. Ask a sample of your student friends to draw mental maps showing the routes from school to each of them. Compare the maps and see if one of the features is perceived to be more distant than the other. If so try to account for the differences.*
3. *A variation of the above exercise is to list fifteen landmarks or buildings which are at varying distances from your school or college. Ask a sample of respondents to rank each building/landmark according to how far they perceive it to be from school/college, i.e. to place the nearest first ranked and so on. Compare the average rank order given by the respondents with the actual rank order. Try to account for any differences in the rank orders.*
4. *How is it possible for space to acquire social attributes?*

C. The Neighbourhood

1. Neighbourhood concepts

The neighbourhood may be regarded as a form of territorial space which has both spatial and social attributes. The inter-relationship between the spatial and the social dimensions is not uniform and is perhaps best explored if the notion of a continuum is used (see Table 5.4).

(a) At its simplest level, the neighbourhood is little more than an ill-defined territory lacking any sort of individual identity or social cohesion. The only feature which distinguishes such an *arbitrary neighbourhood* is one of *propinquity* or spatial proximity; i.e. the people who reside in it all live relatively close to one another but have no real social or communal contact.
(b) The next stage in the continuum is the *physical neighbourhood* which is distinguished by distinct physical characteristics and clearly defined boundaries. For example, the houses may be of similar age and style and the neighbourhood may have boundaries formed by barriers such as a railway line, canal, major road, industrial estate, an extensive public open space, land liable to flood or steep slopes.
(c) The *homogeneous neighbourhood* possesses the attributes of the physical neighbourhood and has a clearly defined territory with distinct physical characteristics. However, it has also acquired certain social characteristics and is occupied by a group of people with common social and cultural attributes, for example people of similar socio-economic status and/or members of an ethnic or racial minority group.
(d) The *functional neighbourhood* possesses all the characteristics of a homogeneous neighbourhood but within it additional activities such as shopping, education, church-going and recreation take place. In other words a local shopping

Table 5.4. The Neighbourhood Continuum (after A. T. Blowers)

	Neighbourhood concepts				
	(a) Arbitrary	(b) Physical	(c) Homogeneous	(d) Functional	(e) Community
Distinguishing characteristics	Propinquity or nearness is the only distinguishing characteristic.	Has distinct physical characteristics with clearly defined boundaries.	Contains a population which is socially and economically homogeneous.	The people are dependent on the services which the neighbourhood provides (i.e. engenders functional interaction).	There is much social interaction within the neighbourhood which forms a distinct and cohesive community.

centre, a primary school, a church and a branch library may act as foci within the neighbourhood, and their catchment areas will broadly coincide with the boundaries of the neighbourhood. Research by R. Glass in Middlesbrough led her to conclude that functional neighbourhoods can be most clearly defined as those parts of a town which are isolated and geographically separate entities, particularly if such areas also form the poorest parts of the town.[20]

(e) At the most sophisticated level, the neighbourhood forms a distinct *community* in which people have 'developed a sense of togetherness and also tend to associate with each other more than outsiders.'[21] Obviously, such a sense of community develops gradually over a considerable period of time and length of residence is clearly an important factor. Thus a neighbourhood will develop a sense of community only where there is stability and limited movement of

143

families into and out of it. Other important factors in the development of community are common social and demographic characteristics. For example, families may have reached a similar stage in the family cycle – there is a preponderance of families with young children, or the elderly, which have shared attitudes.

Class is an important consideration in the development of distinctive, homogeneous neighbourhoods with a sense of community. Long-established, working-class neighbourhoods are likely to be more socially cohesive than their middle-class equivalents. In their study of Bethnal Green, a working-class district in the East End of London, Young and Willmott vividly describe the sense of community that existed there.

> . . . In Bethnal Green the person who says he 'knows everyone' is, of course, exaggerating, but pardonably so. He does, with various degrees of intimacy, know many people outside (but often through) his family, and it is this which makes it, in the view of many informants, a 'friendly place'.
> . . . There is a sense of community, that is a feeling of solidarity between people who occupy the common territory which springs from the fact that people and their families have lived there a long time.[22]

In contrast, in Woodford, an established middle-class suburb on the fringes of London, the social ties are more loose-knit and the sense of community less well developed.

> In Woodford there is not the same gregariousness as in Bethnal Green and parents and children often live at some distance from each other. Although they saw each other less frequently, contact with their families was maintained both by visiting and in many cases by car or telephone. Willmott and Young observed a distinct 'life cycle of kinship' with the generations living apart until the parents reached retirement age at which point they were often reunited with their children.[23]

2. Perception of the neighbourhood

It seems that one of the reasons why a sense of community would appear to be best developed in those parts of the city where the population is stable and well established, is that an individual will often develop a unique relationship with his or her birthplace. This is because 'the immediate physical and social environment is, without doubt, crucially important in the early psychological and social development of the individual.'[24]

Pocock and Hudson suggest that people have three basic psychological needs: identity, security and stimulation; and the local environment or neighbourhood is extremely important in contributing to the satisfaction of these needs. They conclude that people need to identify with a limited territorial space. Certainly studies of the way in which people perceive their neighbourhoods would seem to confirm this. For example there is a tendency amongst those who have lived in the same house for some time who are very familiar with their local areas to 'better' them when describing them to others. If asked to draw a mental map of their neighbourhood they would tend to make it more uniform and attractive than it in fact is. Similarly, surveys of people's perception of neighbourhood facilities have indicated that they perceive the desirable elements, such as the school, library, park, post office, to be closer to their homes than they are in reality while the less desirable elements such as main trunk roads and heavy industrial plants may be perceived to be farther away.

3. Attempts to create new neighbourhoods

As we noted in Chapter 3, the post-war period has witnessed a phase of unprecedented urban renewal and growth. Vast slum clearance programmes in the inner cities have resulted in the destruction of established communities and many thousands of families have been uprooted and rehoused in sprawling suburban estates, new towns or comprehensively redeveloped parts of the city. It is hardly surprising, therefore, that one of the principal planning objectives in post-war Britain has been to recreate clearly defined neighbourhoods within the new housing developments. This has inevitably involved architects and planners in trying to establish what is the optimum neighbourhood design and, in this respect, consideration has been given to the following:

(a) *Layout*: Can housing estates be planned in such a way as to encourage social interaction and engender a sense of community? Probably the major single influence in this respect has been Clarence Perry's Radburn, New Jersey, scheme.[25] This incorporated traffic/pedestrian segregation and a network of footpaths designed to make it more likely that people would meet and get to know each other. At the centre of each neighbourhood was a primary school, and shops and services were built in a cluster on the edge of the neighbourhood. Many of the neighbourhood designs incorporated in British New Towns have been modifications of the Radburn layout. (This point is further developed in Chapter 9.)

(b) *The boundaries of neighbourhoods*: How clear cut should these be? Does spatial isolation enhance the development of functional and social interaction within a neighbourhood? In some British new towns attempts were made to isolate neighbourhoods by using wedges of open spaces to form their boundaries. Peterborough provides a good example of this. Both planned open spaces and the main road networks have been used to separate the new neighbourhoods which have been grafted on to the existing town (see Fig. 5.13). Recent attempts at neighbourhood planning have, however, moved away from this policy, as it is recognized that physical isolation can be achieved only at the expense of convenience.

(c) *The degree of social homogeneity/heterogeneity*: In general within British new towns, planners have attempted to create socially heterogeneous neighbourhoods in which the social balance reflects that in Britain as a whole. The policy has, however, been modified in more recent developments and it is increasingly recognized that the pursuit of social balance may actively inhibit the development of a sense of community within a neighbourhood.

Unfortunately, attempts to create communities have been relatively unsuccessful (see Chapter 9) and, partly as a result of this, the whole concept of the neighbourhood unit is increasingly being questioned. There are those who claim that the neighbourhood has less relevance as the urban population becomes more mobile and is less dependent on spatial proximity for social and functional interaction.

In contrast, others contend that an individual needs to be able to identify with a

145

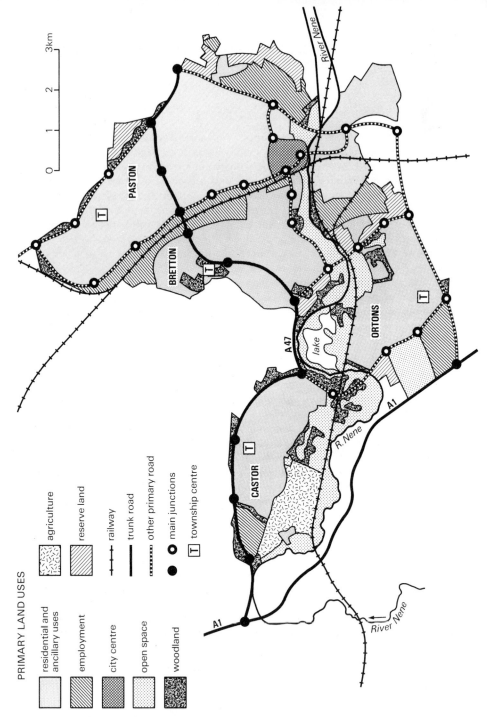

Fig. 5.13   Neighbourhoods in Peterborough. (Source: based on an original plan in *Greater Peterborough Master Plan*, Peterborough Development Corporation)

limited territorial space and failure to do so can create stress and psychological disorder.

ASSIGNMENTS
1. *Find out which districts in your town are perceived by your fellow students as displaying the greatest sense of community. Work through the distinguishing characteristics of neighbourhoods which are summarized on the neighbourhood continuum diagram (page 143) and assess which of these characteristics apply to the community neighbourhoods in your town.*
2. *Conduct a questionnaire survey in your own neighbourhood to find out if there is image agreement over the boundaries of the neighbourhood, i.e. if people living in the neighbourhood perceive it to have clearly defined boundaries. Test the hypothesis that local people have a clearer perception of the boundaries of old, established neighbourhoods than in neighbourhoods in new housing districts.*

D. Processes

Having discussed some of the techniques whereby social areas can be identified (the *pattern*) we can now turn our attention to the *processes* which help to bring these about. The two which will be discussed at some length are residential segregation and residential mobility.

1. Residential segregation

Many studies using multivariate analysis have revealed racial and ethnic status as important variables in accounting for residential differentiation. The segregation of racial and ethnic minority groups into distinctive quarters of towns is not a new phenomenon. A feature of many medieval towns in Europe, the Near East and North Africa was an exclusive Jewish quarter or ghetto. This area was often walled and physically separate and had developed partly in response to the determination of the Orthodox Jews to retain intact their cultural identity.[26] In contemporary cities the segregation is unlikely to be as extreme but will probably be most evident in multi-racial communities or where fundamental cultural differences exist.

(a) Techniques
Studies of residential segregation within towns have demanded precise quantification and a number of methods have been devised for measuring and mapping the distribution of minority groups. These include the *location quotient* and the *segregation index*.

The location quotient indicates the deviation of a minority population from what would be expected if its members were evenly distributed throughout the city.[27]

$$\text{Location quotient} = \frac{\text{observed}}{\text{expected}}$$

Thus if 3 per cent of the population of a city are Poles and they are evenly distributed, then each sub-division of the city will have 3 per cent Poles. In this case the location quotient would be $\frac{3}{3} = 1$. If on the other hand a single ward contained 10 per cent of the Polish population, the location quotient would be $\frac{10}{3} = 3.3$. Thus location quotients in excess of 1 imply that the group in question is over-represented while figures below 1 indicate under-representation. The location quotients for each ward or enumeration district can be mapped to give an indication of the degree of clustering of the minority groups in the city. (For a fuller explanation of location quotients see Bale J., *The Location of Manufacturing Industry*.) The segregation index is also a measure of the extent to which the distribution of a minority population group deviates from a random distribution.[28] The index is applied to small areal divisions of the city such as E.D.s and extends from 0 to 1, where 0 represents an unsegregated population and 1 total segregation. Thus if 25 per cent of a town's population are Asians, an enumeration district which also contained 25 per cent Asians would have a segregation index of 0 whereas enumeration districts containing 100 per cent Asians and no Asians would both have segregation indices of 1. In E.D.s in which the Asian population falls between 0 and 25 per cent and 25 and 100 per cent the segregation index is calculated as a ratio of that distance.

Techniques such as these can be used to illustrate patterns of residential segregation. For example studies of Asian households in Glasgow[29] and the distribution of Commonwealth immigrants in Birmingham have both suggested a pattern of discontinuous clusters in the middle zone of each city. P. N. Jones, in his Birmingham study, found that the distribution correlated closely with a broadly concentric ring of Victorian and Edwardian later by-law houses and modest villas.[30] (See Fig. 5.14.) The type of housing proved an important locating factor as much of the property in the 'zone in transition' which might be expected to be a reception area for newly arrived immigrant families (see page 103) was municipally owned and consequently not freely available to immigrants. This made 'invasion' into the inner city largely impossible and had the effect of pushing it farther out into districts which contained substantial houses, often with short leases, which could be purchased.

In American cities, where the ethnic and racial minorities are of longer standing, sectoral segregation patterns have been observed. For example, Chicago's 'black belt' has migrated outwards in a wedge or sector within which there has been a degree of sifting based on socio-economic status. In other words the poorest families have been left behind near the city centre as the segregated sector has grown outwards (see Fig. 5.7, p. 130).

(b) Functions of segregated areas

Population migration is the principal *raison d'être* for residential segregation based on race or ethnicity. When migrants first arrive in a town or city, they are usually easily distinguishable from the host group and, if it is possible, choose to live in closely knit, socially and culturally distinct neighbourhoods. Increasing tension and, perhaps even conflict, between population groups can also lead to more exaggerated residential segregation. This has been the case in Belfast since the onset of the most recent civil disturbances. Housing areas have become more and more homogeneous as Protestants have moved from predominantly Roman Catholic areas and vice versa.[31] (See Fig. 5.15, page 151.)

F. W. Boal identifies a number of distinct functions that ethnically segregated residential areas fulfil.[32] These are:

   (i) *defensive functions*, the area providing for the migrant, in a strange 'land', psychological security and a secure haven in which language and customs are familiar;

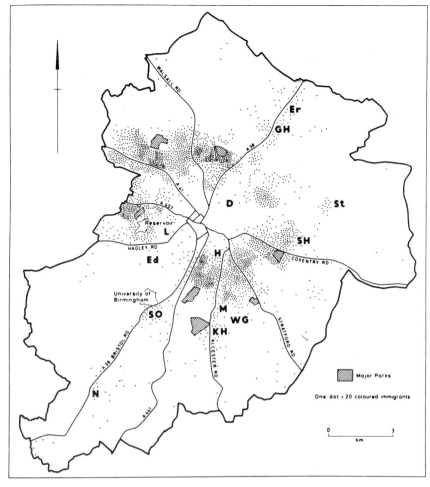

Fig. 5.14   The distribution of Commonwealth immigrants in Birmingham, 1966. (Source:
E. Jones (ed.), *Readings in Social Geography*, OUP, 1975, p. 77)

(ii) *avoidance functions*, allowing the migrant a period of adjustment during
which he can become gradually more familiar with the *mores* of the host
group;

(iii) *preservation functions*, permitting the cultural heritage of the minority immigrant group to be preserved more easily;

(iv) *'attack' functions*, providing a basis for political strength and facilitating joint
action by the minority group members.

The segregated residential area may be a transitory feature of the city which
breaks up gradually as the second and third generation migrants are assimilated and
disperse, or it may become more permanent, developing into an enclave or ghetto.
Boal suggests that the degree of permanence of the residentially segregated area
depends to a large extent on the degree of racial and cultural distinctiveness of the
immigrant group from the host group. The range of possible spatial outcomes of
migration are summarized below. (See Table 5.5.[33]) In cases where the ethnic group
differs little from the host society, the minority group is assimilated relatively

149

quickly. On the other hand, where contrasts are very pronounced, a permanent enclave or ghetto may develop. The diagram also envisages an intermediate stage where a temporary 'colony' is formed allowing the immigrant families gradually to acquire the *mores* or patterns of generally accepted behaviour before they are assimilated.

Table 5.5 The possible spatial outcomes of immigrant ethnic minority groups moving into a city. (After F. W. Boal.)

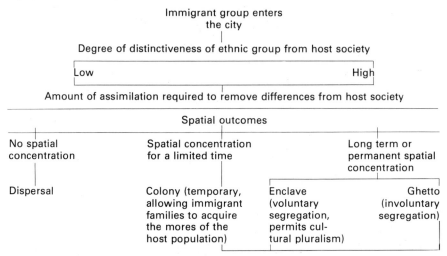

(c) Residential segregation in Belfast

In his study of residential patterns in Belfast, Boal found that, in common with other Western cities, there is an increase in average socio-economic status and decrease in population densities with distance from the city centre.[34] Superimposed on this are sectors of high and low status. A further differentiation in the western low-status sector arises from religious differences. In this sector divisions between the Protestant and Roman Catholic housing areas are very sharp and are often marked by non-residential land uses such as factory sites or railway lines. Where this is not possible the transition occurs within the width of a single street. Boal, conducting his research prior to the outbreak of civil disturbance, analysed site characteristics to define two culturally distinct residential areas; Clonard, in which 98 per cent of the population was Roman Catholic, and Shankill (I) in which 99 per cent of the population was Protestant.[35] The two areas meet in a very narrow band restricted to a single street, Cupar Street (see Fig. 5.15).

Boal then proceeded to examine the activity patterns of the two clearly segregated groups and found these to be extremely territorial. He discovered that 89 per cent of those living in Shankill (I) went to Shankill Road to catch a bus to take them to the city centre, while 93 per cent living in Clonard went to the Falls or Springfield Road, not all minimizing the distance. He also found that shopping trips were strongly focused on each area's 'own' spine road and that visitor connections revealed

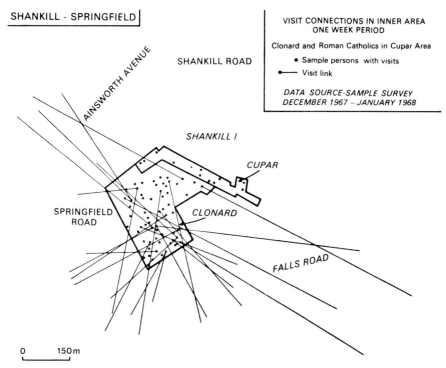

SHANKILL - SPRINGFIELD

AINSWORTH AVENUE

SHANKILL ROAD

SHANKILL I

CUPAR

SPRINGFIELD
ROAD

CLONARD

FALLS ROAD

VISIT CONNECTIONS IN INNER AREA
ONE WEEK PERIOD

Clonard and Roman Catholics in Cupar Area

● Sample persons with visits
●— Visit link

DATA SOURCE-SAMPLE SURVEY
DECEMBER 1967 – JANUARY 1968

0   150m

Fig. 5. 15   An indication of territoriality in Belfast based on local area names in the Shankill-Springfield district. 94% of those in Clonard called the area Clonard, Springfield or Falls and none used the term Shankill. In Shankill I no one used Clonard, Springfield or Falls and 77% used Shankill. In the transitional Cupar St., 37% used Clonard, Springfield or Falls and 26% Shankill. (Source: F. Boal, in N. Stephens & R. E. Glossock (eds.), *Irish Geographical Studies*, Queens University, Belfast, Dept. of Geography, 1970)

mutually exclusive networks (see Fig. 5.16). In other words there was practically no spatial interaction between the two groups. Each group identified with a clearly defined territorial space which gave it security and a sense of belonging. Thus in Belfast cultural and religious differences have caused the Roman Catholics and Protestants to become increasingly segregated and, in effect, enclaves have developed.

(d) The assimilation of the Italian population in Bedford

A study of the Italian population in Bedford provides a useful contrast to Belfast for there is evidence to suggest that this minority ethnic group is gradually being assimilated into the town as a whole.

Bedford is a town of approximately 80 000 inhabitants, about 20 per cent of whom are of immigrant stock. The largest single ethnic minority group is the 8000 strong Italian community which comprises 10 per cent of the total population of the town and is the largest Italian community in Britain outside London.[36] The Italians were first attracted to Bedfordshire during the 1950s and early 1960s when they were recruited by the London Brick Company to work in the local brick industry. Initially they were on four-year contracts and lived in hostels at the brickworks but later moved into lodgings in the town. The first wave of Italian migrants to Britain was, of course, mainly male. They were , however, able to send for their wives and families

151

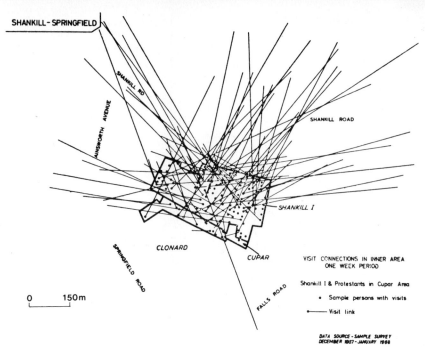

Fig. 5.16   Territoriality in Belfast, visitor connections of Catholics and Protestants in the Shankill-Springfield district. (Source: see caption to Fig. 5.15)

once they had received their employer's certificate of satisfactory conduct and had found a landlord who could guarantee the family suitable accommodation. At the 1961 census there were 3280 Italians in lodgings in Bedford but many of these have since purchased their own houses, particularly in the districts in and around Queens Park; the Ampthill/Elstow Roads; Foster Hill Road and streets leading off Midland Road close to the station (see Fig. 5.17). At present there is still some truth in the assertion that Bedford's Italian community lives in peaceful segregation rather than true integration.[37] But unless for some reason the process is reversed, the Italian families are gradually becoming more widely distributed throughout the town, and it has been estimated that true assimilation will be reached when the third generation of migrants establish their homes.

ASSIGNMENTS

1. *Table 5.3 on page 133 provides data on immigrants from the Indian sub-continent residing in Bedford. Use the location quotient to illustrate spatial contrasts in the distribution of the Asian population. You will need to go through the following stages:*

    (a) *Total the Asian population in all E.D.s and divide by the number of E.D.s in Bedford. This will give you the expected number of Asians in each E.D. if the Asian population were evenly distributed throughout the town. To save you time, this has been done for you. The overall average of Asians residing in E.D.s in Bedford is 1.22 per cent.*

    (b) *The location quotient* $= \dfrac{observed}{expected}$

152

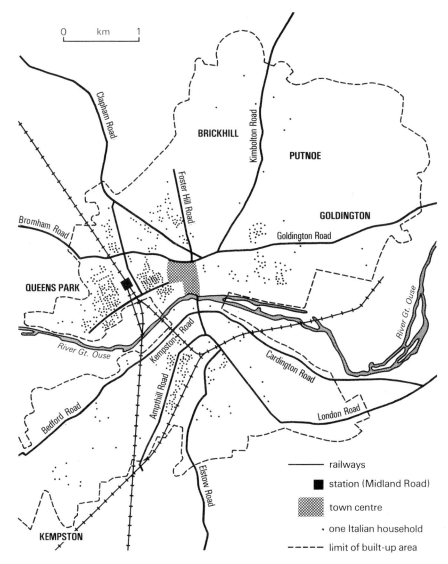

Fig. 5.17   The distribution of Italian households in Bedford. (Source: R. King, 'Bedford, the Italian Connection', *The Geographical Magazine*, London, April 1977, p.442)

Thus for each E.D. you will need to divide the proportion of Asians recorded by the expected, assuming an even distribution.

(c) You will then need to decide on the number of classes, the choice of class limits and method of density shading to be used (see page 131) before you can map the location quotients to illustrate spatial variations in the distribution of Bedford's Asian population.

2.   According to F. W. Boal what functions (at least in the short term) are fulfilled by ethnically segregated areas?

3.   Describe the possible spatial outcomes (i.e. the degree of dispersion or segregation) of a recently arrived immigrant minority group in a town and discuss some of the

153

factors that will influence the extent to which the group will be assimilated by the host community.

2. Residential mobility

Studies which concentrate on the demand side of the housing market must inevitably be concerned with decisions made on an individual, single family basis, for it is at this level that a decision to move house is taken. Each year approximately one in ten households in Great Britain moves house. In the USA residential mobility is even higher and approximately 18 per cent of the households change residence in the course of a year.[38]

(a) Why people move house
The reasons why people choose to move are varied. The principal motivators have been identified as

  (i) *changes in the family size related to the life cycle*, for example, a person is likely to move house on marriage and may move to more spacious accommodation to bring up children, then to a smaller property after the children leave home or on retirement;

 (ii) *career changes*, which account for most of the longer distance moves and involve, in particular, members of the higher socio-economic groups, who constitute a mobile elite;

(iii) *a reassessment of how the family sees itself*, that is brought about through income changes, social aspirations and so on, which may lead the family to consider the house and neighbourhood no longer suitable.

(iv) *the neighbourhood may change in character* and undergo social change through a process of invasion and succession.[39] This may lead on the one hand to an area being downgraded as it is 'invaded' by families of lower socio-economic status and population densities increase as substantial houses are divided for multiple occupancy. On the other hand, there is the possibility of upgrading as homes of artisans are acquired by more affluent middle-class families who make substantial improvement to their properties.

(b) The relocation process
Once the decision to move house has been taken, the relocation process involves three distinct phases:

  (i) establishing the criteria for a different house;
 (ii) the search procedure during which the original criteria may be modified;
(iii) the actual purchase or rental agreement.

When establishing the criteria of choice for a different house, the family will take into account the physical accommodation required (number of bedrooms, whether there is a garden, garage etc.), and the quality of the built environment and the availability of essential services such as schools, shops and public transport. Behavioural factors will also play a significant role at this stage for each family makes an estimate of its social standing and will eliminate districts of the town which it regards as unsuitable or unattainable. These criteria of choice will be constrained by such factors as income, socio-economic status and, in Britain in particular, type of tenure. For in Britain there operates a dual housing market, private and public.

Once a household moves into either sector it rarely moves out, but rather moves within its own tenure.[40]

(c) Effects of relocation constraints

    (i) These constraints give rise to *opportunity space*, and this is obviously much more extensive for a high status, high income family than for a low paid wage earner who lacks job security. This is why the most wealthy families have a wide choice and can afford to live almost anywhere in a city and its surroundings. It also helps to explain why the inner city is characterized by poverty and contains many of the socially and financially most disadvantaged families – the unemployed, single-parent families, recently arrived and migrant families, the elderly, who fail to move out as the area undergoes social change. The opportunity space of such families is very restricted and thus they have little alternative but to reside in the socially and environmentally poorest parts of the city.

    (ii) Once the criteria for a different house have been established the family is in a position to start house hunting. The family defines a *search space*[41] in which to look. This constitutes a sub-set of the family's *awareness space* which will include parts of the town directly familiar to them and other parts of which they have no direct experience but only images which have been derived from the mass media or conveyed to them by friends and acquaintances. (See Fig. 5.18).

    When they start their search, their awareness space may be extremely restricted. For example a commuter may have a dumb-bell shaped awareness of his or her town, being familiar only with the restricted areas surrounding home and workplace and the linear routes which connect them.[42] As we have seen, the work of Lynch and Orleans has demonstrated that, in general, middle-class professional people have more wide-ranging and more accurate mental images of their towns than manual workers. In other words, their awareness space is more extensive. Of course when searching for a different

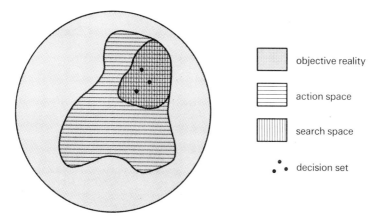

    objective reality

    action space

    search space

    decision set

Fig. 5.18   The spatial context in which residential decisions are made. (Source: after A. L. Backler, *A Behavioural Study of Locational Change in Upper Class Residential Areas: the Detroit Example*, Indiana University, 1974, p.49)

house, a family is likely to extend its awareness space by seeking information from such formal channels as local newspapers and estate agents or simply by either walking or driving round parts of the town unfamiliar to them. The information so acquired may cause them to redefine their search space. Studies by D. T. Herbert and others have demonstrated that formal channels of information are relatively unimportant to families moving to low-cost areas as they are far more likely to rely on casual channels such as information passed on by friends.

In the light of the above comments it is, perhaps, hardly surprising that the average distance of move of the least advantaged families will be short as such families are constrained by limited *opportunity space* and are likely to possess a very restricted *awareness space*.

(iii) A number of studies have also been conducted to establish where people would choose to live if they had the chance; in other words their *preference space*. A survey by D. T. Herbert[43] in Swansea (Fig. 5.19) indicated that the high status western resort districts, Sketty, West Cross, Langland and Oystermouth, were the most sought after and each of these districts was placed in the first three choices of over 40 per cent of the total sample. The survey also revealed, however, that a high level of desirability was attached by the respondents to their existing neighbourhoods so that districts such as Morriston which appeared less desirable to the total sample were often still preferred by the people residing there.

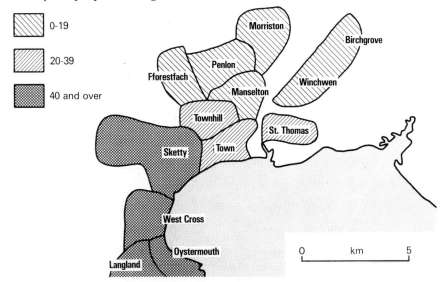

Fig. 5.19   District preferences within Swansea. The map shows the percentage of the total sample placing a district in the first three choices. (Source: after D. T. Herbert, *Urban Geography; a Social Perspective*, David & Charles, 1972)

ASSIGNMENTS

1.   *Explore the inter-relationships of opportunity space, awareness space and search space in the context of someone who is looking for a new house.*

2.   *By what means may an individual extend his/her awareness space?*

Conclusion

In Chapter 3 we traced the growth of towns and briefly examined the supply side of
the housing market and in this chapter we have explored some of the concepts
attached to residential space and the processes which operate when a family moves
house. We have seen that housing space (i.e. the provision of dwellings of different
types and ages), which affects the supply side and housing demand, takes place
within the constraints of social space. It is the interaction of these two that leads to
social segregation within the physical space of towns and cities. B. T. Robson has
summarized the total process in a flow diagram reproduced below.[44]

Fig. 5.20 shows the inter-relationship of the demand and supply side of housing.
Demand is influenced by, among other factors, income, lifestyle and family size.
Supply is influenced by factors operating at a local scale, such as land ownership and
planning restrictions, and those operating at a national scale, such as the availability
of mortgages and interest rates. The diagram also suggests that house tenure and
ethnicity act as further filters, restricting an individual family's choice of where to
live. These collective processes are responsible for social patterning or *social ecology*
within a town.

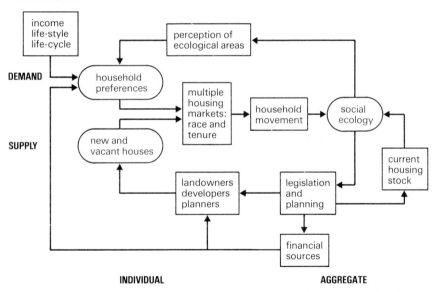

Fig. 5.20   Interaction between supply and demand in the British housing market. (Source:
B. T. Robson, *Urban Social Areas*, OUP, 1975, p.29)

Key Ideas

A.   Social patterning: quantitative approaches
1.   In most towns it is possible to distinguish comparatively homogeneous social
sub-areas.

2. A number of techniques have been developed to distinguish these sub-areas, the most effective of which involve a wide range of variables rather than a single one.

B. *Social space: behavioural approaches*
1. The urban ecologists considered that the principles and processes of plant ecology could be applied to a study of city structure. (See also page 87.)
2. They examined how the forces of competition led to dominance and segregation, thereby creating distinctive sub-areas.
3. Culture and tradition also exert powerful influences and certain parts of a town may acquire sentimental and symbolic connotations which may counteract the forces of competition.
4. Social space is a synthesis of objective, physical space and the perceived dimensions of space.
5. Social space includes both activity space and awareness space.
6. A person's activity space is the area in which he or she lives and moves.
7. Awareness space is the perception that an individual or group has of its environment.
8. Groups and individuals acquire mental images of their environment which are influenced by their values, aspirations and cultural traditions.
9. An individual's images of the urban environment form a link between reality and behaviour.

C. *The neighbourhood*
1. A neighbourhood is the local area with which a group is most familiar and with which its members can most readily identify.
2. It is a form of territorial space with both spatial (physical) and social attributes.
3. The balance between spatial and social attributes varies between neighbourhoods.
4. At the simplest level of definition, propinquity or nearness is the only distinguishing characteristic of the neighbourhood.
5. At the most sophisticated level, the neighbourhood forms a distinct, cohesive community in which there is much social interaction.
6. Neighbourhoods with social attributes tend to have clearly defined boundaries.
7. Length of residence, class and, possibly, physical isolation contribute to the development of community neighbourhoods.
8. One of the prime planning objectives in post-war Britain has been the establishment of neighbourhoods in new housing areas.
9. In the initial stages, the layout of housing estates may influence the development of a sense of community.
10. Homogeneous neighbourhoods are more likely to develop a sense of community than heterogeneous neighbourhoods.

D. *Processes*
   Residential segregation
1. Residential segregation fulfils a number of functions: defensive, avoidance, preservation, and 'attack', facilitating joint action.

2. The extent to which ethnic and racial minorities will be assimilated in the host community depends partly on the degree of distinctiveness of the ethnic group from the host community.

Residential mobility

3. A person selecting a new housing area must work within the constraints of opportunity space. This is most limited for certain sections of society such as the low paid and unemployed.
4. A person's search for a new house is further restricted by his/her limited awareness of the town in which he/she is moving.
5. The search space is a sub-set of a person's awareness space.

Additional Activities

1. (a) Examine P. H. Rees's model of the social areas of metropolitan Chicago (see Fig. 5.7) and compare it with the Burgess model of Chicago shown on page 86. (Fig. 4.2.)
   (b) In what respects does Rees's model incorporate elements of both the concentric zone and sector models?
2. In a recent study of people's perception of Hull, two groups were chosen, one local with first-hand experience of Hull and the other consisting of people from other parts of Britain whose mental images of Hull have been derived indirectly (for example through what they watch on television or read in their newspapers). Each group was asked to select ten terms from a list of forty-eight which best described Hull. The table below summarizes the results of the survey and indicates the percentage from each group which listed the various terms. Describe how the local and non-local groups perceived Hull and try to account for differences in the responses.

Table 5.6 Leading characteristic attributes of Hull as perceived by inhabitants and outsiders. (Source: E. W. Burgess, and reproduced in Pocock & Hudson, *Images of the Urban Environment*, Macmillan, London and Basingstoke, 1978.)

Inhabitants	%	Outsiders	%
Good shopping centre	85	Docks	90
Working-class city	84	Working-class city	85
Docks	81	Ships	79
Large council estates	75	Fishy	75
Friendly	74	Heavy industry	67
Trees, parks	74	Slums	63
Ships	65	Large council estates	59
Low wages	61	Unemployment	57
Fishy	58	Cold	56
Congested traffic	57	Smoke	53
Tower block flats	56	Congested traffic	50
Redevelopment	55	Drabness	49

Responses in percentages. $N = 180$ for both groups.

3. If you live in a town which attracts tourists, you could attempt a similar exercise and try to compare the composite perceptions of the town of samples of local people and tourists.

4. If you live in a new housing area, conduct a questionnaire survey to try to discover if the layout of houses exerts an influence on the development of a sense of community. Are there contrasts in the degree of social interaction in streets of differing layout? You can test this by constructing restricted surveys in (a) a cul-de-sac, (b) part of a main road, (c) a pedestrianized housing district and (d) a minor road which also takes through-traffic. In each of these find how many of their neighbours each person can name, or how many neighbours' houses they have visited. The data can be presented on sociograms as illustrated in Fig. 5.21.

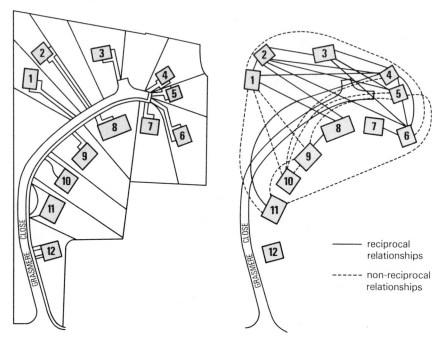

Fig. 5.21   Sociogram of visiting relationships on an estate in the North Midlands. (Source: L. Carey & R. Mapes, *The Sociology of Planning*, Batsford, 1972)

5. Examine B. T. Robson's flow diagram which summarizes the structure of the British housing market (Fig. 5.20) and then answer the following questions:
    (a) What factors influence an individual's housing demands?
    (b) What factors influence the availability of housing?
    (c) Why is it necessary to distinguish multiple housing markets based on tenure?
    (d) How do social sub-areas develop in a town?

Reading

A. KNOX, P. L., *Social Well-Being: a Spatial Perspective*, OUP, 1975.
    JONES, E. & EYLES, J., *An Introduction to Social Geography*, OUP, 1977, Chapters 3 and 4.

DAVIES, P., *Science in Geography 3, Data description and presentation*, OUP, 1974, in particular Chapters 5 and 6.

B.   JONES, E., *Readings in Social Geography*, OUP, 1975. In particular, BUTTIMER, A., 'Social Space in Interdisciplinary Perspective', pages 128–137, and FIREY, W., 'Sentiment and Symbolism as Ecological Variables', pages 138–148.

JONES, E. & EYLES, J., *op.cit.*, Chapters 1 and 2.

LYNCH, K., *The Image of the City*, MIT Press, 1960.

C.   HERBERT, D. T., *Urban Geography, A Social Perspective*, David & Charles, 1972, pages 225–237.

D.   *Residential segregation*

JONES, E. & EYLES, J., *op.cit.*, Chapter 7.

KING, R., 'Bedford: The Italian Connection', *Geographical Magazine*, April 1977, pages 442–9.

SMITH, D. M., *Patterns in Human Geography*, Penguin Books, 1977, pages 161–171 for a full discussion of location quotients.

Residential mobility.

HERBERT, D. T., *op.cit.*, Chapter 8.

# The central business district

Introduction

The one feature common to all the models of city structure discussed in Chapter 4 was a Central Business District where commercial activities such as specialized shops and offices are dominant. The CBD is at the very heart of the urban system, the commercial hub about which the rest of the city is structured.[1] In its most pronounced form it is essentially a twentieth-century phenomenon. Developments in construction technology have led to the erection of multi-storey buildings, and in transport technology have meant that people can reach shops, offices and places of entertainment relatively swiftly. These factors combined to make the centralization of activities feasible.

The CBD has traditionally been *the most accessible part of the urban system*, at the focal point of the transport network. It is accessible not only to those living in the built-up area but also to those residing within the town's urban field. It is often ringed by bus termini, suburban railway stations and extensive off-street car parks. Its position at the centre of the urban and regional communications network greatly influences the type of development located there. As we saw in Chapter 4, commercial activities compete with one another for the most accessible sites located within the relatively confined space of the town centre. The competition for space pushes up land rent and rateable values so that they are at their highest within the CBD, reaching their maximum at what is described as the *peak land value intersection*[2] *(PLVI)*, and declining fairly rapidly with distance from that point. This is because, within the town centre, most movement must necessarily be on foot and walking distance from the PLVI is, therefore, a critical factor. Pedestrian densities are extremely high at and near to the PLVI. If the area has not been pedestrianized, the pavements are often very wide so that they can accommodate the many shoppers and office workers who use them. Pedestrian densities decline rapidly with distance from the PLVI and are reflected in a parallel decline in rateable values.

Not only is the CBD the most accessible part of the urban system but it also provides commercial enterprises with unique linkages with other businesses and the public.[3] Shops benefit from *cumulative attraction* if their potential customers are concentrated into a limited area. A number of similar retail outlets confined to a specialized area can each expect to attract more customers than an equivalent number of isolated stores. The customers also benefit from such a concentration because this makes comparison shopping easier; that is the possibility of inspecting the quality and price of similar goods being offered in several shops. Offices benefit because the CBD, more than anywhere else in the urban system, offers the possibility of rapid personal contact with ancillary services such as legal advisers, advertising agencies and accountants, as well as banks, stockbrokers and the Stock Exchange.

It is the combination of maximum accessibility and the unique linkage it offers commercial activities that gives rise to the distinctive characteristics of the CBD. We shall now discuss this in greater detail.

A. The Characteristics of the CBD

1. Concentration of department stores, variety goods stores and specialist retail outlets

The accessibility of the CBD attracts those retail outlets which provide goods and services which have a wide range and a high threshold population (see page 191) and, therefore, depend upon customers being drawn from a very extensive catchment area[4]. This accounts for the specialized nature of retailing. Department stores and variety goods stores such as Marks and Spencer, British Home Stores and Woolworth are likely to be located at the 'node' of the CBD occupying the most desirable sites at the intersection of the busiest thoroughfares (see Plate 6.1.), while specialist shops such as book shops and jewellers will occupy less expensive sites. There will also be a number of shops and retail services which cater specifically

Plate 6.1   Department stores, Oxford Street, London. *(Author's photograph)*

for the many people who work in the CBD. These will include men's and women's outfitters, office stationers and cafés and will be located mainly amongst the offices (see Plate 6.2). The extensive catchment area enables the specialist shop to carry a wide range of goods, including high quality, expensive items.

Plate 6.2   Shops and retail services on the ground floors of office blocks in Kingsway, London, which cater for the needs of office workers, *(Author's photograph)*

2. Concentration of offices

In a large city these will include the principal regional, or even head offices, of a number of companies which must be accessible to as many potential clients as possible (see Plate 6.4). A central location also makes it easier for offices to assemble their labour force, drawn from middle-class workers who often live in peripheral suburban locations.

3. Absence of manufacturing industry

There are, however, a few specialized manufacturing activities such as the *publication of periodicals and newspapers* which find it desirable to locate at least some of their processes here. In the publication of periodicals and daily newspapers speed in production is crucial. Immediate access to contributors, illustrators, photographic agencies and other relevant services is vital. Likewise speed of despatch is

Plate 6.3   Harley Street, London, renowned for its concentration of medical specialists. *(Author's photograph)*

essential, particularly with morning newspapers which need to be sent out nationally during the previous night. Only a CBD location can meet these exacting requirements.

4. Functional zoning

Similar activities tend to be concentrated into distinct areas and it is often possible to distinguish concentrations of offices, places of entertainment and one or more shopping districts. In addition, there is often a certain degree of specialization within these functional zones. For example, in the office zone it is often possible to delimit a financial quarter where there is a concentration of banks and stockbrokers. In a similar way, insurance company offices and legal firms may well be grouped together in different parts of the office zone; while within the retail shopping zone the department and variety goods stores are often close together and it is sometimes possible to distinguish a street dominated by more expensive specialist shops. Regent Street, in London, provides a good example of this. At a more detailed level of specialization, certain streets or parts of streets become renowned for a particular activity. Many city centres include an 'automobile row' where car dealers are concentrated or a street where medical specialists are clustered (see Plate 6.3).

5. Multi-storey development

The high land and rent values in the town centre encourage multi-storey development and multi-storey buildings will often occupy the most expensive sites, giving

Plate 6.4   Multi-storey development; the City of London. (*Aerofilms*)

the CBD a three-dimensional quality (see Plate 6.4). In this way the effective floor space in the CBD can be greatly increased and is generally much greater than the ground space. Thus the 'real area' of the CBD is often considerably larger than it appears on a map; it might, in fact, be four or five times greater than the ground space (see Fig. 6.1).

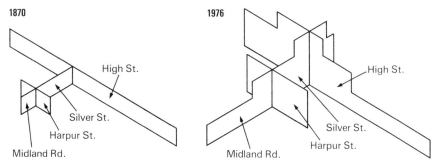

Fig. 6.1   The increasing three-dimensional quality of Bedford's CBD. (Source: R. Hardaker)

6. Vertical zoning

Within the multi-storey blocks in the CBD the same use is generally not made of each floor. Those activities which need maximum contact with the public such as retail shops and services, building societies and banks tend to occupy the lower, more accessible floors where the rents are higher. Other users who need a central location, but do not require sites which will attract passing trade, such as solicitors, architects and advertising agencies, are often found on the higher, less expensive floors (see Fig. 6.2).

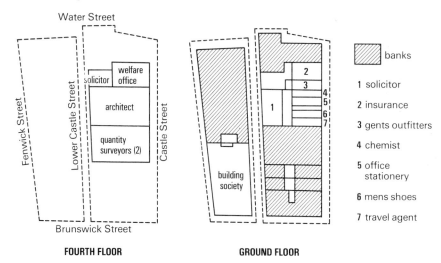

Fig. 6.2   Vertical zoning in an office block. (Source: M. F. Cross & P. A. Daniel, *Fieldwork for Geography Classes*, McGraw-Hill, 1968, p.53)

167

7. A low residential population

The high land values within the CBD dictate that commercial enterprises dominate to the virtual exclusion of certain other functions. In particular, the CBD tends to be characterized by a low residential population. Some dwellings may survive around the fringe of the CBD and it is possible that a few blocks of luxury flats may recently have been built in the city centre itself, but generally the residential population of the CBD is very small. This has encouraged some geographers to describe the CBD as the 'dead heart' of the city[5] but such a description applies only at night-time. During each working day, the CBD becomes the focus of an intense concentration of people.

ASSIGNMENTS
1. *List the features characteristic of a CBD as illustrated in Plate 6.5.*
2. *Explain the distribution of offices in the office block illustrated in Fig. 6.2.*

B. The Delimitation of the CBD

Many of the earliest studies of the CBD by geographers were concerned with attempts at areal definition, that is to delimit the precise extent of a town's CBD. Such studies have been justified in that they make possible comparisons between the CBDs of a number of towns. These, in turn, permit generalizations to be made about the CBD as a concept of universal application at least within the Western city.[6] Precise definition also facilitates studies of the processes of change and evolution through time within a single CBD.

Within American cities the CBD might well end abruptly in what has been described as a 'cliff-line' which marks a sharp break between the distribution of commercial and non-commercial activities. In most Western European cities, however, the edge of the CBD is not so distinct. It tends to be gradational and fragmented, more of a zone than a line, and any attempts at areal definition must take this into account.

1. Some techniques of delimitation

(a) Pedestrian flows

During the working day, pedestrian densities tend to be greatest at the peak land value intersection (PLVI) and, very approximately, decline with distance from it. It is thus possible to use pedestrian density data, collected at intervals throughout the central area, to gain some idea of the extent of a town's CBD. The pedestrian counts should, of course, be made at judicial times of the day, such as mid-morning or mid-afternoon when few non-central business pedestrians, such as school children returning home, will be included. The recorded values can each be converted into percentages of the highest pedestrian count and an isopleth map constructed to distinguish surfaces of varying degrees of pedestrian intensity.

◀ Plate 6.5   Liverpool's CBD. (*Author's photographs*)

(b) Restricted parking zones

Traffic congestion in city centres has for long posed a problem and traffic management schemes and parking restrictions have been in operation for many years. In some British towns the extent of the parking meter zone or parking disc zone (where drivers must display discs indicating their time of arrival) provides a useful indication of the extent of the CBD. In some instances restrictions of traffic in town centres are even more acute. For example, Central Göteborg, Sweden, is divided into five separate traffic zones which are surrounded by a circular route from which there are special entrances to each zone. To travel from one zone to another it is usual to use the circular route (see Fig. 6.3). Within these zones parking spaces are limited and generally restricted to short stay parking (as little as fifteen minutes in some cases). For longer stay parking there are extensive car parks beyond the circular route. The extent of the traffic zones provides a useful indication of the extent of Göteborg's CBD.

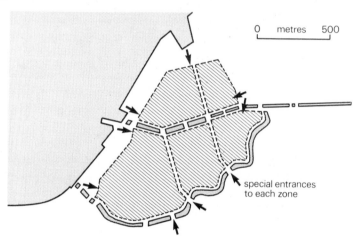

Fig. 6.3   Traffic zones in central Göteborg.

(c) The rate index

Rates, which contribute towards local finances, are payable on all properties. Gross rateable values reflect the rent at which the properties might reasonably be let and, therefore, provide a good indication of the considered commercial advantages of a particular site. A number of studies have used rateable values in attempts to define a 'hard' commercial core within a CBD. These have generally taken into account variations in total floorspace of different premises by standardizing the data through the application of a rate index.[7]

$$\text{Rate Index (R.I.)} = \frac{\text{Gross rateable value (in £s)}}{\text{Ground floor space (in sq. feet or sq. metres)}}$$

The R.I. is expressed in £ per sq. foot or metre of ground floor space.

The information thus obtained can be mapped (see Fig. 6.4) using somewhat arbitrarily defined categories or by the use of isopleths which join points of an equivalent rate index (see Fig. 6.5).

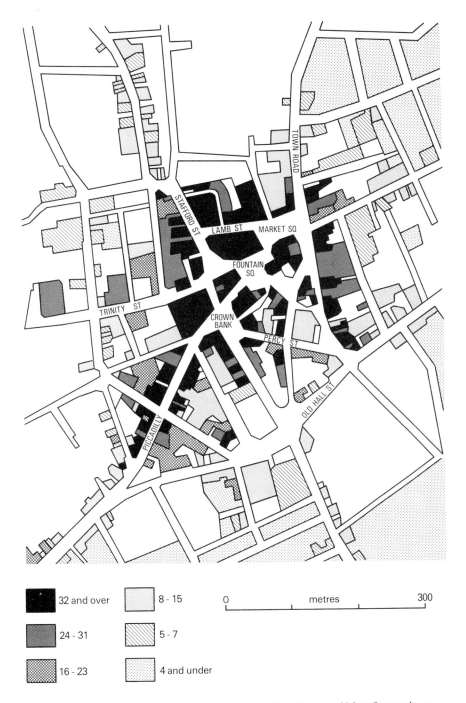

Fig. 6.4   Rate index scores, Hanley, Staffs. (Source: D. T. Herbert, *Urban Geography; a Social Perspective*, David & Charles, 1972, p.82)

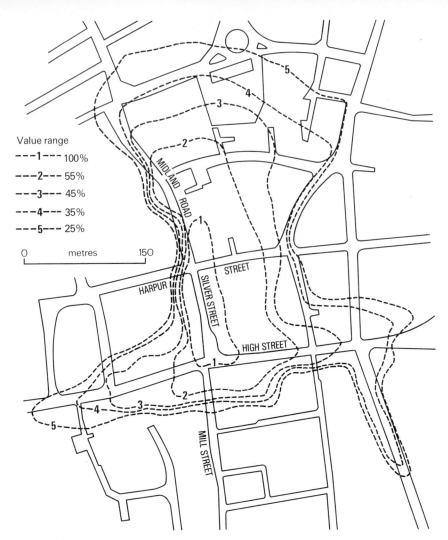

Value range
- - -1- - - 100%
- - -2- - - 55%
- - -3- - - 45%
- - -4- - - 35%
- - -5- - - 25%

0   metres   150

Fig. 6.5   An isopleth map showing shop values in the central area of Bedford. (Source: after *The Bedford Study: Central Area Shopping*, Beds. County Planning Office, 1967, p.26)

(d) The Central Business Index (CBI)

This is a technique of CBD delimitation devised by R. E. Murphy and J. E. Vance in the 1950s.[8] The technique involves determining for blocks and premises within the central area of a town the proportion of floor space which is in central business use.

To apply the CBI, the following steps must be taken:

(i) On a large-scale plan of the whole of the central area record central (C) and non-central business (X) functions for each floor of each building. Murphy and Vance distinguish the following non-central business functions:
Permanent residences.
Government and public buildings and open spaces (including civic buildings, schools and parks).
Organizational establishments (churches, colleges, etc.)

Wholesaling and commercial storage.

Vacant premises and building sites.

Railway lines and yards.

Other functions, such as shops, offices and other commercial activities, are distinguished as central business functions.

(ii) For each block of buildings within the central area calculate the proportion of the total floorspace in central business (C) and non-central business district (X) uses. (This method is more easily applied in North American cities which are invariably planned on a grid basis.)

(iii) By applying the following formulas the Central Business Height Index (CBHI) and the Central Business Intensity Index (CBII) can then be calculated for each block.

$$CBHI = \frac{Total\ C\ floor\ space}{Ground\ floor\ space}$$

Thus a CBHI of 1 indicates a complete ground floor or equivalent coverage in commercial or central business uses.

$$CBII = \frac{Total\ C\ floor\ space}{Total\ floor\ space} \times \frac{100}{1}$$

The CBII measures the proportion of the total available floor space within the block which is in commercial or central business uses. Thus if a block has a CBII of 50 per cent, central business uses occupy at least half the total floor space of all storeys.

(iv) Murphy and Vance suggest that, in order to be included within the CBD, a block must have a CBHI of at least 1 and a CBII of at least 50 per cent (see Fig. 6.6).

The Central Business Index has been criticized because of the subjective nature of the non-central business functions listed by Murphy and Vance. Certain functions, such as garages and hotels, do not fit easily into either central or non-central business categories. A second criticism concerns the apparent degree of subjectivity used in determining the limiting values which qualify a block for inclusion within the CBD, although Murphy does claim that they are based upon reasoning and empirical research.[9]

One of the great virtues of the CBI is that, in common with pedestrian densities and rateable indices, it can be used to distinguish, within a town's CBD, a commercial 'hard core' from the 'frame'. D. H. Davies, in his study of land use in central Cape Town, adopted a CBHI of 4 and a CBII of 80 per cent in his delimitation of the 'hard core' of the CBD of Cape Town[10] (see Fig. 6.7).

2. The CBD core-frame model

The methods described above by which the CBD may be delimited have been selected because they can be adapted to distinguish a highly concentrated central area within a CBD, the 'core', from its bordering area, the 'frame'. The 'core-frame' model of CBD structure was proposed by E. M. Horwood and R. R. Boyce in 1959[11] (see Fig. 6.8). The core is the area of the greatest concentration of daytime population and most intensive land use. Land values are at their highest and multi-storey buildings dominate. Within the core it may be possible to distinguish districts where particular activities are concentrated and which form sub-functional zones.

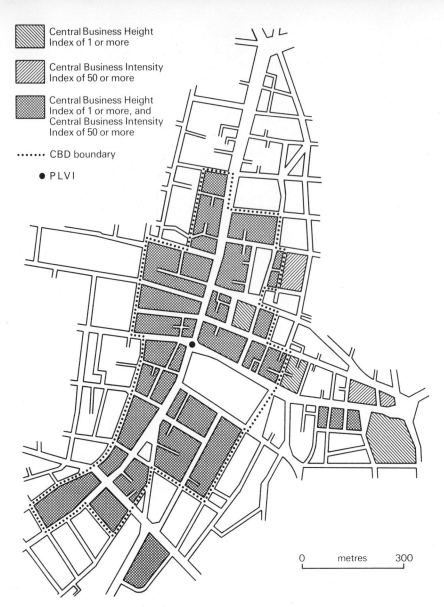

Central Business Height
Index of 1 or more

Central Business Intensity
Index of 50 or more

Central Business Height
Index of 1 or more, and
Central Business Intensity
Index of 50 or more

······· CBD boundary

● PLVI

0   metres   300

Fig. 6.6   The CBD of Worcester, Massachusetts, USA, delimited by applying the Central
Business Height and Intensity Indices. (Source: after R. E. Murphy, 'Delimiting the CBD',
Economic Geography, 1954, Fig. 6)

The frame is less intensively developed; land values are lower and functions more
varied. There are, however, clusters of functions derived from linkages and the
model identifies such sub-zones as car sales and services and specialist medical
facilities. As conceived by Horwood and Boyce, the frame comprises peripheral
districts of the CBD but overlaps into Burgess's 'zone in transition'.

Blocks omitted from hard
core after application of
exclusion rule

Blocks retained
under this rule

—— Final hard core
boundary

----- CBD boundary

● PLVI

0   metres   200

Fig. 6.7   The 'hard core' of Cape Town's CBD. (Source: after D. Hywel Davies, 'The Hard
Core of Cape Town's CBD: An Attempt at Delimitation', *Economic Geography* **36**, 1960)

3. The CBD and the Zone in Transition

Once the notion of a clearly defined CBD is relaxed and replaced by a core-frame
concept, it is pertinent to reconsider the surrounding Zone in Transition. This is
essentially an area of conflict and adjustment which aptly demonstrates the dynamic
qualities of the modern city. As city centres expand, CBD functions may be
extended into this transitional zone. This process has been referred to as 'invasion-
succession' (see page 91) and has been summarized in a model developed by
D. W. Griffin and R. E. Preston (1966)[12] which recognizes the interaction of the CBD
and the Zone in Transition (see Fig. 6.9).

Thus, within the Zone in Transition Griffin and Preston distinguished sectors of:
(a) *active assimilation* where new CBD functions are in the process of development,
such as an extension of the shopping floorspace.
(b) *passive assimilation* where there is less new development and this tends to be of
a non-CBD character, such as warehousing.
(c) *general inactivity* where there is little change.

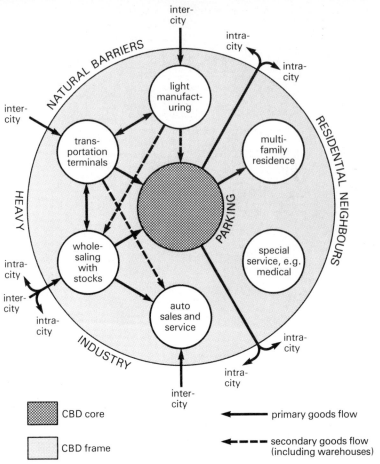

Fig. 6.8   A CBD core-frame model. (Source: E. M. Horwood & R. R. Boyce, *Studies of the Central Business District and Urban Freeway Development*, University of Washington Press, 1959)

4. The perception of the city centre

We have seen in the previous chapter that individuals form images of their urban environments and it can be argued that in many respects people's perception of the CBD is of more relevance than attempts at objective definition and delimitation. A town's residents will have their own mental images of what comprises the commercial core of the CBD. Brian Goodey's study,[13] investigating Birmingham residents' perception of their city centre, recognizes this (see Fig. 6.10). Readers of the *Birmingham Post* were asked to send in sketch maps, compiled without reference to accurate street maps, that conveyed their broad impressions of the city centre. The sketch maps summarized the images that people carried in their heads and which they used to find their way about on visits to the city centre. The individual responses were combined to build up a composite map illustrating people's prefer- ences for features in Birmingham's centre. Perhaps not surprisingly, the responses demonstrated a clear preference for developments on a small and more personal

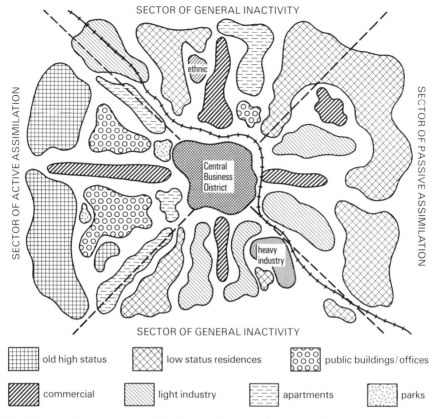

Fig. 6.9   A schematic pattern of land use in the zone of transition for the American city. (Source: after D. W. Griffin & R. E. Preston, 'A Restatement of The Transition Zone Concept', *AAAG*, **56**, 1966)

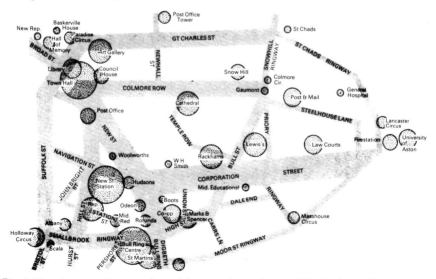

Fig. 6.10   A composite map of people's perceptions of central Birmingham. (Source: P. Gould & R. White, *Mental Maps*, Penguin Books, 1974, p.29)

scale. Some of the tall, skyline features were far less prominent than might have been expected. Such a map provides useful information to planners whose role it is to influence the nature of central area redevelopment.

ASSIGNMENTS
1. Using the evidence presented in Fig. 6.5, try to distinguish a 'hard' commercial core within Bedford's CBD. Why is it difficult to delimit the CBD definitively?
2. Compare the core-frame concept outlined by Horwood and Boyce with the CBD and Zone in Transition envisaged by Burgess.
3. Ask everyone in your group to use their knowledge of the local town to:
   (a) Delimit a CBD.
   (b) Distinguish a hard commercial core within the CBD.
   (c) Locate the PLVI within the CBD.
   (An estate agent's map might be used as a base map.)
   Use these individual mental maps to compile a composite map to illustrate the group's perception of the extent of the CBD.
4. Use the CBHI and CBII to delimit the CBD of your local town. Use the criteria suggested by D. H. Davies to distinguish a 'hard core'. Compare this map with the mental map and attempt to account for any discrepancies.

C. Analysing the Internal Structure of the CBD

In order to gain some insight into the internal structure of the CBD of a city it is necessary to identify and delimit functional districts, and determine the degree of clustering of different shop and office types. It has long been recognized that certain types of shops and offices such as shoe shops and stockbrokers tend to cluster while others such as newsagents and travel agents are usually more widely distributed. A number of techniques have been devised which quantify the degree of clustering of CBD functions, and the *Centre of gravity* and *Index of dispersion* are amongst the most useful of these. The *Centre of gravity*, as the term suggests, defines the most central point of the distribution of a particular functional type, while the *Index of dispersion* measures the degree of clustering within the distribution. They are derived as follows:

(a) Draw horizontal (x axis) and vertical (y axis) lines to contain the distribution in question, representing each unit of floorspace by a point plotted at its centre.

(b) Measure the shortest distance from each point to the x and y axes.

(c) Work out the mean of the distance to the x and y axes (i.e. total the distances to the x and y axes respectively, and divide by the number of points in the distribution).

(d) The *Centre of gravity* of the distribution occurs where the two means intersect. To obtain a more accurate result, a weighting factor should be introduced to take into account variations in floorspace, i.e. some shops will be bigger than others.

(e) The *Index of dispersion* is obtained by measuring the distance from each point to the centre of gravity and determining the mean of all the distances.

(f) Some indications of the boundary of the cluster may be gained if a circle is drawn from the centre of gravity, of radius equal to the mean of all the distances from each point to the centre of gravity.

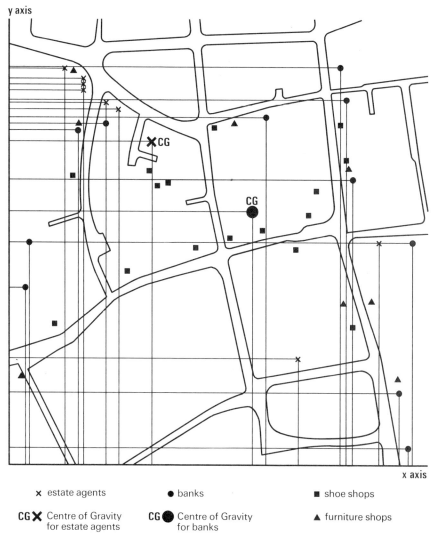

y axis

x axis

| x estate agents | ● banks | ■ shoe shops |

| CG ✗ Centre of Gravity for estate agents | CG ● Centre of Gravity for banks | ▲ furniture shops |

Fig. 6.11   The method used to calculate the centre of gravity and index of dispersion of estate agents and banks in a given urban area.

From Fig. 6.11 the centres of gravity and indices of dispersion have been worked out for banks and estate agents in central Bedford. They are as follows:

Banks: *Centre of gravity* is at the intersection of the mean distance from the *y* axis (6.7 cm) and the mean distance from the *x* axis (6.7 cm).
Index of dispersion = the mean distance from the centre of gravity for the distribution of banks = 4.9.

Estate agents: *Centre of gravity* is at the intersection of the mean distance from the *y* axis (3.9 cm) and the mean distance from the *x* axis (8.7 cm).
Index of dispersion = the mean distance from the centre of gravity for the distribution of estate agents = 3.3.

Note that it is the relative figures, rather than the absolute ones, which are important.

179

The indices of dispersion indicate that estate agents demonstrate a greater degree of clustering than do banks. Why do you think this might be?

This is a somewhat crude method of determining the location and extent of the cluster boundary. Far more sophisticated techniques of cluster analysis have been adopted by researchers such as D. H. Davies in his study of Cape Town's CBD.[14]

It is possible to study trends in spatial patterns within the CBD if changes in the centre of gravity and size and shape of clusters are monitored. This may be done with the help of earlier editions of street directories and large scale Ordnance Survey plans.

A number of recent studies of the internal structure of the CBD have suggested that it is necessary to go beyond the delimitation of land use patterns in the CBD to attempt to gain some understanding of the processes which bring these about. In other words to identify and analyse the related linkages and activity patterns. In this respect, however, data can be difficult to collect and appropriate research techniques are still being developed.

ASSIGNMENTS

Table 6.1. The degree of scatter of selected activities in Central Manchester.
(After R. Varley (1968), Unpublished M.A. thesis, and reproduced in H. Carter, *The Study of Urban Geography* page 224.) Note that the lower the figure the greater the degree of clustering.

Type of establishment	Index of Dispersion
Stock and share brokers	1.77
Barristers	2.33
Building societies	3.24
Insurance offices	3.28
Solicitors	3.36
Estate Agents	4.03
Travel agents	5.95

1. Suggest reasons for the variations in the indices of dispersion for functions in Central Manchester summarized in the table.
2. Work out the centres of gravity and indices of dispersion for the distributions of furniture shops and shoe shops in central Bedford (see Fig. 6.11) and compare them with those for banks and estate agents. Try to account for any differences.

D. Change Within the CBD

1. The evolution of the CBD

(a) Constraints to development
We have already seen that the areal extent of the CBD is determined in part by the distance the potential customer can be expected to walk to obtain the goods or services required. Historically, the development of the CBD may also have been constrained by the location of the historic core of the town. Limitations may also have been imposed by the town site and certain physical barriers such as a river, land liable to flood and steep slopes. Land ownership and lines of communication such as canals and railways may have imposed other constraints on development.

H. Carter and G. Rowley in their study of the nineteenth-century limitations to the expansion of central Cardiff[15] demonstrated how, by the 1840s, the medieval kernel which comprised the city centre was surrounded on all sides by marked physical barriers. To the north lay the Castle and the adjoining extensive estate, owned by the Bute family and preserved from development; to the west was the River Taff; to the south was the South Wales Railway and to the east were the successive lines of the medieval town walls, the Glamorgan Canal, the feeder to the Bute Dock (constructed in 1839) and the Taff Vale Railway which was opened in 1841 (see Fig. 6.12). These physical barriers effectively restricted the location of commercial development in central Cardiff and resulted in enormous pressures being exerted in the central area as the population of Cardiff increased from 10 000 in 1841 to 277 000 in 1971.

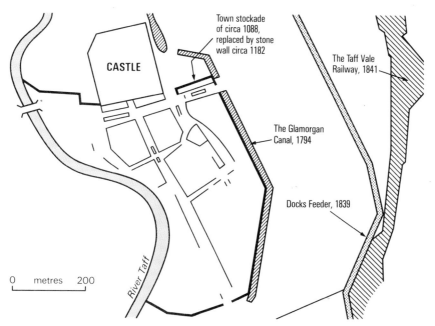

Fig. 6.12   Nineteenth-century limitations to the expansion of central Cardiff. (Source: after H. Carter & G. Rowley, 'The Morphology of the Central Business District of Cardiff'; in *Trans. Inst. Br. Geogr.* **38**, 1966 and reproduced in H. Carter, *The Study of Urban Geography*, Edward Arnold, 1972)

(b) Incentives to CBD expansion
Centrality is obviously the key factor in controlling the expansion of the CBD. Central business functions will move into only those districts which are accessible to potential customers. The direction of expansion of the CBD may, however, have been influenced in the past by the suitability for conversion to commercial use of existing buildings. The substantial eighteenth- and nineteenth-century villas were particularly suitable in this respect and often became available for conversion as the middle classes moved to more peripheral suburban locations. Carter and Rowley demonstrate how the CBD of Cardiff was extended eastwards along what is now Queen Street, 'following the line of least resistance and easiest conversion.'[16]

2. The redevelopment of central areas

The redevelopment of town centres is not only a twentieth-century phenomenon. For example, during the nineteenth century the centres of many of Britain's rapidly growing industrial towns underwent substantial renewal. One example is provided by Birmingham, where a brand new central shopping street, Corporation Street, replaced slum property.[17] However, there has been nothing comparable with the scale of post-war redevelopment and many of the central areas of British towns and cities have been, or still are, the focus of comprehensive redevelopment schemes. For the most part, this redevelopment has been part of a coherent plan which has been gradually implemented. The overall aim of such schemes has been to maintain and strengthen the CBD's regional role as a shopping, business and cultural centre and place of employment, by endeavouring to improve both the functioning of the centre and its physical environment. Attempts have been made to ensure that any increase in shop and office floorspace and employment opportunities is accompanied by appropriate improvements in public and private transport provision.

The specific objectives of central area redevelopment may be summarized as follows:[18]

(a) To exaggerate the zoning of commercial functions by:
    (i) defining areas for the expansion of shop and office floorspace,
    (ii) securing the redevelopment of physically and functionally obsolete areas such as those of poor quality housing, obsolescent warehouses and small workshops,
    (iii) relocating outside the town centre those activities which are undesirable and do not require a central location.

(b) To maintain, and, where possible, enhance the environmental quality of the central area by:
    (i) conserving districts and buildings of architectural value and character. In this respect many local planning authorities have designated a number of specific Conservation Areas within the town centre,
    (ii) ensuring that any new development is carefully designed and in harmony with its surroundings, and that carefully landscaped open spaces and precincts are provided.

(c) To improve accessibility to and movement within the town centre by:
    (i) implementing a transport and car parking policy designed to improve public transport and increase parking provision,
    (ii) easing traffic congestion within the town centre by adopting road improvement and building schemes. This may include the construction of an inner ring road to improve cross journey traffic flow,
    (iii) maximizing pedestrian/vehicular segregation and, possibly, developing a network of pedestrian precincts and walkways.

A close examination of the redevelopment of the central area of most large British towns will illustrate the implementation of some, if not all, of these broad aims. For example, in Liverpool's CBD commercial activities are being increasingly concentrated into clearly defined functional zones (see Fig. 6.13) while non-CBD functions such as wholesaling are being moved to other parts of the city. The wholesale fruit and vegetable market is a case in point. This used to be in the very heart of the city centre, but a few years ago was moved to a less congested suburban site. In the

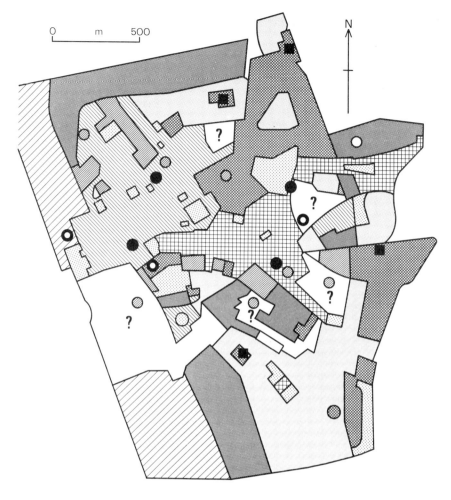

0   m   500

N

PROPOSED PRIMARY LAND USE PATTERNS

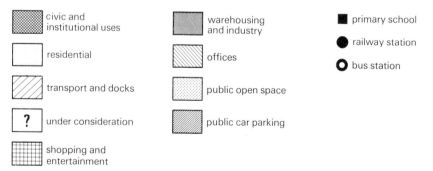

civic and institutional uses

residential

transport and docks

? under consideration

shopping and entertainment

warehousing and industry

offices

public open space

public car parking

■ primary school

● railway station

O bus station

Fig. 6.13   Proposed primary land use patterns, central Liverpool. *(Liverpool City Planning Department)*

comprehensive redevelopment of central Liverpool, attempts have been made to conserve districts of architectural interest and three conservation areas, William Brown Street, Castle Street and Rodney Street have been designated. Redevelopment proposals have also included attempts to improve the environment for shoppers. The main shopping street (Church Street) is now totally pedestrianized. Access to the CBD has been improved by the provision of additional car parking space, major road improvement schemes and the completion recently of an underground rail loop which connects all the main line and suburban stations.

3. Future prospects

One of the features of recent urban development has been the increasing tendency to decentralize commercial activities.[19] Retailers in particular have been quick to see the advantages of developing vast out-of-town centres incorporating extensive parking space and providing the advantages of economies of scale and more efficient operating which can be passed on to the consumer in terms of lower prices[20] (see Plate 7.3). Such developments have generally taken the form of 'superstores', often located in suburban sites and concentrating on the sale of convenience goods, and 'hypermarkets' which may have a rural location and trade in both convenience and durable goods. It is the latter, in particular, which pose a threat to town centres as they compete directly with department stores, variety goods stores and the specialist shops which are so characteristic of town centres. It is hardly surprising, therefore, that the development of out-of-town hypermarkets is a contentious issue. Each planning application is keenly debated and may become the subject of a public enquiry. Some of the arguments used by the protagonists and opponents of out-of-town shopping centres are summarized below:

(a) *Arguments in favour of the development of out-of-town hypermarkets*
   (i) The hypermarket provides a convenient form of retailing. The consumer is able to park easily and can purchase a wide range of goods at competitive prices under a single roof.
   (ii) The increase in car ownership (now over half British families have regular access to a car) means that, even if the out-of-town hypermarket is not served by regular public transport, a high proportion of shoppers can visit the centres.
   (iii) Technical innovations, for example refrigerators and deep freezers, make frequent shopping trips less essential and make possible bulk purchases of perishable goods.
   (iv) The development of suburban and ex-urban shopping centres eases traffic congestion and parking problems in town centres by siphoning off a significant proportion of the customers.
   (v) Throughout the inter-war and post-war periods, urban population has been decentralizing to the sprawling suburbs, and, as a result, average journeys from home to town centres have increased. This process has accelerated in recent years. For example, in the single decadal period 1961–1971 the population of Manchester declined from 662 000 to 543 000. The development of suburbs which in a large city may be situated some kilometres from the town centre has had the effect of increasing average

journey distances from home to the central shopping area. The decentralization of certain commercial functions can reduce the frequency of shopping trips to the town centre and thereby conserve energy by reducing petrol consumption by private motorists.

(b) *Arguments against the development of out-of-town hypermarkets*

(i) The out-of-town hypermarket is likely to comprise a vast, single-storey building with extensive associated car parking facilities. It is likely to consume a considerable area of land which formerly will have been used for agriculture or some other non-urban purpose. It will also make considerable demands on public services which cannot easily be satisfied. Pressure will be exerted on immediate access roads which are unlikely to have been built to cope with the density of traffic which may be generated.

(ii) The building of a hypermarket in a rural setting implies the relaxation of planning restrictions and may act as a precedent for further development.

(iii) Hypermarkets favour a certain type of consumer, namely the car owner who provides for a family and can benefit from making bulk purchases. Such developments militate against the non-car owner who may find the hypermarket inaccessible and the elderly who may need to make small purchases frequently. The social implications of the large scale decentralization of shopping facilities are, therefore, considerable.

(iv) Hypermarkets may pose a threat to the continued viability of town centres as potential customers are drawn to them from the CBD shops.

(v) The over-provision of shops is an inefficient use of limited resources. Investment should be channelled into those sectors of the economy engaged in production rather than servicing.

(vi) The development of an ex-urban hypermarket will encourage cross-town journeys which may greatly exceed average journey distances between homes and the town centre. The generation of additional traffic is wasteful of energy.

ASSIGNMENTS

1. (a) *Draw an annotated sketch map of a town centre that is familiar to you to illustrate how physical barriers have constrained the development of the CBD. Consider:*
   (i) *Fortifications (castle, defences).*
   (ii) *Natural features such as a river, land liable to flood and steep slopes.*
   (iii) *Lines of communication such as canals and railways.*
   (iv) *Land ownership.*

   (b) *Discuss more recent constraints to development such as arterial roads and, possibly, urban motorways and planning restrictions. The Town Plan almost certainly reinforces functional zoning within the town centre and restricts commercial activities to certain parts of the central area.*

   (c) *Assess how far the distribution of middle-class housing areas influenced the direction of any later extensions to the town's CBD.*

2. *Discuss how far the aims and objectives for central area redevelopment have been achieved in the CBD of your nearest regional centre.*

3. *Helicol Parks Ltd. applied for planning permission to develop a large hypermarket in the Bedfordshire village of Husborne Crawley.*

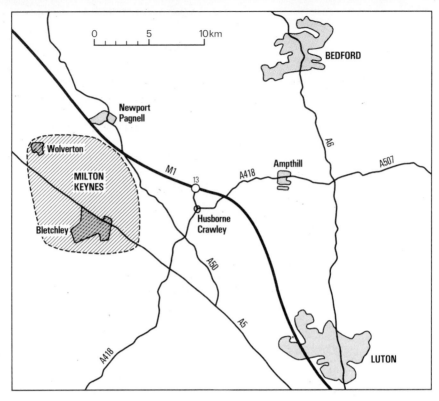

Fig. 6.14 . The proposed site of Helicol Parks development.

(a) *Examine Fig. 6.14 and summarize the advantages of the situation for the proposed development.*

(b) *A planning committee has been invited to consider whether the proposed development should receive planning permission. The committee consists of the following individuals:*

   (i) *an unemployed young person residing in Husborne Crawley.*

   (ii) *a retired military gentleman who has recently moved to Husborne Crawley and would like to see the village conserved.*

   (iii) *a working woman with three children living in Milton Keynes New Town. (The family owns two cars.)*

   (iv) *the manager of a supermarket in the centre of Bedford.*

   (v) *a young executive representing the developers.*

   (vi) *an old age pensioner, without a car, living in Luton.*

Write role profiles for each of the committee members and give each one a brief or an indication of the interests he or she represents. The role profiles and briefs can then be given to members of your group who will become a simulated planning committee. The committee members should each in turn put their case and the committee eventually arrive at a consensus of opinion which should be reported back to the rest of the class. If you have a large enough class it will be interesting for more than one committee to discuss the planning application. The groups can then compare decisions and the processes by which they were reached.

Key Ideas

Introduction

1. The CBD develops at the most accessible part of the urban system.
2. Competition for CBD sites results in high site values, higher than in any other part of the urban system.
3. These high land values dictate that commercial enterprises dominate to the virtual exclusion of other functions.
4. The CBD provides commercial enterprises with unique linkages with other businesses and the public.
5. Shops and other commercial activities benefit from cumulative attraction within the CBD.

A. The characteristics of the CBD

1. Certain types of retail outlets, such as department stores and variety goods stores, which have a wide range and high threshold population, are likely to occupy the most central space.
2. Offices may occupy rather more peripheral sites within the CBD.
3. There is a marked absence of manufacturing industry within the CBD.
4. The potential linkages with other business and the public which a CBD site provides, encourages the development of distinctive functional zones such as shops and offices.
   Within these broad functional zones marked sub-sections can often be identified, e.g. a financial quarter within the office zone.
5. High site values within the CBD encourage multi-storey development.
6. Within individual office blocks, activities which need maximum contact with the public usually occupy the lower floors.
7. Within the CBD there is a low residential population.

B. The delimitation of the CBD

1. The boundary of the CBD is generally gradational rather than clear cut.
2. In general, pedestrian densities and rateable values decline with distance from the CBD.
3. An examination of parking restrictions within the town centre may provide some indication of the extent of the CBD.
4. It is often possible to distinguish a 'hard core' of commercial activity within a town's CBD.
5. The core-frame model distinguishes a core, a district of intensive land use where land values are highest, from a less intensively developed frame.
6. CBD functions may be extended into the Zone in Transition where it may be possible to distinguish sectors of active and passive assimilation and general inactivity.
7. Individuals will have their own mental images of what comprises the commercial core of a town. A composite map of these will provide an indication of the perceived extent of the CBD.
8. Individuals' mental maps of town centres would seem to indicate a preference for developments on a small and more personal scale.

C. Change within the CBD

1. The development of the CBD may have been constrained by limitations imposed by the site of the town's historic core and by certain physical barriers.

2. The direction of expansion of the CBD may have been influenced by suitability of buildings already in existence for conversion to commercial uses.
3. The objectives of central area redevelopment are concerned with functional zoning; environmental quality and movement to and within town centres.
4. The decentralization of commercial activities poses a threat to the continued viability of town centres.

Additional Activities

1. Describe the features which distinguish the CBD of a large city.
2. Critically examine the techniques you would adopt to:
   (a) delimit the CBD of a large town,
   (b) analyse the internal structure of a town's CBD.
3. Write an essay on 'The CBD in twenty years' time', incorporating a reasoned account of the changes you envisage taking place.

Reading

A. JOHNSON, J. H., *Urban Geography: An Introductory Analysis*, Pergamon, 1972, Chapter 6.
B. MURPHY, R. E., *The Central Business District*, Longman, 1972, Chapter 3.
C. CARTER, H., *The Study of Urban Geography*, Arnold, 1976, Chapter 10.
D. PARKER, A. J., 'Hypermarkets: the changing pattern of retailing', *Geography*, **60**, April, 1975, pages 120–124.

7 Central place theory

A. Economic factors: supply, demand and choice

1. The need to choose

Suppose that you decide, whilst reading this section, to have a cup of coffee, only to discover that there is none in the kitchen. Assuming that you have some money and that the shops are still open you could either (a) go out and buy some coffee, come home and make a cup or (b) if it's late, or you live in a large enough town, go and buy a cup of coffee at a coffee bar. These choices assume the *availability* of what you want, if you are prepared to travel to get it. Our reluctance to travel is an aspect of *friction of distance*. Alternatively you could stay at home and make a cup of tea or open a bottle of coke, in other words accept *substitutes* for what you want. Thirdly you could forget the whole idea and carry on with your reading.

Which of these alternatives appeals to you will depend in part upon your personality, but it will also be conditioned by how strong your desire is to obtain the commodity in question and by the means available to satisfy it. The variety of choices available each time we want something illustrates fundamental concepts of supply and demand which become more apparent if we explore further. The need or *demand* for coffee is only one of a whole group of needs which are satisfied by the *supply* of some item or service. How much effort we are prepared to expend upon satisfying the need will depend upon how important it seems to be, relative to all the others. Generally speaking, the keenness of our *demand* for goods or service declines with a rise in its cost. This cost may be the actual price we are charged, but it also includes the cost of time and effort expended in satisfying the need. If this cost is too high we may turn to a substitute or abandon the demand altogether. Diagrammatically this may be represented as in Fig. 7.1 where the DD^1 demand curve increases in quantity with a decrease in price, indicating that we are prepared to buy more goods if prices are reduced. The steepness of the demand, and indeed the supply, curve indicates how much more or less people will buy or sell as prices change. This steepness is referred to as the *elasticity* of demand. A steep curve is said to be elastic, and a shallow curve, indicating little change in quantity with price is said to be inelastic. Goods for which there are easily available substitutes will have very *elastic* demand.

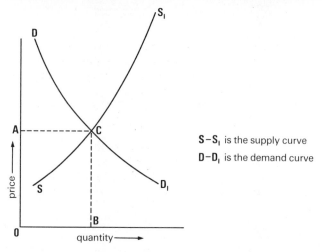

S–S₁ is the supply curve

D–D₁ is the demand curve

Fig. 7.1   A supply and demand curve. At price A, quantity B will be supplied, and the intersection Point C is the equilibrium point. If the price falls, the excess demand will force it back up and if it rises the decline in demand will force the price down again.

2. How do we choose?

A manufacturer is likely to be more willing to supply goods when the price obtained for them is high, and when a greater profit is made. The coffee bar will make a greater profit if it is either selling a lot of coffees, or charging a high price for them; because overheads such as staff, wear and tear on equipment, rental and so on will remain fairly constant so that the marginal return on each extra item sold is greater to the owner. The compromise position will be reached in something of the manner of the diagram, where the public are prepared to pay price P and consume quantity Q of a given commodity at that price (see Fig 7.1).

This analysis of supply and demand is, of course, over-simplified. In reality the price of goods is also conditioned by manufacturing costs (for raw materials, transport, power etc.). At the same time the public's willingness to pay is influenced by their ability to change from one commodity to another – i.e. to substitute satisfiers. In some circumstances we can change fairly easily if the price becomes too high – from potatoes to rice, butter to margarine, coffee to tea. However, with more specialized services such transfer is less possible, and consequently, the most essential of these are generally run as legalized monopolies in the form of public utilities; hospitals, schools, postal service. Clearly in understanding the working of the interactions of supply and demand in the urban landscape we must take account of the urgency and frequency of specific needs. It should also be remembered that suppliers may not be able to change their levels of output easily. Supply may also be inelastic and shortages or gluts can thus occur, because of the time lag in manufacturers' reaction to changes in demand. From what has been said so far, it seems evident that there are various categories of goods which we use frequently and expect to find conveniently near. On the other hand, we are prepared to travel farther to obtain the goods which we purchase rarely, especially if they are expensive. Also we like to have a greater choice with important purchases – this may help to explain the grouping of particular shops into districts. Obviously we do not expect small shops or groups of shops to stock every item we might require. They

190

could not afford to do so and they would make only a very small profit on items that were rarely asked for. The underlying idea that there are different *orders* of goods is basic to an understanding of how a hierarchy of shopping centres or settlements develops.

3. The application of supply and demand in the landscape

If we can now generalize about how far people are likely to travel so as to obtain goods or services of different orders, we can see why 'urban fields' are of different dimensions. This average distance from which people will come to use a particular service or purchase a particular good is more briefly defined as the *range* of that good or service.

So far we have looked at the business of trading only from the viewpoint of ourselves as consumers. From the suppliers' point of view, a minimum number of purchasers is necessary before it is worthwhile setting up a supply outlet. The less frequent the average purchase of the good or service, the greater the 'market population' needed in order to ensure that the supplier receives an adequate level of demand to remain in business. The 'minimum level of demand necessary to sustain a service' is referred to as the demand *threshold*, above which a particular facility will be profitable and thus come into existence. Examples of the threshold population of different suppliers are given in Table 7.1.

Table 7.1. Thresholds of Several Well-known Shops. (Source: M. Collins, 'Fieldwork in Urban Areas', in R. J. Chorley & P. Haggett, *Frontier in Geography*, 1965, p.227.)

Shop	Threshold
Boots the Chemists	10 000
MacFisheries	25 000
Barratts Ltd (Shoes)	20-30 000
Sainsbury's (Grocers)	60 000 (for medium-sized self-service store)
Marks & Spencer's	50-100 000
John Lewis	50 000 (for a supermarket)
John Lewis	100 000 (for a departmental store)

We can begin to see that some towns will provide smaller or greater varieties of services than others on the basis of the threshold population available to utilize them. That there may be a statistical relationship between the size of a settlement and the amount of trade it attracts is an idea which we will examine in Chapter 8. If centres are reasonably close together and transport is fairly cheap, it is likely that people will 'shop around' for the best value in a particular commodity. Hence the range of a particular service from an urban centre is limited by competition from other places supplying the same or similar services. The range of a service is controlled at the lower level by the minimum threshold population necessary to sustain it.

As a result of the interaction of threshold and range it can be shown that a hierarchy of central places supplying goods of different orders will emerge. Although an individual service such as a shoe shop may have a unique threshold and range it will be located in an urban centre where it benefits from the proximity of

191

other services. As a result distinctive groups of services will develop in settlements which provide the right threshold for their survival within the range of urban field appropriate to them. As we have already surmised a ranking of settlements in order of the number of services they offer demonstrates that small centres (villages) provide a limited number of facilities accessible locally. The majority of the population requiring greater choice or higher order goods may have to travel considerable distances to larger centres to obtain them. This has implications for the land values in the more favoured centres. These larger centres serving extensive urban fields are commonly called *central places*.

ASSIGNMENTS
1. *Using a local map, preferably at 1:250 000 scale and a tracing overlay, plot the distribution of settlements of different sizes, using the type face of the place names as a guide to their relative importance. Graph the relative numbers of each type. By reference to the Yellow Pages of the local Telephone Directory, plot the number of facilities (e.g. banks, estate agents, public houses) and compare the ranking of settlement size and range of services. The maps of Lincolnshire at a scale of 1:100 000 and 1:250 000 would provide a suitable case study area in which to try this exercise, but a more detailed survey could be undertaken using larger scale maps and population figures from the Bureau of Population and Census Reports. If a large number of settlements is studied it is worth ranking them in order and applying a correlation coefficient test to the two rankings. The simplest formula to apply is Spearmans Rank:.*

$$r = 1 - \frac{6\Sigma d^2}{(n^3 - n)}$$

where r is the coefficient of correlation,
d is the difference in ranking, and
n is the number of cases ranked: in this case settlements.

For example:

Town	Population	Pop. rank	No. of facilities	Facilities ranked	d	d²
a	25 000	8	45	7	1	1
b	35 000	7	27	10	3	9
c	130 000	3	200	3	0	0
d	23 000	9	35	8	1	1
e	22 000	10	30	9	1	1
f	250 000	2	400	2	0	0
g	75 000	4	92	4	0	0
h	320 000	1	420	1	0	0
i	65 000	6	78	5	1	1
j	68 000	5	68	6	1	1

$n = 10$ $\Sigma d^2 = 14$

Substituting in the formula:

$$r = 1 - \frac{6 \times 14}{1000 - 10} = 0.92$$

If we compare the figure obtained for r with the table below we find that in 99 cases out of 100 such a correlation is likely to be the result of factors other than chance; in other words one variable is likely to vary with the other. This does not mean that one variable, in this case population size, actually causes the other, but we can claim that the relationship between the two is of statistical significance. This statistical significance at particular levels (or percentage of cases) is a convenient method of measuring how far two quite different characteristics are related, because the test does not rely upon their being measured in the same units. The frequency with which this is likely to prove a correlation is termed the 'confidence level' and normally geographers aim at confidence levels of 95 or 99 per cent.

Table 7.2 Statistical Significance and Confidence Levels for Spearman Rank Correlation Coefficient.

Number of Items	Values of r at Confidence Levels	
	95%	99%
10	0.564	0.746
15	0.440	0.620
20	0.377	0.534
25	0.336	0.475
30	0.306	0.432

2. Which of the following products do you think will have 'elastic' demand and which 'inelastic' demand: salt, butter, cornflakes, fuel oil, coffee, frozen peas, newsprint, disposable nappies? Give reasons for your answers, bearing in mind that the substitutability and the relative proportion of our average expenditure which these items comprise will be important factors.
3. Which of the following services and goods do you think will have elastic and which inelastic supply: beef production, dishwashers, new houses, motor cars, package holidays, soap powder? Bear in mind that the capacity for suppliers to change output at short notice will be important. Will any other factors affect supply levels (e.g. advantages of large scale production, government restrictions on production)?
4. A special offer of 40 per cent reduction is advertised on one of the following items at a store 30 kilometres from your home. Which item would you feel most anxious to obtain in order to take advantage of this offer, and why: radio-cassette recorders, current Top Ten LP records, tights (packs of two dozen only), shoes, your favourite range of perfume or aftershave?

B. Central Places: the Christaller Model

As we saw in Chapter 2 there tends to be a pattern of declining intensity of land use around rural settlements. This can also be noted as one moves away from lines of communication, and is attributable in part to increased problems of accessibility of land and thus its relative unattractiveness for development. These ideas, originally applied to the changing value of agricultural land as one moved outwards from a market centre, were put forward in the eighteenth century by Ricardo and Von Thünen. An extension of this thinking was put forward in 1933 by Walter Christaller,[1] who noted the relationship of threshold and range of settlements of different orders in Southern Germany. In order to express his ideas he simplified the land-scape which he was describing. Hence the rather formal and unrealistic nature of the diagrams, which are not intended to be maps.

Table 7.3 The Urban Hierarchy in South-west Germany (after Christaller). (Source: E. L. Ullman, *Amer. Jour. Sociology* **46** (1941), page 857.)

Settlement form	Distance apart (km)	Population	Tributary area size (km²)	Population
Market hamlet (Markort)	7	800	45	2 700
Township centre (Amtsort)	12	1 500	135	8 100
County seat (Kreistadt)	21	3 500	400	24 000
District city (Bezirksstadt)	36	9 000	1 200	75 000
Small state capital (Gaustadt)	62	27 000	3 600	225 000
Provincial head capital (Provinzhaupstadt)	108	90 000	10 800	675 000
Regional capital city (Landeshaupstadt)	186	300 000	32 400	2 025 000

1. The underlying assumptions

Christaller realized that it is possible not only to view the rural landscape as serving its local centre with produce but also to see the area around each town as the recipient of services produced in the town. However, these tributary areas or urban fields were not uniform in size, nor were the settlements, and the comparative growth of some at the expense or stagnation of others demanded explanation. The relative sizes of the settlements and their tributary areas in the region Christaller studied are shown in Table 7.3. In order to explain the variations in settlement size and importance in the area about which he was writing Christaller envisaged an homogenous plain, sometimes referred to as an *isotropic surface*, upon which early settlement was evenly distributed in the form of small nucleated hamlets. If it is assumed that the landscape quality is everywhere similar and that each settlement has the same number of farming families gaining their livelihood from the land, then a regular distribution of hamlets may be expected. The spacing in the diagram (Fig. 7.2) is at two-mile intervals (3.2 km) approximately similar to that in some areas of Saxon lowland occupance, but inferior or superior conditions of terrain and productivity would alter this distancing. After some time, as technology and road transport improve, specialization of production is able to develop and trade bet-ween the towns increases. If 3.2 km is as far as a farmer is willing to walk to market, the more enterprising or better favoured population in 'central place' villages can expect to share in the trade of six surrounding hamlets in addition to their own. In a similar way other centres are likely to develop, and if the whole area is covered in 'market areas', a pattern of hexagonal networks may grow up, with each central village receiving a total trade allegiance of three times its own population $(1+(6\times1/3)=3)$. This total trade allegiance which a market centre received from surrounding hamlets, Christaller expressed as its k value. He then went on to consider alternative ways in which small settlements might depend upon larger ones, and to devise k values to describe these relationships as well.

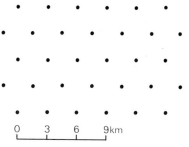

Fig. 7.2   The hypothetical spacing of settlements.

2. The determining of *k* values

In establishing a hierarchy of central places based on marketing Christaller envisaged a '$k = 3$ network', and he suggested that once a k value has become developed within an area it would apply to all the levels in this hierarchy; i.e. the k value was fixed. However, he recognized that marketing might not be the only factor distinguishing service centres from their neighbours, and he developed two other network patterns: one based on the most efficient system of transport between centres where the ratio of orders or k value $= 4$ to 1. The k value is simply the number of other settlements which a central place is able to serve (see Fig. 7.3). If a settlement is

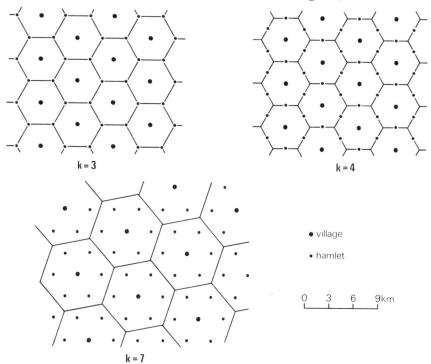

Fig. 7.3   The pattern of $k = 3$, $k = 4$ and $k = 7$ hierarchies applied to a landscape of regularly spaced settlements.

195

located between two or more central places it is likely that its inhabitants may be divided in their allegiance, so that the k value may be composed of the 'fractions' of many village populations. Such 'sharing' is more likely for purposes of trade than for purposes of transport. Christaller also envisaged a pattern of settlement networks where the $k = 7$. This he called his defensive or administrative principle, implying that a town responsible for acting as the military focus of surrounding territories would not share that control with another town but rather keep control entirely within its own hands. Once the principle by which the ratio between towns of different levels of importance or orders was established, Christaller argued, then the whole range of settlements in that area would relate to each other in accordance with that ratio as the settlements grew. In time a hierarchy of settlements would develop based upon the ratio, and these he believed could be identified in various parts of Western Europe. Examples of the hierarchy he envisaged as existing are given in Table 7.4. Whilst k values of 3, 4 or 7 produced the basic lattice work connecting centres, the system could be expanded in complexity over time while retaining the basic ratio: hence values of $k = 3, 9, 27$, etc., would be produced.

Table 7.4 Inter-urban and intra-urban hierarchies. (Based on diagram in J. A. Everson and B. P. FitzGerald, *Settlement Patterns*, Longman, 1969, page 92)

General hierarchy	Special hierarchies for the highest level of central function			Centres within a city	
	Entire settlements				
	Christaller (Germany)	G.B. scale	Switzerland scale	Scale for Zurich centres	Scale for G.B. centres
First Lowest		Roadside hamlet (Chippenham)	Dorf	Local business district	Local centre
Second Low order	Marktort	Village (Old Buckenham)	Marktort	Neighbourhood business district	Neighbour-hood centre
Third Middle order	Amtsort Kreisort Bezirksort	Town (Thetford)	Stadt	Regional business district	Community or District centre
Fourth High order	Gauort Provinzhauptort	City (Norwich)	Grossstadt		Regional centre
Fifth Higher order	Landstadt	Metropolis (Bristol)	Metropole	Central business district	The CBD of large town or city
Sixth Highest order	Reichsteile	Super Metropolis (Manchester)			Super metropolitan centre
Seventh World wide order	Reichstadt	World metropolitan centre (London)			

3. Applications of Christaller's theory

On the basis of the theoretical network system, Christaller developed a hierarchy of settlements, related to their population, and their range in tributary area.

Whilst this model may seem inflexible and theoretical, it did apply well to the uniform landscape of South Germany in the 1930s. Although increased industrialization, specialization and mobility have rendered it less satisfactory in the west as time has passed, it has been shown to be applicable in rural societies, such as contemporary China.[2] In suitable terrain, the regular pattern of settlement arrangement may be demonstrated in Britain, especially in pre-industrial landscapes such as those of Eastern England in the nineteenth century. (See Fig. 7.4.)

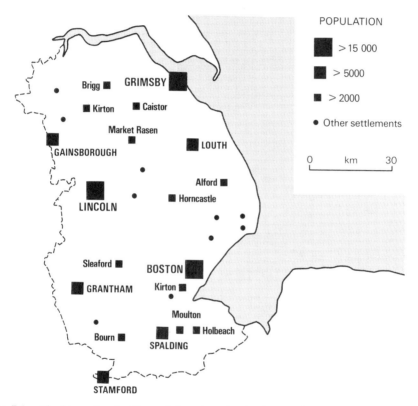

Fig. 7.4   The hierarchy of settlements based on size in nineteenth-century Lincolnshire.

C. Development of the Theory: The Lösch Model

1. Making the theory more flexible

It is obvious that although the different orders of settlement which Christaller identified may well exist in many areas, it is unlikely that they will relate to each other in the neat inflexible ratios of fixed k values. Before criticizing the theory on these grounds it is perhaps valuable to consider the work of another German writer, some twenty years later. August Lösch[3] in 1954 used the same hexagonal networks or *lattices* for his theoretical landscape. He took Christaller's model and developed a more sophisticated form by superimposing all the various hexagonal systems so far mentioned – and many others. By superimposing all the lattices on one point and rotating them he achieved a pattern of sectors. You can do this yourself if you trace the $k = 3$, $k = 4$, and $k = 7$ hierarchies on to transparent film or thin tracing paper and then rotate them keeping the centre point uniform. Six of these sectors have many relatively high order settlements – these he called *city-rich* sectors, and six were relatively sparsely settled or *city-poor* (see Fig. 7.5). Hence we should not dismiss the application of central place theory if we find that a particular area is lacking in the 'correct' number of subsidiary settlements; at least not until we have examined adjacent regions – for these may compensate for the sparsity of settlement that we have found.

Under this system of a variable k hierarchy the pattern of settlements appears much more 'realistic' with a continuum of settlement size, rather than distinct tiers or orders as in the earlier model. This is true not only of the population size but also the functional variety of the settlements in terms of services supplied there. There has been considerable discussion by geographers as to whether Lösch's 'continuum' or Christaller's 'tiered' system of urban centres is more closely approximate to reality.

ASSIGNMENTS

1. (a) *Using the O.S. map and the overlay from Assignment 1. on p.192, measure the average distance between settlements of the same size or order.*
   (b) *Taking this distance as the diameter, draw circles with their centres based upon these settlements.*
   (c) *Attempt to explain areas of overlap, or where there are gaps between the circle boundaries. You should refer to both physical and human map evidence in your explanation.*

2. *Rank in order how frequently you obtain or visit the following:*

a pair of shoes	*a part for*	*a library*
a packet of sweets	*car, bicycle*	*a restaurant*
an LP record	*or moped.*	*a pair of jeans*
a magazine or paper	*a cinema*	*aftershave or*
a soft drink	*a football*	*perfume*
a new coat	*match*	*a present for*
	a bus pass	*someone else.*

   (a) *Try to explain any correlation you notice between the price of these goods or services and the frequency with which you replace them or make a return visit.*
   (b) *Indicate whether there is any relationship between these two factors and the distance you are prepared to travel.*

3. *With reference to the map of Lincolnshire (Fig 7.4) draw boundaries around the higher order settlements to take in the ones of the order immediately below. Does the resultant pattern bear any relationship to Christaller's model?*

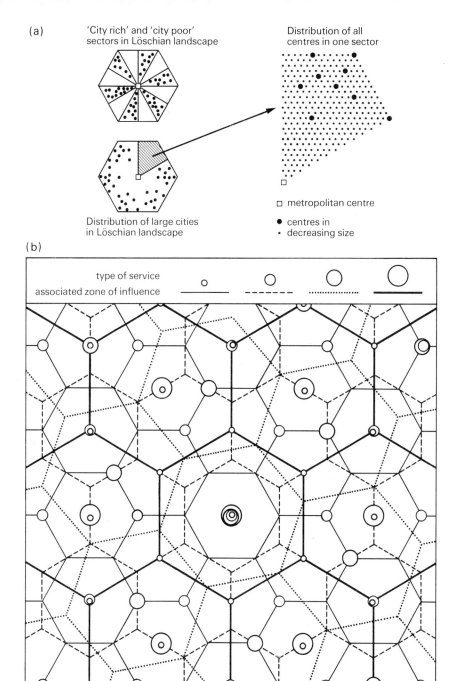

(a)

'City rich' and 'city poor' sectors in Löschian landscape

Distribution of all centres in one sector

Distribution of large cities in Löschian landscape

□ metropolitan centre

● centres in
· decreasing size

(b)

type of service

associated zone of influence

Fig. 7.5   (a) Löschian landscape developed by the rotation of a number of k system hexagons, developing 'city rich' and 'city poor' sectors. (b) The Löschian landscape applied to several orders of centre.

2. Limits to Central Place theory

There are obvious simplifications in the basic theory of Christaller which he did not intend to be overlooked. *Distortion* of the hexagonal pattern of lattices due to irregular terrain, and variations in distances and direction as a result of landscape configuration and differences in soil fertility and of mineral deposits, are ones that will immediately come to mind. In addition there is the factor of *temporal change*. Settlements once founded do not disappear but rather stagnate or decline when their role is challenged by later technology. For example a change in transport technology may make them more, or less, effective service centres. But it would be unreasonable to dismiss Christaller's theory on the basis of simplifying real world situations, for those simplifications are necessary in order to render the development of theory possible. In other words, we endeavour to remove the background noise which prevents us from perceiving the plain ideas of the theory. This method of eliminating the distracting 'noise' in a model theory is quite valid, as long as we are careful to reintroduce the 'noise' gradually to see how the model stands up to real world situations. However, a serious criticism of the theory so far discussed is that not all towns came into existence as, or indeed presently function as, service centres for the surrounding rural area. As well as market towns with dependent villages linked to them by public transport services, there are many examples of ports, mining towns and oddly or badly sited settlements which do not approximate to the service centre pattern. If we leave out deliberately planned towns to which consideration will be given in Chapter 9, we can recognize with Johnson three groups of factors responsible for settlement siting which are not dealt with by Central Place theory:

(1) those cities or towns that have grown because of a location that links an area to the outside world or with certain types of manufacturing;
(2) the availability of highly localized physical resources;
(3) the chance element or 'human whim' in urban location and development, a factor which is often overlooked because it is so difficult to assess.[4]

These factors give rise to important exceptions to Christaller's theory which will be considered in the following section.

ASSIGNMENT
Figure 7.6 illustrates the settlement pattern of villages in an imaginary landscape. What effect will the following events have upon the pattern?
(a) the granting of a Charter in 1500 for a market to be held weekly at **A**.
(b) discovery of coal in 1700 at **B** *in small quantities.*
(c) building of a canal along the line indicated in 1785.
(d) coming of the railway along route indicated in 1856.
(e) establishment of a trading estate at **C** *in 1955.*
(f) closure of the railway in 1964.
(g) opening of motorway in 1970 along route indicated, with access at **P**.
(h) scheduling of upland area as greenbelt in 1975.
It is suggested that you redraw lines of communications and relative sizes of settlements (**A, B, C, D,** *and* **E**) *at each period.*

200

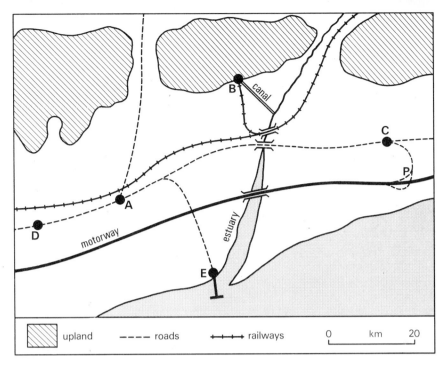

Fig. 7.6   The settlement pattern of villages in an imaginary landscape.

D. Exceptions to the Theory

1. Transport centres

Many towns developed either as staging points or stations on road or rail routes. The existence of 'way traffic' as it is called helps generate demand for retail services, accommodation and some employment as in the case of railway workshops or transport depots. Similarly, break of bulk points, where cargo is transhipped from one form of transport to another, are often nodes for settlement development. Examples of such centres can be found in most industrialized countries, and their relative importance changes with shifts in transport technology. A city such as Chicago where twenty-one rail lines terminate at the Great Lakes railhead is a good example. It is also a city which has kept pace with transport innovations, now possessing the internationally important O'Hare airport. In Britain we can find examples of settlements created by transport – the railway towns of Crewe and Swindon, and the more recent container port of Felixstowe. The important factor, however, is not the number of routes which focus upon a centre, but the amount of interchanging of goods and passengers that takes place there. Such centres are of several types, depending upon the amount of traffic and the trade they generate:
(a)   small wayside centres which service transport or act as collecting points in otherwise empty areas, e.g. elevator and service station points on trunk routes across the Canadian Prairies;
(b)   break of bulk points where refining or distribution is concentrated, as at major ports;

(c)   major redistribution centres, where goods are stored and where wholesaling is an important commercial function. Often settlements which owe their origin and growth to forms of transport also suffer if that medium is superseded. In its location, plan and history Winnipeg fits this pattern very well.

Originally sited by the Hudsons Bay Company, the town attracted two rival railways and grew up between their respective stockyards and hotels. In the late nineteenth century it was the fastest growing city in Canada; now it is among the slowest, as the 'frontier' has passed it by. Its role as a centre for immigrants has largely been superseded, the streets around the railway lines are rundown and the station hotels dilapidated. Grain and fur traffic still flows through the city but the new wealth of western Canada is to be found north and west of the prairies in the tar sands of northern Alberta. The new growth cities of the Canadian west are Edmonton and Calgary, (Plate 7.1) which provide the financial and technical services for exploiting these new resources.

Plate 7.1   The CBD of Edmonton, Alberta, Canada. (*Author's photograph*)

2. Towns located in relation to physical resources

Frequently urban clusters grow around some physical resource, where *manufacturing* is the dominant occupation. In England the textile towns of Lancashire and Yorkshire are examples of this, where coal has been the major locating factor. Of the numerous towns on the Lancashire coalfield only one, the glass manufacturing centre of St. Helens, failed to develop a textile industry, and almost all the textile towns are coalfield based. In Germany the process has developed further: the Ruhr coalfield led to the development of steel producing centres, these in turn led to textile machinery and cloth, thence to dyestuffs, and eventually perfume and cosmetics, all utilizing coal byproducts (Fig. 7.7). But physical resources do not necessarily generate manufacturing enterprise. Holiday resorts utilizing the attractions of sandy beaches, spa water, or a combination of transport links and dramatic scenery have

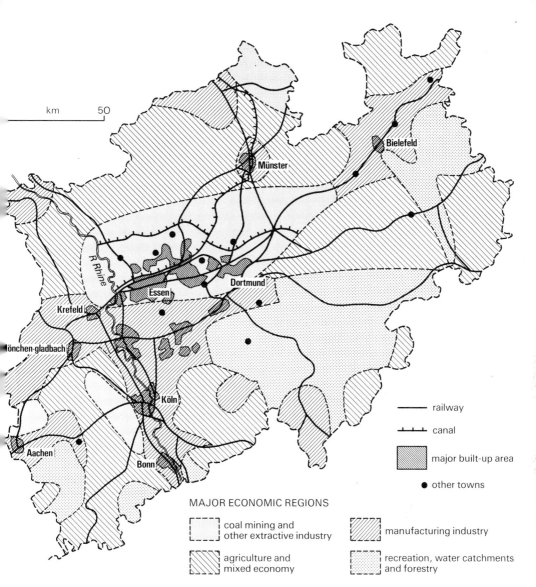

Fig. 7.7   The Ruhr, West Germany. (Source: based on an original Fig. in s.v.r. Regional planning (Atlas), 1960)

been equally significant in causing a new settlement pattern to emerge in the last two centuries. The street pattern of nineteenth-century holiday resorts is highly individual; and is related to the growing promenade or sea front, backed by shops and boarding houses (see Plate 7.2). A municipal park and railway station are often important elements too and these are located near the centre of the town. This was possible because there was frequently little growth of these settlements before the advent of cheap rail travel. A few more isolated settlements have endeavoured to capitalize on their lack of development in more recent years, by exploiting their unspoilt image.

Plate 7.2   Southend in the nineteenth century. (Source: Callcut & Beavis, *32 Views of Southend-on-Sea and District*, Supplied by Southend Central Library)

The distribution of physical resources may be important in locating a cluster of settlements, whilst not affecting their subsequent growth or specialization. Industrial concentrations in areas like the Potteries, or the metal manufacturing towns of Birmingham, may well be due to agglomerative factors more adequately explained by Weber's theory than by Central Place concepts (see John Bale, *The Location of Manufacturing Industry*[5]). As Pred has argued, the very existence of specialist towns encourages their further development.[6] Local industries become increasingly enmeshed by the system of linkages that develops between them, and this makes the prospect of relocation unattractive, whilst new firms join those already there because of the locational advantages of existing services and allied activities. Over time the region becomes the accepted centre of a particular group of trades, even after the initial advantages of the site have disappeared.

This pattern of self-sustaining urban concentration has led to our recognition of urban clusters around large metropolitan centres, resulting in city regions. This process may culminate in a 'megalopolitan' situation as in the North Eastern USA where an interconnecting group of towns and their attendant suburban satellites stretches along the coast. If deliberately planned, the process may produce a combination of established, new and expanded towns located in an economically favoured situation, as in South Eastern England. Here the economic potential of location close to London and the EEC leads to a competition for space which has only partially been overcome by planned dispersal of settlement and employment farther afield. Hence we find a variety of groups of industrial centres:

(a)   those related to a mineral or power resource which in turn have attracted related industrial enterprises to the initial site.

(b)   groups of towns, each of which specializes in a particular aspect of a trade, as is often the case in textile-producing areas.

(c)   planned industrial estates, designed to reduce congestion in old centres and to encourage relocation of firms to sites designated by government or the local authority.

(d) declining industrial complexes which, despite the gradual slipping away of their initial site advantages, remain because of the cost of re-establishment elsewhere. Such agglomerations often seek to retain their importance by pricing agreements on their products which safeguard their position, or by obtaining government aid. The 'phantom freight' system operated by the Pittsburgh steel makers in the USA before the Second World War is a famous example.

Whatever the reason for the continued existence of industrial urban concentrations such as these, it is clear that they provide exceptions to a pattern of market centres based upon spatial principles such as those contained in Christaller's model. In such cases the *interrelationship* of the individual settlements, and their reliance upon interconnecting transport links and high levels of mobility on the part of their populations has enabled specialization of functions – e.g. 'dormitories', 'shopping centres', 'light industry' on a large scale. A special case is the deliberately planned retail centre, often located outside established urban areas, which acts as a focus for the car owning shopper (see Plate 7.3). These are considered in more detail in Chapters 6 and 9.

Plate 7.3   Rheinpark Hypermarket, St. Margerethen, Eastern Switzerland. Opened in 1974 at the side of the Rhine and affording easy access along the valley and from across the border with Austria, this site prospered because almost half the customers came from across the river to take advantage of cheaper Swiss prices. Since then the change in currency exchange rates has meant that fewer find the visit worthwhile.

The colonization of areas of land at motorway intersections by such hypermarkets is relatively new to Europe although the process has been going on for many years in North America.

3. Towns established by whim or chance

It is likely that the original choice of almost all early settlements had a strong element of personal decision, as nomadic or invading groups would have limited knowledge of their new terrain. (This point has been discussed in Chapter 2.) In later times and with improved knowledge and techniques of decision-making, the choice of sites for industry, or even whole settlements on a large scale, is likely to be at once more informed and more serious in its consequences. Despite the gradual improvements in our ability to determine good settlement locations, and the operation of economic forces to 'weed out' the settlements that are unlikely to survive, examples of 'historical accidents' in settlement development based upon whim or local initiative occur, for example, Morris at Oxford, and Boeing at Seattle. Also the decision to choose a new centre for settlement may in fact be almost a chance one.

> Madison, Wisconsin, provides an interesting example of the actual factors which influenced the founding of an individual city. At first sight the location of this city, on what now seems an accessible and attractive site, seems a good instance of the role of the physical environment; but the history of the choice of site reveals that other forces were at work. . . . The decision to locate the capital on its present site was taken by 15 votes to 11, and this decision owed more to intrigue by the most subtle of the speculators than to any careful assessment of site and situation.[7]

It is worth remembering that few totally unsuitable sites survive even when local invention had made them famous; thus no planes are now built in Dayton, Ohio despite the Wright Brothers' epoch-making flight.

It might seem likely that in looking at actual settlement distribution there is considerable deviation from the theoretical distribution, as envisaged by Christaller and Lösch. However, the models do isolate some of the factors involved in this distribution. We can refine our understanding of settlement pattern by considering the individual circumstances conditioning the location of specific towns.

ASSIGNMENT
For an area of about 500 km² with which you are familiar, map and describe the changes that either the coming of the railway, or a bypass road has had upon the shape and development of towns.

E. The Rank-Size Rule: Urban Hierarchies

Earlier we mentioned that Christaller's theory was concerned not only with the pattern of settlement distribution, but also with the different orders of settlement and their relationship to each other. In many countries this relationship approximates to a situation where the size of a settlement is inversely proportional to the number of settlements of a similar size: i.e. there is a 'pyramid' something like this. The vertical axis of the pyramid indicates the order or 'ranking' of the settlement (see Fig. 7.8).

Capital

Regional Administrative Centres

Large manufacturing towns and commercial centres

Smaller commercial, retailing and market towns in provinces

Large numbers of small, old-established villages with local services

Numerous hamlets, isolated groups of habitation, without many service functions.

Fig. 7.8   Pyramid of settlement ranking.

The example of Great Britain bears some relation to this:

Table 7.5. Urban areas of Great Britain. (Source: Philip's, *Geographical Digest*, 1978.)

Settlement size	Number of settlements
Above 1 million	2
500 000–1 million	3
250 000–500 000	20
150 000–250 000	34
100 000–150 000	25
75 000–100 000	35
40 000– 75 000	133
20 000– 40 000	185
10 000– 20 000	220
2 000– 10 000	305 (approx.)

G. K. Zipf explained the relationship between settlement *rank*, and *size*.[8] He stated this connection as a rule, given by the formula:

$$P_n = P_1(n)^{-1}$$

where P_n is the population of the nth town in the series 1, 2, 3, . . ., n, in which the towns are arranged in descending order of size of population, and P_1 is the population of the largest or primate town. Thus if the largest town were of a population size of 100 000 (P_1) then the second town in rank would, by this formula have a population of

$$100\,000\,(2)^{-1} \text{ or } \frac{100\,000}{2} \text{ which is } 50\,000$$

This formula may be expressed verbally thus: *if all the urban settlements in an area are ranked in descending order of population size, the population of the nth town will be 1/n the size of the largest city, and the population of the other urban settlements will be arranged in the series 1, ½, ⅓, ¼, . . . $\frac{1}{n}$.* Thus we should find a fixed ratio between the few large settlements and the many smaller ones. If we know the population of the largest or primate city, we should be able to work out the number of settlements of a given smaller size that there should be in the country or region. When this rule is tested against real world examples, there are variable degrees of correspondence in the results. The graph (Fig. 7.9) demonstrates the application to England and Wales, and shows that London is larger than the rule suggests it should be (see Fig. 7.9). Otherwise the facts 'fit' the formula remarkably well, but we may wonder if the graph supports the argument that too great a proportion of the nation's wealth is now concentrated in the London area, at the expense of the regions.

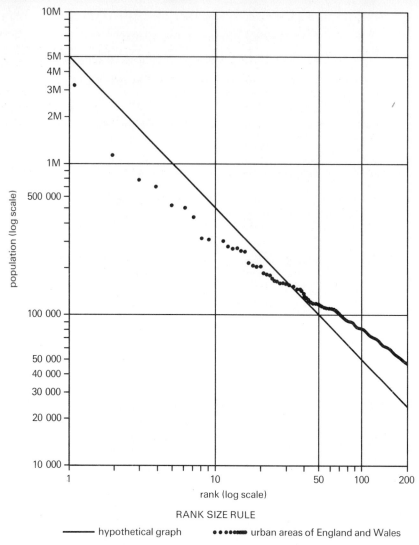

RANK SIZE RULE

——— hypothetical graph   •••••••• urban areas of England and Wales

Fig. 7.9   The rank-size rule in England and Wales. (Source: J. H. Johnson, *Urban Geography: An Introductory Analysis*, Pergamon Press Ltd, 1972, p.107)

As the population of the Greater London area is some three or four times larger than the Administrative County of London shown at 3.2m in Fig. 7.9, the 'error' of the graph in its upper reaches is in fact even greater. This situation of an overlarge *primate city* is often found in underdeveloped countries, and a lack of correspondence between a country's real profile and the hypothetical one is sometimes used as an argument for a more even spread of development in peripheral regions by development-economists. However, whilst the rank-size rule may approximate to the pattern of city size in a 'balanced economy', it should be remembered that these discrepancies are to be expected. The rank-size 'rule' is merely the formulating of a generally observed phenomenon. In this it differs from the Christaller-Lösch model which sought to explain rather than merely demonstrate an orderly pattern within the landscape. Despite this difference in approach there are obvious connections between the two ideas, concerned as they are with a situation where the size of settlements is inversely related to their number and distance apart.

When all is said and done, we may feel that the existence of Central Place theory is helpful in explaining the rank-size connection of settlements, even allowing for individual discrepancies. This is the view of the American geographer William Bunge (1966) who comments that:

> an argument rages as to whether there is in fact a hierarchy of settlements (hamlets, villages, towns, etc.), or only a continuum of various sized and functional places.
> The debate has split between evidence offered for low ranked cities as opposed to high ranked ones.
> It may well be that local discontinuous hierarchies blend into a continuous distribution for a country taken all together.[9]

Whilst much work on the pattern of settlements remains to be done, the application of this useful theory to individual regions, and at a smaller scale *within* towns, has demonstrated the interactions taking place in and between urban settlements. It is to the spatial patterns within towns that we turn next.

ASSIGNMENT
Reference to Philip's Geographical Digest *(published annually) will enable you to draw rank-size graphs for developed and underdeveloped countries. Alternatively an atlas with detailed population statistics will provide suitable data. Choose one example of a developed and one of an underdeveloped country and describe what your graph shows.*

F. Hierarchies within the Town: Retail Shopping

1. Hierarchy of shopping centres

American and British studies have shown that a distinct hierarchy of shopping centres exists within an urban area. A shopping hierarchy arises because of the differing ability of varying shop types to pay high rents. Convenience goods shops sell necessities, basic foodstuffs like bread, meat and vegetables which must be purchased frequently. Those goods have a low *range*, that is customers are not prepared to travel far to obtain them. Convenience goods shops also have a low *threshold population*, the minimum number of customers needed for a shop to be profitable, and, therefore, are most likely to be situated in small local centres. 'Shoppers' goods' shops and specialist stores on the other hand, both sell consumer durable goods which are bought less frequently than convenience goods, e.g., furniture and electrical goods, Shoppers' goods shops also include clothes and shoe shops which tend to group together in the larger centres. Specialist stores include book and sports equipment shops which do not need to group together and do not require a location quite so near the centre of the town. Both categories of shops, however, offer for sale higher order goods and services which have a wider range and a higher threshold population than convenience goods shops. Shoppers' goods shops and specialist stores, therefore, compete for the more advantageous sites in the larger or higher order shopping centres in a town.

Thus there develops a continuum from convenience goods stores, dependent on access to a small tributary population, to department stores requiring access to a vast population. The shops, in turn, are organized into a distinct hierarchy of shopping centres, ranging from a cluster of a few convenience stores serving a restricted neighbourhood to the CBD of a large city serving not only the built-up area but the city's entire urban field. The following types can be identified:

(a) Local centre
This is the lowest order centre and consists of a small group of low order shops selling convenience goods. The shops are complementary rather than competitive and it is unlikely that there will be more than one of any given shop type.

(b) Neighbourhood centre
This contains more shop types than a local centre. There are likely to be a few shoppers' goods shops and specialist stores but convenience goods shops will predominate. There may be branches of small supermarket chains.

(c) Community or district centre
This contains more shop types than a neighbourhood centre. There is a higher proportion of shoppers' goods shops and specialist stores selling goods and services with a wider range, because people are prepared to travel farther to obtain them.

(d) Regional centre
This contains more shop types than a district centre. Shoppers' goods shops and specialist stores predominate and the convenience goods shops are confined to the cheaper and inferior sites on the periphery of the shopping centre (see Plate 7.4).

(e) The CBD of a large town or city
This contains more shop types than a regional centre. Convenience goods shops are unlikely to be able to afford to occupy the valuable sites in a CBD where shoppers' goods shops and specialist stores will congregate. Many of these will sell high order goods with a very wide range which customers will be prepared to travel some distance to obtain.

(f) Super metropolitian centre
This is a more specialized CBD which attracts customers from a very wide area indeed. The West End of London probably constitutes the only example of a super metropolitan centre in the UK. It serves, to a greater or lesser degree, not only everyone living in the UK but, to some extent, its influence extends throughout much of the world.

Note that:
  (i) Some of the larger shopping centres may have developed from old village nuclei which have been absorbed as the town grew.
  (ii) Lower order shopping centres are unlikely to be distributed evenly through- out a town and are often absent near the CBD.
  (iii) As well as there being both more shops and a greater variety of shop types at successively higher levels in the hierarchy, existing functions become

Plate 7.4   Shops on the edge of the CBD. *(Author's photograph)*

progressively more specialized and the shops frequently carry a greater range of stock. Thus a jeweller in a CBD location will be able to offer for sale much more expensive items of jewellery than will a counterpart with a shop in a district centre. This is because the jeweller with the CBD site has a much wider potential trading area.

The number of levels in the hierarchy of a given town depends on the size of its CBD. The central area of a market town may be equivalent either to a regional centre or a district centre depending on the size of the town and its urban field. If it is equivalent to a district centre, then at best other shopping centres in the town will be neighbourhood or local. Such a town will contain examples of only three levels in the intra-urban shopping hierarchy.

Central Place theory assumes that consumers go to the nearest outlet to obtain a particular item or service. In other words it takes account of 'convenience' as measured in terms of physical distance from home to service centres. If the concepts embodied in Central Place theory are applied to intra-urban shopping centres one would expect shoppers to use the shop nearest their homes that provides the item or service required. While, however, convenience is still an important factor in determining which shopping centre is visited, it is by no means the only consideration. Many shoppers rate 'selectivity' as expressed through the competitiveness of the prices, the quality of the goods for sale, the service provided and the cleanliness of the shop, higher than convenience. It should also be recognized that convenience is relative and means something quite different to a car owner, as opposed to a non car owner. A car owner is able to travel much farther to obtain even relatively low order goods and services and the assurance of a parking space might outweigh all other considerations in his or her choice of shopping centre. Furthermore, shopping may

211

be done on journeys that have been made principally for some other purpose. Some shoppers may make most of their purchases near to their place of work during lunch breaks, or shopping may be combined with a visit to a relative or a day out in an attractive town. Thus in practice shopping habits tend to be quite complex and weaken the assumption that the consumer will go to the nearest outlet to obtain an item or a service.

Contrasts have been observed in the hierarchical structure of shopping centres in predominantly middle-class and working-class areas in a large town or city. Working-class families are often less mobile than their middle-class counterparts. They are less likely to own a car and many are, therefore, more dependent on public transport for shopping trips. The restricted mobility of many less affluent families makes them more likely to purchase goods and services at the nearest shop or outlet. As a result, a concentration in one area of working-class housing may produce a bottom-heavy hierarchy with many small local and neighbourhood centres. Conversely in more affluent areas, where car ownership is more common, a top-heavy hierarchy has been recognized, where local and neighbourhood centres are less common. Furthermore, B.J.L. Berry working in Chicago, noted that in the higher order shopping centres situated in predominantly working-class areas there was a greater duplication of shop types, while in comparison with equivalent centres in more middle-class parts of the city, some more specialist shop types were absent. Berry also discovered that planned centres would tend to provide more functions than their unplanned equivalents.[10]

With the predicted increases in affluence and car ownership and the innovation of aids such as a deep freezer which makes frequent shopping trips less necessary, consumers' habits are likely to change considerably in the future. These changes are already causing the shopping hierarchy of towns to be modified and the number of local and neighbourhood centres is being reduced. In addition, new forms of retail shopping are being pioneered. These include the out-of-town hypermarket, which is discussed on pages 184–185. As we have seen, the less well off and elderly, who are the least mobile members of the community, are unfortunately generally unable to take advantage of bulk purchases made at discount prices at an out-of-town hypermarket, and must often still rely heavily on the local shops. Such people may suffer great inconvenience and hardship if the hierarchy of shopping centres which exists at present breaks down completely.

The hypermarket and the very large urban shopping centre may grow to assume importance beyond the towns they originally served. The Luton Arndale Centre, one of the largest covered shopping malls in Europe, has begun to attract shoppers from across the North Sea who come on day excursions to the nearby airport with the object of stocking up on British goods to take advantage of favourable exchange rates. In the Rhine valley, Swiss hypermarkets (see Plate 7.3) sited to take advantage of cross-border trade from Austria, are now increasingly dependent upon this trade. As exchange rates rise and Austrian shoppers are fewer in numbers they are finding difficulties in obtaining enough trade from their own Swiss nationals. Another interesting case is that of the 'Asda' hypermarket which was permitted to build as a peripheral supplier to Billericay in Essex, so that it would provide a trading focus around which the new town of South Woodham Ferrers could be built. As the new town grows, more customers will come from nearby housing and intensify demand 'Asda' will underwrite early losses in hopes of long term profits. (See Chapter 9.)

ASSIGNMENTS

Choosing the area for investigation

A survey of the hierarchical structure of shopping centres can be done only in a town large enough to possess a number of separate shopping centres in addition to the main concentration of shops in the town centre. In a market town with a population of about thirty to forty thousand it should be possible to conduct a comprehensive survey of all the centres in the town. In a large city you will have to limit your study to compare the hierarchical structure of shopping centres in two socially distinct parts of the city to see if the expected contrasts do in fact exist. You will need a map to help you fix the location of the service centres. In this respect the Ordnance Survey 1:10 000 (6 inches to 1 mile) is the most useful scale, but a Geographia *town plan may be used as an alternative.*

1. The morphology of service centres

Draw sketch plans to illustrate the arrangement of shops and other commercial premises in each of the service centres.

Discover what facilities, if any, are provided for vehicles delivering goods to the shops. To determine this you will need to look at the rear of the shops. If no such facilities exist find out if any restrictions are imposed on the time deliveries can take place. (You will need to look at the parking restriction signs to discover this.) Note the width of the street; is it sufficiently wide to be able to cope with stationary vehicles or are they a cause of traffic congestion?

At each of the centres record the car parking facilities available for shoppers. If an off-street car park is provided, find out if parking restrictions apply along the adjoining roads, and, in ribbon centres, if the restrictions also apply in the side roads.

Look carefully at the buildings in the centre and estimate their age. Are the shops purpose built, or have they been converted from some other function? Photograph or sketch any interesting examples of building conversion and add suitable annotations.

2. The hierarchy of centres

Copy the logging sheet shown in Table 7.6, which distinguishes broad categories of shops and shop types. Head the columns with the names of the service centres you are to investigate. Visit each centre and record the types of shops and retail services contained there. If there is more than one shop of a particular type also record this. For each centre add up the number of shops and different shop types and draw a scatter graph to show their relationship. This will enable you to classify the service centres and distinguish first order (local centres) from second order (neighbourhood centres) etc. B. J. Garner suggests the data should be plotted on log normal graph paper with the number of shops and retail services (establishments) placed on the y axis and the number of shop types (functions) on the x axis. The advantage of using log normal graph paper is that it minimizes the effect of the number of shops in a centre. The crucial factor in distinguishing the order of a shopping centre is the number of shop types contained rather than the number of shops. In fact it is possible to find centres of a similar order in which the number of shops varies quite considerably.

Work out the average number of shops and shop types in each order of service centre (i.e. local, neighbourhood, district, regional, CBD) and summarize this on a matrix.

Draw histograms to illustrate the average number of convenience goods shops, shoppers' goods shops, specialist stores and department and variety goods stores in each order of service centre.

Table 7.6. Logging sheet for field study of suburban service centres.

Type of Service	Suburban Service Centres				
Public Houses and Off licence					
Cafés					
Food shops: General					
Supermarket					
Fresh Fruit and Vegetables					
Freezer Centre					
Grocery					
Bakery					
Fishmonger					
Fish and Chips					
Butchers					
Delicatessen					
Sweets and Tobacco Newsagents/Stationery/Fancy Goods					
Pharmacy					
Clothing: Men's					
Women's					
Children's					
Babywear and wool					
General					
Footwear Cooperative Store Multiple Department Store					
Services: Filling Station, Car spares					
Hairdresser, Men's					
Women's					
Cleaners					
Shoe repair					
Banks and Insurance					
Betting Shop					
Furniture Electrical, radio, TV. Sports goods Luggage, leather goods Books and records.					
Other retail (specify)					
Other services (specify)					

3. The extent of the market areas of shopping centres

Determine the market area of the shopping centres by using a simple questionnaire. In the smaller centres, ask a minimum of 25 shoppers the name of the road in which each lives. If the road is a very long one you will need to locate the shopper's home rather more precisely.

On an O.S. 1:10 000 map or Geographia *town map, fix the location of each of the centres and mark in the homes of the shoppers. Draw lines from the shoppers' homes to the shopping centre at which they were interviewed. Use different coloured lines to distinguish home/shop links of each centre (see Fig. 8.5). You will probably find that your map includes some apparent anomalies, for example shoppers who have travelled some distance to visit a small, local centre. The shoppers may have made multi-purpose trips, combining shopping with some other purpose such as a visit to relatives. You can, however, eliminate this possible source of error when you attempt to delimit the market area of the centre by disregarding the most distant homes. The following method should be adopted:*

(a) *Draw two lines at right angles through the shopping centre.*
(b) *Add up the number of shoppers' homes in each quadrant.*
(c) *Draw lines to include three-quarters of these ('the upper quartile line') in each of the segments.*

You can check on the accuracy of your results by working out the theoretical breaking point between two neighbouring centres by using the formula outlined on page 229. In the formula, substitute the number of shop types in each centre for the total population. Measure the road distance separating the two centres.

When you have delimited the extent of the market area, it is possible to obtain an approximate idea of the number of customers residing within it by counting the number of houses enclosed by the line and multiplying this figure by three (the approximate number of people living in the average household). Remember that this method will only give you a rough and ready total which will be invalidated if there are a number of blocks of flats contained within the market area.

Finally, you should analyse your market area maps. You might discover that trunk roads, railways, canals and rivers act as barriers and exert a considerable influence on movement within the town.

Key Ideas

A. *Economic factors: supply and demand*
1. The basis of economic activity lies in the need to make choices among scarce goods.
2. These choices are affected by the prices of goods, which are a reflection of our ability to substitute one good for another, as well as the cost of manufacture and the intensity of our need for a particular item.
3. This balance of supply and demand has an influence upon the landscape, and its visible expression is the market centre and its retail establishments.
4. The distance we are prepared to travel for goods and the number of people needed to make retailing or manufacture worthwhile will influence the number and type of facilities in a town or village.
5. The range of supplies and the threshold of demand are competing economic

215

forces which find expression in the landscape as the 'market area' of a firm or town.

B. *Central Places: the Christaller Model*
1. To explain the variations in intensity of land use, Christaller developed models or idealizations of the landscape based upon an homogenous plain.
2. He suggested that fixed ratios of population would be needed to sustain the growth of 'central places' which would provide them with services. These ratios he called k values.
3. Central places would become the important marketing, transport and administrative centres in an area, around which smaller settlements would be grouped in a regular manner.

C. *Development of the theory: the Lösch Model*
1. Subsequently August Lösch suggested refinements of Christaller's theory which allowed for greater flexibility in the determining of the k values.
2. Application of the theory often depends upon our ignoring local effects of history and terrain in modifying the landscape.

D. *Exceptions to the theory*
1. Certain types of urban landscape are not explicable in terms of Central Place theory.
2. Examples include some transport centres, manufacturing and mining towns, holiday resorts or settlements located by chance or on the basis of unusual historical decisions.

E. *The rank-size rule: urban hierarchies*
1. In many areas there appears to be an inverse relationship between the number or frequency of settlements and their individual population size.
2. This is not a theoretical proposal but an observed phenomenon, and variations from the norm are sometimes taken to indicate weakness or imbalance in the economy of an area.
3. The variety of functions that settlements of different sizes contain tends to demonstrate the importance of urban functions in influencing the size of settlements.

F. *Hierarchies within the town: retail shopping*
1. It is possible to distinguish different levels of retail centres within towns as well as a system of ranking or ordering as between towns.
2. Shopping centres and their catchment areas provide good examples of urban hierarchies. So do educational establishments and the distribution of other public facilities.
3. There is often a connection between the size of a centre and its economic competitiveness; for example the cost of similar goods or services may be higher in smaller shopping centres which have fewer customers.

Additional Activities

Consumers' shopping habits

Use a more detailed questionnaire, such as the one outlined below, to obtain additional information about consumers' shopping habits. This should be used with a smaller sample, perhaps one in five of the shoppers you stop to determine where they live. Use logging sheets as illustrated below to record their replies.

Suburban shopping centre questionnaire

1. Where do you live? (street name)

2. How often do you visit this shopping centre?
   (a) Daily
   (b) At least twice weekly
   (c) Once a week
   (d) Occasionally

3. How have you travelled here?
   (a) Foot
   (b) Car
   (c) Bus

4. What is your average journey time from your home to this shopping centre?
   (a) Less than 5 minutes
   (b) 5–10 minutes
   (c) 10–15 minutes
   (d) 15–20 minutes
   (e) Over 20 minutes

5. Have you ever bought any of the following types of goods here?
   (a) Food
   (b) Clothes and/or shoes
   (c) Furniture
   (d) Retail services (e.g. launderette)

6. What attracts you to this shopping centre?
   (a) A wide range of shops offering a good selection of merchandise
   (b) Is it economical to shop here (competitive prices)?
   (c) Convenient (i.e. close to home)
   (d) A parking space is assured
   (e) The shops offer a good service
   (f) There are good quality shops here

7. Which other shopping centres do you use?
   List these a, b, c, d, e.

8. Where did you make your last purchase of:
   (a) food
   (b) clothes
   (c) shoes
   (d) furniture?

List shopping centres rather than individual shops.

Example

Name of shopping centre: Allerton Road. Date: 3 Jan. Time: 10.30–11.30 a.m.

LOGGING SHEET		*ADDRESS* (STREET)	
1. Calderstones Road	**(m)**	26. Taggart Avenue	**(y)**
2. Dovedale Road	**(y)**	27. Heathfield Road	**(y)**
3. Druidsville Road	**(y)**	28. Kingsdale Road	**(e)**
4. Allerton Road	**(e)**	29. Queens Road	**(y)**
5. Pitville Avenue	**(m)**	30. Herondale Road	**(m)**
....		....	

Every fifth shopper should also be asked to answer questions 2 to 8. The letter in brackets after each street name refers to the approximate age of the interviewee (y – young, m – middle aged, e – elderly).

Analyse the replies to the questionnaire to find out:
(a) If shoppers visit the lower order, local centres more frequently than the higher order centres.
(b) If shoppers are prepared to make longer journeys to the higher order centres.
(c) If the shopping habits of the young, middle aged and elderly are significantly different.
(d) If shoppers buy convenience goods as well as shoppers' goods and specialist goods at the higher order centres.
(e) The factors which attract shoppers to a particular centre.
(f) If shoppers use centres at different levels in the hierarchy to obtain goods and services of different orders.

If you live within the area in which you are conducting the survey, ask whoever shops most often in your family and perhaps one or two of the neighbours or relatives who also live in the district to record all their purchases for the space of one week. e.g.:

Example

Date	*Goods/services purchases*	*Type of shop visited*	*Location*
3 Jan.	Groceries/bread	Supermarket	Allerton Rd.

These case studies will help to demonstrate the complex pattern of consumer behaviour. You must, however, be careful not to generalize from the results.

Reading

A.   TIDSWELL, V., *Pattern and Process in Human Geography*, University Tutorial Press, 1976, Chapter 12.
B.   BLUNDEN, J. R., 'The size and spacing of settlements,' *Spatial Aspects of Society*, Open University Press, 1971.
C.   JOHNSON, J. H., *Urban Geography*, Pergamon, 1969, pages 76–109.
D.   DAVIES, R. L., *Marketing Geography with special reference to retailing*, Methuen, 1976, Chapter 4.

8 The urban field and inter-urban movement

Introduction

Mention has already been made of the relation between towns and their surrounding areas. Whilst it is obvious that towns do serve the surrounding rural landscape and (especially in pre-industrial societies) receive produce to sustain them, the size of the area tributary to a particular settlement will vary with the level of technological development in the country, and more especially with the quality of transport services. Moreover, when a fully urbanized society has developed, there will often be competition amongst towns for the trade in the area between them.

If we are interested in determining how far the influence of a settlement extends we may approach the question in two alternative ways. The first way is to ask firms and public utilities in the town about the boundaries of the areas to which they send out their goods or services. Alternatively we may ask individuals in rural villages to tell us which centre they use to supply their day to day and, indeed, their occasional needs. In neither case will we draw very precise boundaries around the sphere of influence which we distinguish and the process, though interesting, is time consuming. Recently geographers have begun to devise statistical models of how population and trade will be attracted to towns. These can provide us with an overall pattern which is appealingly simple. Care must be taken in the use of these models, however, as we shall see.

The sphere of influence around a town is commonly referred to as the *urban field*. The use of the term 'field' is in this case analogous to that of a magnetic field, in that the degree of attraction is greatest close to the centre, and may diminish farther away, so that if more than one centre of attraction exists, there may be overlapping at their borders.

A. Provision of Urban Services

Methods of urban field delimitation based on field survey which try to find out about the *supplying* of services from a central point to a surrounding community include the following:

1. Analysis of local bus services

All that is required for this is a bus timetable and an O.S. map of the area to be studied.

One of the earliest attempts at working out the network of urban fields was applied by Green.[1] Amongst the techniques that Green utilized was the mapping of bus routes, by lines of proportional breadth from the centre he was investigating out to the peripheral villages which the bus routes served. This can be done for several adjacent centres of similar sizes, or indeed the transport links for a hierarchy of places can be established, giving a vivid impression of the way that smaller urban fields 'nest' within larger ones. Unfortunately, present-day bus services may be a poor indicator of traffic flows because of increased car ownership; but suburban rail services still provide a valid measure around metropolitan centres. Fig. 8.1 is a map of bus services from Ballymena and demonstrates the gradual deterioration of the service with distance from the centre.

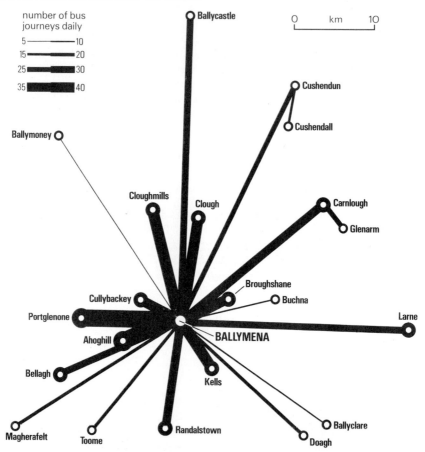

Fig. 8.1   A flow-line diagram showing the number of daily bus journeys from Ballymena to surrounding settlements. (Source: Joyce Wylie)

2. Local delivery areas

An alternative method of measurement is to plot the distribution of local delivery services, or the number of mentions that villages receive in local town newspapers, which may allow 'contours' of influence to be drawn up. The construction of such contours, more properly termed *isolines*, is based upon joining together all points with equal values. Hence all villages with, say, ten news items in the county newspaper in a given month would form one set of points for an isoline. One would expect that the more distant and isolated the villages the less frequently would be their mention in papers, or their record of deliveries from local stores. It is desirable to look at several criteria in determining upon what the isolines should be based, and as the urban field served by centres may overlap, it is also useful to consider the newspapers or delivery areas of stores in other towns in the region, so that a composite view may be built up. This is a point which we will refer to again later.

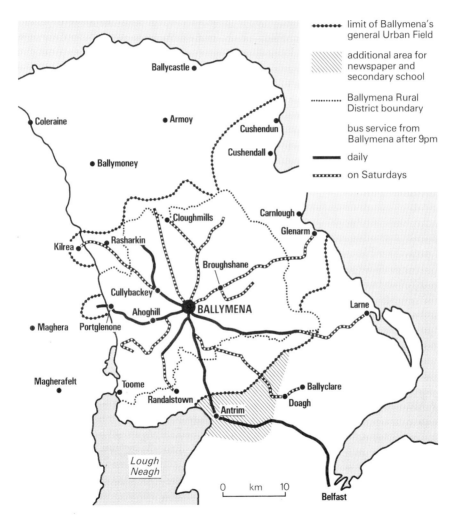

Fig. 8.2   The catchment area of Ballymena. (Source: A. E. Smailes, *Geography of Towns*, Hutchinson, 1953)

3. Catchment areas

Some organizations have official boundaries to the areas which they serve. In rural areas the catchment area of secondary schools and the zones controlled by statutory bodies such as police, fire service, electricity, gas and water boards, can be determined by local enquiry and mapped. It should be remembered that boundaries imposed by external authorities may be drawn for their convenience, rather than to reflect the influence of the town upon which they are centred. Although these methods have been in use since Smailes studied Ballymena in 1953[2] they provide a sound basis for delimiting the urban field of the individual settlement, and if applied over a period may show how the boundaries of the area change (see Fig. 8.2).

However, when the map of the urban field is drawn for a particular town, there is always some confusion over where the boundaries lie.Three zones are normally discovered: (a) one of *dominance* in which all the criteria proposed to test the field are satisfied; (b) one of *competition* included in the boundaries produced by some criteria and excluded by others. This may be a broad zone, and if we wish to delimit our area exactly, this is a weakness (see Fig. 8.3); and (c) one of *marginal influence* (*indifference*), beyond all the isolines drawn upon the map and where we may assume that the town exerts no influence (although we cannot be sure that visitors from farther afield do not come into the town).

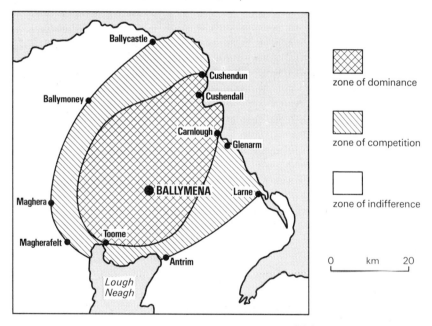

Fig. 8.3   The zones of influence of Ballymena. (Source: Joyce Wylie)

ASSIGNMENT
Figure 8.4 shows the trading area which the Chamber of Trade of a small Canadian town, Neepawa, drew up on the basis of their surveys of shoppers.

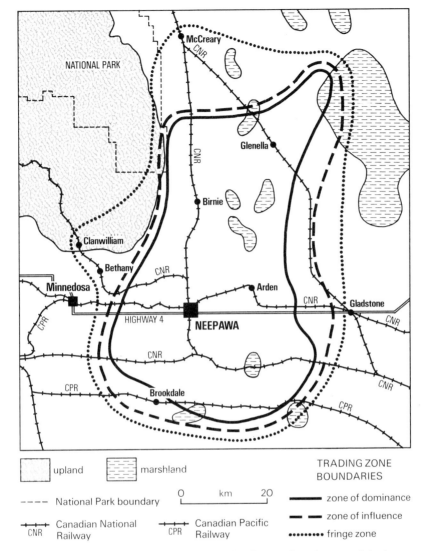

| upland | | marshland | | TRADING ZONE BOUNDARIES |

---- National Park boundary

+--+--+ Canadian National Railway CNR

+--+--+ Canadian Pacific Railway CPR

O   km   20

——— zone of dominance

— — zone of influence

••••••• fringe zone

Fig. 8.4   The trading areas of Neepawa, Manitoba. (Source: based on an original map produced by the Neepawa Chamber of Commerce)

The trading area is divided into three zones of decreasing influence. The population of the 'area of dominance' is about 10 500 people, including 3200 who live in the town itself. The populations of the areas of 'competition' and 'marginal influence' are 3300 and 1200 respectively. The definition of these areas is as follows:

1. *Within the area designated as the 'area of dominance', residents do at least 50 per cent of their shopping in Neepawa.*
2. *Within the 'area of competition', residents do between 25 per cent and 49 per cent of their shopping in Neepawa.*
3. *Within the 'area of marginal influence', residents do between 1 per cent and 24 per cent of their shopping in Neepawa.*

It can be assumed that because of the distances involved in travelling to larger centres only the very highest order goods are bought from far outside the area of the map by residents within that area, and most of these will be mail order purchases. Study Fig. 8.4 and Tables 8.1 and 8.2. Write a report to the Chamber of Trade suggesting what could be done to extend the urban field of the town. Explain alternative ways in which this could be measured.

Table 8.1. Shopping done by Neepawa Area residents in other centres.

| | Times mentioned | |
Centres	Number	Percentage
Brandon	62	29
Dauphin	2	1
Portage la Prairie	5	2
Winnipeg	42	20
Mail Order (Winnipeg and Regina)	31	14
Local town or hamlet in Neepawa area	73	34
Total	215	100

When asked for their reasons for shopping outside Neepawa, replies from residents were as follows:

Table 8.2. Reasons for shopping outside Neepawa.

| | Times mentioned | |
Reasons	Number	Percentage
1. Generally not enough variety, and prices are too high	28	17
2. Insufficient professional services	27	16
3. Poor selection of clothing	27	16
4. Desire to support a town other than Neepawa (their home community)	26	16
5. Live closer to another town	24	15
6. Dislike Neepawa's parking meters	8	5
7. Shop in Winnipeg while there for another purpose, i.e. visiting, business, etc.	7	5
8. Dislike Neepawa's Monday closing by-law	5	2
9. Better selection and price from sales catalogue	5	2
10. Lack of courtesy from Neepawa businessmen	3	1
11. Miscellaneous	8	5
Total	168	100

B. Utilization of Urban Services

As an alternative we may go into the rural area and take a sample of the population to find out where they go to utilize various urban services. This will enable us to find out about the demand side of our rural-urban service equation. A variety of methods can be used but most involve interviewing individuals about their needs and preferences, which constitute the 'demand' side of the equation.

1. Questionnaire surveys

There are certain basic rules in the use of these. It is necessary for the sample to be a sufficiently large one in order to obviate error, and that the questionnaire be drawn up to include a variety of goods and services.

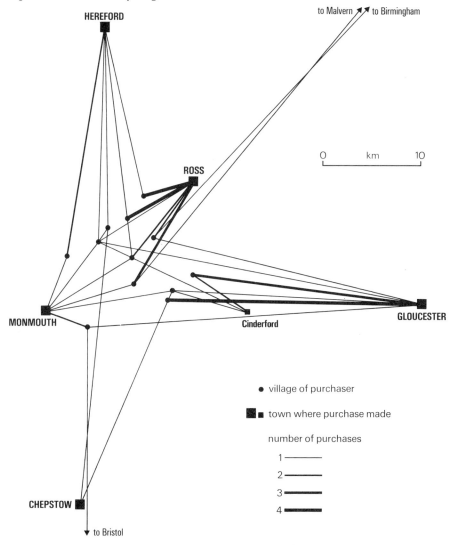

Fig. 8.5   A desire-line diagram related to the purchase of furniture.

What is being done here is to establish the range of influence of the town by drawing upon the experience of its users. Our map will look rather different from the isoline type because we shall insert a line, connecting all the correspondents with the centre that they claim to use (see Fig. 8.5). Such lines are termed 'desire lines' and it is possible to draw boundaries for several urban centres around the outer limit of the desire districts so constructed. Normally the furthest 10 per cent of points are excluded when the map is drawn, to avoid overlap. As Johnson states:

> One of the problems of this method is that the service areas for towns often overlap . . . Whilst the area close to the town may be said to be dominated by that town for the supply of goods and services, farther away there is competition for trade between one town and the next, until at some point another town begins to dominate the trade pattern of the landscape.[3]

In administering questionnaires we must be careful to include a valid sample of people – that is to say our sample should reflect the population we are seeking to find out about. Whether we go to every tenth house, or every tenth name on the electoral roll, we should check the overall composition of the village from census schedules if possible. Detailed consideration of sampling techniques is beyond the scope of this book but the following general points should be remembered if samples are to be selected from the population for study:

(a) Samples may be *random*, where we make no assumptions about the nature of the total population but merely extract data on a percentage of its members. Most street interviews are of this type.

(b) Alternatively, the sample may be *stratified*, that is it may be chosen in order to represent a particular group or to ensure cross-coverage of several sub-groups in the population. A study of immigrants or schoolchildren would be of this type, as would an attempt to interview members of different ethnic or social groups in proportion to their share in the numbers of the total population. Care must be taken not to allow stratification to creep into our sampling unintentionally, for example by conducting interviews only in school holidays or when wage earners are at work.

(c) The sample should be sufficiently large to give a meaningful set of results: this is especially important if samples for different areas or periods are to be compared.

(Further details on the methodology of statistical work in geography can be found in texts such as G. B. Norcliffe, *Inferential Statistics for the Geographer*.[4])

ASSIGNMENT

An early attempt at using questionnaire surveys to establish the trading areas of towns was undertaken by H. E. Bracey in Somerset in the 1950s.[5] A total of fifteen services were specified on his form and those questioned were asked where they usually obtained these. Those villagers who obtained more than eleven of the fifteen items at a particular town were mapped as living in the area dependent upon that town. Thus he was able to draw maps similar to those of Ballymena and Neepawa which you have met in this chapter.

Which of the following constraints on his method do you think might hamper the accuracy of his research, and how could a more satisfactory result be obtained?

(a) Only fifteen services investigated: clothing, household goods shops and professional and medical services.

(b) People questioned in each village were 'schoolmaster, clergy, chairman of parish council and other responsible persons'.

(c) Each village was given a score for the overall shopping pattern of its residents.

(d) Goods might be obtained in more than one town.

(e) Villagers were asked where they usually obtained items or services.

(f) Village size was not considered, all settlements were counted as of equal importance.

(g) All services were regarded as of equal importance despite the fact that some would be visited more often than others.

C. Rural-Urban Interaction

1. The friction of distance

Although the supply and demand approaches to the study of the urban field differ in the areas which they investigate, they have one idea in common. This is that the degree of attraction to a town will be proportional to the ease with which it can be reached – a concept sometimes referred to as the *friction of distance*.

We have seen the operation of this factor within the central business district (page 162). Originally the model of declining intensity of land use with distance from the centre was proposed by Johann Henrich Von Thünen, an agriculturalist, who had studied the working of the eighteenth-century economist, Ricardo. The accompanying diagram demonstrates how he envisaged a decline in intensity of land use as one moved away from a market or other centre. (Fig. 8.6.) His model of concentric rings

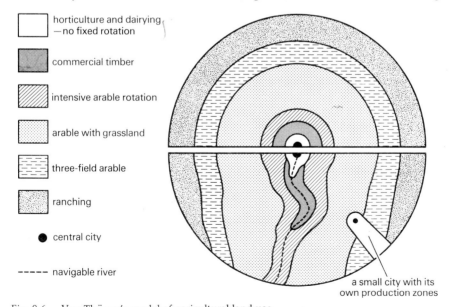

horticulture and dairying — no fixed rotation

commercial timber

intensive arable rotation

arable with grassland

three-field arable

ranching

● central city

----- navigable river

a small city with its own production zones

Fig. 8.6   Von Thünen's model of agricultural land use.

of decreasing intensity around a market may be combined with the idea of the attraction of a three dimensional object to produce a 'gravity model'. Gravity is the force which attracts objects towards the centre of a planet. If the object can overcome resistance it will be drawn inwards, as with a ball dropping through the air, or falling through water, until it encounters a surface which it cannot penetrate. The strength of gravity can be overcome, but even a rocket has to expend energy to overcome the earth's gravitational pull, and will ultimately be drawn into another planet's orbit. The great distance between the planets will mean that they are not drawn to each other – in this sense it acts as a resistance or form of 'friction', keeping everything in its proper place. Perhaps we can apply this theory in a geographical context.

2. Methods of measuring interaction: mathematical models

(a) Gravity models
If we take the physical or 'gravity' model and apply it to the landscape, we could express it in terms of likely or expected movement between two towns (A and B).
   (i) The movement between A and B would be proportional to their respective populations and inversely proportional to the distance between them. If we assume that the larger the population the greater the activity and hence movement towards a centre so the greater the isolation of the centre the less will be its attraction to other people. Hence our base model would be formulated:

$$\text{Movement A}-\text{B} = \frac{\text{population A} \times \text{population B}}{(\text{distance})^2}$$

Hence the larger the centres and the greater the disparity in size the more movement there should be between them. However, if we are concerned with trading movement it may not be appropriate to think in terms of raw population numbers.

We might try to give a value to the town not of population but of its 'centrality' or 'level of attraction' based upon points scored for specific criteria. For example we might consider a major branch of a supermarket chain worth ten points, a bank worth two and so on. This would enable a total points score for each town to be calculated on a comparative though subjective basis and this total could be used in calculations.
  (ii) Alternatively one might measure 'centrality' by comparing the share that different towns have of the total number of enterprises or shops of a specific type that the whole group of towns possesses in the area under investigation. Hence we would be endeavouring to determine the relative functional importance of particular places in a system. The formula for this calculation is as follows:

$$C = \frac{t}{T} \times 100$$

where t = number of outlets of a particular function (e.g. shoe shops) in one town.
and T = total number of outlets of this function in the group of towns under review.

C, the level of centrality, can be calculated using data from the Census of Distribution or from the yellow pages of the telephone directory, although this will not distinguish the relative size of particular shops, merely the number. Comparison of the ranking of average *C* values for towns, taking into account a range of functions, with the ranking of those towns in population numbers, will indicate how far we are 'safe' in using population statistics as an indicator of the functional importance of settlements.

(iii) Another way of measuring the relative attractiveness of settlements as centres of commerce is the calculation of the boundaries of their spheres of influence. This is often done by establishing a so-called 'breaking point' between two settlements; this being the point at which, in theory, the allegiance of shoppers changes and they tend to travel to one town rather than the other. W. J. Reilly expressed the the idea in the terms,

> Two centres attract trade from intermediate places in direct proportion to the size of the centres and in inverse proportion to the square of the distances from these places to the intermediate place.[6]

Hence the limit of the trading areas of two settlements A and B can be calculated thus:

$$\text{Breaking point AB} = \frac{\text{Distance A B}}{1 + \sqrt{\dfrac{\text{Population A}}{\text{Population B}}}}$$

The breaking point will be given in terms of distance from the smaller of the two centres (see Fig. 8.7).

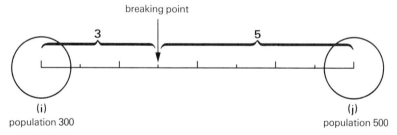

Fig. 8.7 The 'breaking point' between two centres, i and j. (Source: J. A. Everson & B. P. Fitzgerald, *Settlement Patterns*, Longman, 1969, p.97)

(b) Behavioural or probability models

Convenient though these gravity models undoubtedly are, they are over simplistic. They assume that the distance people are prepared to travel for goods of different types is the same; and that different people are all prepared to travel the same distance for similar goods.

Neither assumption is true. For example, in some instances choice of goods is immaterial: e.g. in the case of purchasing postage stamps, or payment of certain statutory bills. In other cases where prices are competitive and the purchases are of major importance, it is worthwhile to shop around; and this may involve extensive travel before a purchase is made. Moreover the degree of mobility of different customers varies greatly and may influence how far they are prepared to travel to satisfy a particular need (see Chapter 7). One attempt to rationalize these differences and to determine the probability of people going to a particular town is Huff's model. Simply stated, it argues that the probability (P) that a purchaser will purchase something in his or her own town (1) rather than in another is related to the number and variety of shops in that town, compared to those in other towns and the comparative ease with which they can be reached. Thus it may be expressed by the formula:

$$P_1 = \cfrac{\cfrac{\text{No. of shops in centre 1}}{\text{Distance or time travelled to reach them}}}{\cfrac{\text{Total N of shops in whole study area}}{\text{Total distance or time travelled to reach them}}}$$

Thus $P_1 = \cfrac{\frac{N1}{\Sigma T^1}}{\frac{NX}{\Sigma TX}}$

Obviously we can compare any number of towns, although for practical purposes three or four is often as many as shoppers will reasonably consider. Or we could compare shopping centres within the same town. Similarly, whilst we could establish probability values for shopping using all types of retail establishment, we might prefer to concentrate only upon one kind, e.g. clothing shops (see Fig. 8.8). Before

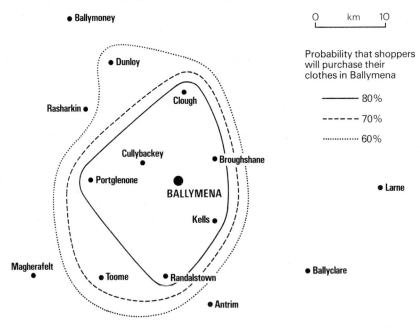

Fig. 8.8 Huff's probability, according to the annual turnover of clothes shops in the Ballymena area. (Source: Joyce Wylie)

applying the formula however it is necessary to bear in mind the following cautionary points:

(i) distance is a less accurate, but a more easily calculated variable than time, as journey times other than by public transport are difficult to establish;

(ii) in comparing towns it may be wise to exclude shops outside the town centre as these may be unlikely to attract out-of-town visitors, but, there remains the problem of the out of town hypermarket or suburban shopping precinct;

(iii) the formula takes no account of shop size, nor of the fact that in many towns, the customer is merely offered a duplicate of facilities in his or her own centre: another branch of Marks and Spencer, Dolcis, and so on.

These problems and the factor of non-rationality on the part of shoppers are considered in the next section.

(c) Problems posed by the use of interaction models

As Carter[7] has pointed out, even if Huff's probability model incorporates a concept of variable consumer behaviour, it still assumes that travel time or distance are always of the same significance in discouraging purchasers. Recent researchers into the area of behavioural geography would dispute this, arguing that perception of the town by rural dwellers will be as important in determining movement from the urban field to the centre as perception of the town by its inhabitants will in influencing social zoning (see page 137).

A simple example of a group of people whose cultural perceptions influence their movement are the Hutterites in Canada. They maintain several small retail service centres by their reluctance to follow the pattern of other Canadians in their search for high order shopping centres. The Hutterites are a group of German-speaking Protestants who live on collective farms and avoid all use of modern machinery, especially motor vehicles. By patronizing small town stores they disrupt the general pattern of American and Canadian retailing, especially in parts of the Prairies where they form an important element in the agricultural population.

If the population of a particular urban field is significantly different in characteristics from the national average, it is reasonable to assume that the size and shape of the area of their urban field will also be different. Also, if people perceive some stores or shopping centres as particularly attractive, this may distort their perception of the real distance involved in reaching them. The setting up of out-of-town shopping centres, and the revitalization of down-town precincts are often attempts to encourage shoppers away from their own town to patronize distant higher order centres for all their purchases. Competitive advertising is similarly designed to overcome the friction of distance. We must realize that a whole range of factors – price, fashion, popularity, variety – influence the individual choice of shops and services and in turn this determines the general pattern.

ASSIGNMENTS

1. Using the data for the total number of retail outlets given in Table 8.3 calculate the degree of centrality for Bournemouth, Southampton and Lymington.
   Apply the formula: $C = t/T \times 100$
   (For a full explanation of the formula, see page 228.)

Table 8.3. Retailing data for Bournemouth, Southampton and Lymington.
(Report on the Census of Distribution and Other Services 1971, Part 8, Area Tables London and South East Region, Table 5, HMSO, Department of Industry. Business Statistics Office (1975.)

Town	No. of retail outlets	Total retail turnover (£000)	Total retail floor space (sq.ft. '000)
Bournemouth			
(entire town)	2 275	79 975	2 004
Central Area	341	27 308	835
Footwear (central area)	17	925	28
Southampton			
(entire town)	1 732	90 543	1 739
Central Area	245	41 686	901
Footwear (central area)	22	1 613	49
Lymington	396	12 494	267
Footwear	11	277	7

2.   (a) *Using the 1971 population statistics provided in Table 8.4, work out the position of the breaking points between Luton and each of the towns listed. (Use Reilly's Breaking Point formula.)*
     (b) *Substitute 1971 retail turnover statistics for population in the formula and repeat the exercise. Compare these results with breaking points derived from population statistics. Which will provide the best indication of Luton's catchment area as a central place?*
     (c) *Briefly describe what the results you obtain show about these centres.*

Table 8.4. Population and retail turnover data for towns in the vicinity of Luton, Bedfordshire.
(Report on the Census of Distribution and Other Services 1971, Part 8, Area Tables London and South East Region, Table 5, HMSO, Department of Industry, Business Statistics Office (1975).)

Town	Distance from Luton (in km)	Population (1971)	Total Retail Turnover (£000s in 1971)
Luton	—	161 178	49 486
Bedford	30	73 064	33 347
Letchworth	18	30 884	7 726
Hitchin	13	28 680	11 764
Stevenage	21	66 918	22 186
Welwyn Garden City	21	40 369	14 696
Harpenden	10	24 161	7 364
St. Albans	19	52 057	22 862
Hemel Hempstead	19	69 371	21 453
Dunstable	8	31 790	12 435
Leighton Buzzard	21	20 326	5 553

3.   *Lymington (1971 population 35 644) is a small market town situated between the large regional shopping centres of Bournemouth (153 425) and Southampton (214 826). It is approximately 30 kilometres from Bournemouth and 27 kilometres from Southampton by road. Using the data provided in the Table 8.3, apply Huff's probability model to work out the likelihood of people living in Lymington shopping in their home town or travelling to Bournemouth and Southampton to*

shop. It is reasonable to assume that people travelling from Lymington to shop in Bournemouth or Southampton will use only the shops in the town centres. It is, therefore, best to use the Central Area figures for Bournemouth and Southampton rather than the figures for the entire towns. Assume the average distance people residing in Lymington have to travel to shop in their home town to be 2 kilometres.

Use in turn figures for the total number of shops, the total retail turnover and the total floor space. Which data will give the most meaningful results?

Remember that the sum of probability values must always equal 1 so that when you have completed your calculations you will need to add together your raw figures and express each as a percentage of the total and then divide by 100.

D. The Rural-Urban Fringe

So far we have considered ways in which the perimeter of urban fields may be delimited either by field study or theoretical measurement. Now we turn our attention to the *character* of these areas outside the municipal boundary but within the zone of influence of the town, large parts of which form what has been termed the 'rurban' fringe.

1. Population

As the urban sociologist R. E. Pahl suggested in *Whose City?*[8] there are many different sorts of occupiers of the rural-urban fringe. Nearest the town are the 'urbanized' residents, commuting to the city daily. For them the villages are a retreat with an artificially rustic life style. But at the edge of the town's zone of influence, the rural population may still live a predominantly agricultural life-style with little contact with the city. Where one group impinges on another there is often conflict between the indigenous population and the 'newcomers'. In Pahl's words:

> Middle-class people come into rural areas in search of a meaningful community and by their presence help to destroy whatever community was there. Part of the basis of the local village community was the sharing of the deprivations due to the isolation of country life and the sharing of the limited world of the families within the village. The middle-class people try to get the 'cosiness' of village life, without suffering any of the deprivations, and while maintaining a whole range of contacts with the outside world by means of the greater mobility afforded by their private transport.

This zone of villages which look for urban services and provide the town with labour, is characterized by residents who live in the countryside but who are not socially or economically part of it. The newcomers are prepared to isolate their living space from their workspace. As Mayer[9] describes it, the *community of propinquity* (those amongst whom one lives) is different from the *community of interest* (the work group, or others of similar interests). If the newcomers are a sufficiently large group in the village population they may develop social activities, e.g. golf clubs, coffee mornings, dinner dances, which enable them to combine the two communities in one place. The risk is that the established villagers will feel excluded or 'taken over' and resent interference in their traditional activities.

2. Social characteristics

In trying to define the social characteristics of the rural-urban fringe, Pahl[10] proposed four main headings, which have been adopted by subsequent writers.

(a) Segregation
Private new housing in villages, often built by national developers (Wimpey, Barratt) rather than by local firms, is often expensive. It is bought by relatively high wage earners for whom it is either more attractive or cheaper than city centre accommodation. However, local people, who have first claim on public housing, will be physically segregated from these new developments. Similarly as the rural-urban fringe is often regarded as a 'greenfield' site it is possible for planners to allocate land for schools, light industry and housing so that there is functional as well as social segregation of land use here.

(b) Selective immigration
The rural-urban fringe attracts mobile middle-class residents who form a small but powerful and economically important proportion of the city population, amongst which they work. One effect of their choosing to live beyond the city is that their financial contribution in the form of rates is denied to the city which they patronize for subsidised services such as public transport, social services and cultural amenities. Such dormitory dwellers may still retain strong social linkages with the city which provides their income, but may have opted out of the problems of urban change and decay.

(c) Commuting
The journey to work of large numbers of people from rural areas has obvious effects in terms of traffic congestion in the city, the lack of activity in the dormitory villages during the day, and the problems of providing transport services capable of handling peak loads which are not much used during the rest of the day.

(d) Collapse of geographical and social hierarchies
Because the rural-urban fringe is being occupied by very mobile residents, normally one or two-car families, the traditional hierarchy of retail services tends to be replaced by specialist ones. One village shop may become an off-licence, another a delicatessen, each with catchment areas beyond the limits of the village in which they are located. The problems of villagers who are unable or can ill afford to travel long distances are gradually increasing with the withdrawal of rural bus and train services. A spiral develops: new residents with urban ties are prepared to drive considerable distances back to town for shopping and entertainment, demand for local facilities declines and these are withdrawn as being uneconomic. This may encourage the elderly to move away to town, thus making way for more newcomers. Economies of scale also force the closure of rural schools and cottage hospitals, and as church attendance falls and parishes are amalgamated to reduce the cost of maintaining old vicarages and churches, the social life which was associated with these institutions also fades away. The village becomes a suburb in style of building and style of life. If these changes in the rural-urban fringe are recognized we may agree with Carter that:

. . . the argument has moved far away from the concept of a fringe as a physical area to one associated with particular social processes. One view considers the rural-urban fringe as identified by static features, a mix of land uses brought about by the incomplete extension of the city as well as the demands which it makes on its marginal areas. The other view sees the fringe as showing distinction in the nature of the communities which occupy it, brought about by the migration of mobile, middle-class families orientated to the city and dominated by urban life styles.[11]

3. The rural-urban fringe and land use

Another way of looking at the rural-urban fringe is to see it as an area where there is no clearly defined land use, where agriculture has given way to ill-disciplined and wasteful settlement sprawl (see Plate 4.5). This is the view of the Director of the Second Land Utilization Survey, Dr. Alice Coleman. When reviewing the changes revealed in comparing land use in Britain in the 1970s with that at the time of the First Survey in 1933, she comments:

> The planned separation of town and country, in order to integrate townscape and conserve the farmland resources, does not seem to have been achieved. There has been a rapid and accelerating farmland loss and in addition to this, there is also much land fragmented and subjected to urban pressures by new sprawling development. Far from attaining its objective of eliminating the 'rurban fringe' of incompatible use mixtures, planning often seems to have actively encouraged its proliferation. On the urban front, the land-use maps reveal that the failure to provide an adequate housing stock appears to be mainly due to the widespread premature demolition of housing. This is explored by examining before-and-after uses of 1000 square kilometres in south-east England. The largest new use proves to be waste land while roads and tended open space have each consumed 15 to 16 times as much new land as residential uses.
>
> The picture of continuing land misuse is surprisingly similar to that of the 1930s. Planning seems to be permitting the same abuses as non-planning, and we must seriously address ourselves to the question: 'Can we afford the vast expense of a planning establishment when free enterprise will do the same job free?'[12]

The Coleman model of land use is to designate urban settlement as 'townscape', agricultural land as 'farmscape' and areas of natural vegetation as 'wildscape' (see Fig. 8.9). In transitional zones between different 'scapes', 'fringes' can be recognized. The zone between vegetation and farmland is referred to as the 'marginal fringe' and if farming becomes more efficient and conservation more deliberate this motley zone should decline in area. The 'rurban fringe' is typified by piecemeal urban development and it is argued that the containment of settlement by green belts and planning constraints is an objective for planners. This objective seems to have failed – there is now more derelict land than forty years ago, and, because of degeneration of land around settlements, three times as much farmland area has been lost in Britain as has been occupied by new building. The blame for the increase in urban sprawl is placed at the door of planners as any change in land use requires planning permission. To quote Dr. Coleman again:

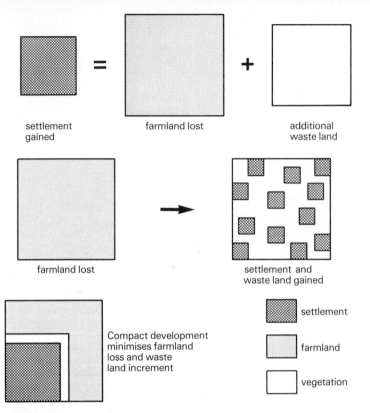

Fig. 8.9   The land-loss equation. (Source: A. Colemen, 'Is Planning Really Necessary?', *Geographical Journal*, **142**, Nov. 1976)

Rurban fringe usually has a greater variety of uses than other environments, and more uses that are mutually incompatible. Apart from a fragmented mosaic composed of all three super-categories, there is also an emphasis on those settlement types that are so coarse in scale or barrier-like in function that they would disrupt the texture of townscape if located within it. Airports, power stations, quarries, marshalling yards, 'spaghetti' junctions and large golf courses are examples, as well as less useful items such as derelict land. Such an environment is far from ideal for urban residents, while they in turn often make farming impossible, by trespass, damage, theft, fire setting and so on. Even the house sparrows that come with a new rurban-fringe building estate can devour up to half the grain in an adjacent field of wheat. These conflicts can be kept to a minimum where the interface between town and country is short and straight, but some planners advocate that it should be deliberately lengthened in the form of green wedges. [13]

Whilst one might discuss whether the environmental quality of the landscape suffers by the spread of low density 'urbanite' settlement, the 'scapes-fringes' model at least serves to enable clear identification of the type of land use in a particular area (see Fig. 8.10). The conflict of interests engendered by pressure on the land for new housing and services form the subject of the activity at the end of this chapter.

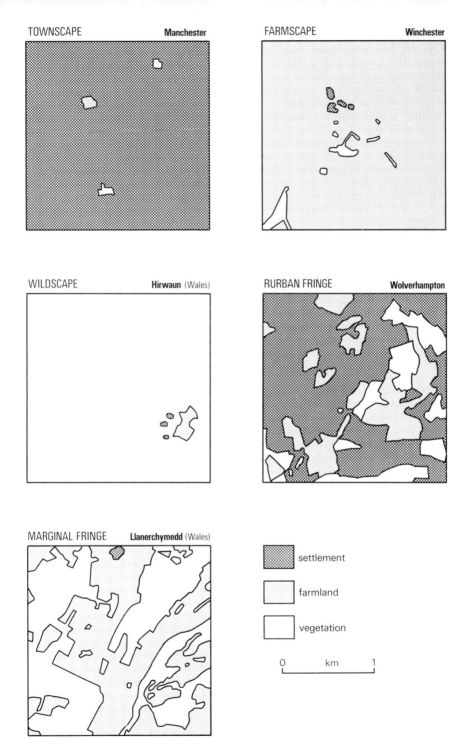

Fig. 8.10   Simplified examples of scapes and fringes. (Source: see caption to Fig. 8.9)

ASSIGNMENT

1. *For a village in your own area, choose a site for the building of new houses and a shop or filling station. Put forward arguments for the houses being either for rent from the Council or for purchase by executive commuters. Then outline the kinds of issues and opinions that such a proposal would be likely to arouse locally.*

2. *Apply Coleman's classification to the area of the O.S. land use map in two contrasting districts (e.g. Sheet 158 Dover and Sheet 207 Gravesend). On the basis of the generalized map which you draw as a result, allocate areas where development should and should not be permitted.*

3. *Prepare a list of ways in which the countryside adjacent to towns could be used to provide recreation for town dwellers without hindering agriculture. Check to see what is being done in your own locality.*

Key Ideas

A. *Provision of urban services*

1. Urban centres are dependent upon and in turn serve an area around them which we term the urban field.

2. The urban field may be delimited by a variety of techniques: those relating to the services the town supplies, those relating to the area from which the town draws custom, and by theoretical measures based on trade statistics.

B. *Utilization of urban services*

1. Urban fields may also be determined by investigation of the area in which demand for urban services is generated.

2. Field techniques of this sort rely upon survey questionnaires which assume the impartiality of their structure and the randomness of the samples to which they are applied for their success.

3. The strength of attraction of an urban centre is diminished by the distance which people have to travel in order to use it.

C. *Rural-urban interaction*

1. Statistical attempts at measuring the urban field rely upon a knowledge of the relative size and distancing of settlements.

2. To refine these techniques further, the concepts of probability and change over time are introduced to the model.

3. Despite these refinements there are problems in the crudity of application of such techniques in the real world.

D. *The rural-urban fringe*

1. The rural-urban fringe can be identified spatially, and by the social activities of its inhabitants.

2. The rural-urban fringe is an inefficient user of land, and there is pressure for its rationalization.

3. Conflicting interests in land use in this area can be examined by the use of role-play games.

Additional Activities

Ways in which we can measure the urban field when we are working outwards from the town to the rural area are given below. Select *one* criterion from sections 1 to 8 and apply it to your own urban area. On this basis construct a map of the town's urban field, indicating the zones of dominance, competition and marginal influence. Suggest reasons for the size and shape of the zones you distinguish.

Measures of the urban field

1. Newspapers
Provide an excellent index for this. Very large centres may have a morning daily (Liverpool, Manchester); large towns have evening papers; while smaller centres have weekly papers. The area they cover can be measured by:
(a) News coverage areas. Map each place for which news items are supplied.
(b) Advertisements. Map places listed in Sales, Vacancies, Houses for sale, etc.
(c) Circulation. Map the limits within which the paper is sold (enquire at office).
(d) Local groupings. Sports leagues, etc.

2. Distribution
(a) Map area of shoppers' homes, preferably by sample on market day. It is usual to omit the farthest 10 per cent or 20 per cent of respondents' locations as these are not likely to be typical of the general area from which shoppers come. If you draw lines from respondents' homes to the town centre these 'desire lines' give an indication of the pattern of movement of people – especially if you can complete them for more than one town.
(b) Map the area within which a furniture store makes deliveries.
(c) Map the area within which a wholesale grocer supplies shops.
(d) Map the area within which mail is delivered from the local Post Office sorting office.

3. Administrative areas
Make maps of areas served by local police, fire, ambulance, hospital, employment exchange, telephone directory.

4. Social areas
Map the area of primary schools supplying secondary schools (i.e. the catchment area of these schools). Likewise for technical colleges, art schools, and other institutions of a specialized nature.

5. Transport flow lines
Traffic reflects movement between a centre and its field. Bus flow line maps which illustrate bus frequency may be drawn. Distinguish: (a) late evening buses (after 21.00 h, returning people to their homes from entertainment centres); (b) early morning and evening services for commuters; (c) 'in between' services for shoppers. Also use the timetables to plot settlements most accessible by bus, i.e. in the area surrounding the main settlement. Note the limitations of this approach. It takes no account of other forms of transport. Car ownership increases annually and more people living in the villages are now able to use private transport.

6. Entertainment areas

Find out the catchment areas of theatres, football grounds, etc. The local supporters club may be able to help you.

7. Catchment areas of principal industries and services other than retailing

Find out the catchment areas of the firms themselves. Some of the larger companies may operate works buses. The routes followed by these will give some indication of the catchment area of these firms.

8. Livestock market

Map the distribution of firms which send livestock for auction at the livestock market. You will probably find that the buyers (who will include butchers as well as farmers) will come from farther afield and will not necessarily provide such a useful index for delimiting the urban field.

Reading

A. CARTER, H., *Study of Urban Geography*, Arnold, 1974. Chapter 6.
B. SMAILES, A. E., *The Geography of Towns*, Hutchinson, 1953. Chapter 7.
C. GREGORY, S., *Statistical Methods and the Geographer*, Longman, 1963,
    HUFF, D. L., 'Defining and estimating a trading area', in AMBROSE, P., *Analytical Human Geography*, Longman, 169.

9 Planned settlements

Introduction

Although all town development is in some sense planned, there were few attempts before the beginning of the last century to go beyond designing individual buildings or groups of buildings. Occasionally complete settlements were built for defensive purposes, as were the 'new towns' of Edward I referred to in Chapter 3, or the 'grand designs' for building terraces and crescents in fashionable parts of London, Bath, Newcastle and Edinburgh, but there was little attempt to regulate the quality of town design for ordinary people before the nineteenth century.

A. Principles of New Town Development

1. The origins of New Towns in Britain

The idea of building complete New Towns came as a response to the industrialization and rapid urbanization of the nineteenth century, which had led to the creation of appalling slums and a high incidence of disease together with low expectation of life in the cities (see pages 61 to 64). The 'new town movement' of the nineteenth century was based upon a concern for the situation of industrial populations in the conditions of housing and work thrown up by the sudden growth of factory towns. By 1840 the average life expectancy in the worst urban areas was around twenty-five years compared to a national average of forty-one years. Philanthropic employers were among the first to endeavour to produce an improvement in conditions out of the profits of their enterprises. Many contemporary reformers saw a solution to the problems of urbanization in the creation of new settlements. Amongst the most important were the following people:

(a) Robert Owen (1771–1858)
Owen took over a cotton mill and industrial village at New Lanark in Scotland in 1799 and devoted all the surplus profits of the enterprise to the provision of social services. He enlarged houses to minimize overcrowding, opened a co-operative shop, abolished child labour in his mills and also set up a school. Owen's writings included *Villages of unity and mutual co-operation* in which he proposed model villages of 800–1200 inhabitants, but only New Lanark (now a museum), was ever built.

(b) James Silk Buckingham

Buckingham published in 1849 an elaborate proposal for a new town of not more than 10 000 called Victoria, in his book *National Evils and Practical Remedies*. The settlement was not built because of lack of finance.

(c) Titus Salt

Salt established a factory employing 3000 people on a site near Bradford in the 1840s. He provided housing, water supply and drainage, a chapel, church, club, library and many other public buildings. Saltaire, as the village was named, is still occupied (see Plate 9.1).

Plate 9.1   Saltaire: a north east view of the village and works in 1895. The settlement is still occupied, and almost all of Sir Titus Salt's original dwellings and social buildings have survived; together with the original lions from Trafalgar Square. *(Bradford Central Library)*

Robert Owen's experiment at New Lanark (1799) and Titus Salt's model village near Bradford were designed to accommodate relatively small numbers of people, but by 1875, B. W. Richardson had proposed a city of 100 000 people – Hygea, the City of Health. He aimed to provide a healthy city, large enough to contain a cross-section of the national population and offering a wide range of employment opportunities. It is interesting to notice that at this early date there was already realization that the *size* and *self-sufficiency* of any new towns were to be important factors in their chance of development. Finance was also a stumbling block to building. In the meantime it remained for individual enlightened factory owners to provide for their workers. This was done by the Cadbury family at Bournville, in the Midlands and by W. H. Lever, who established Port Sunlight (Plate 9.2) near Liverpool in 1889. Lever wanted to socialize and Christianize business relations and get back again in the office, factory and workshop to the close family brotherhood that had existed in the days of hand labour. Inspired by the 'model cottages' built for workers at the nearby Price candle factory, he constructed 900 houses with a church,

242

Plate 9.2   Port Sunlight. The model village with its church, adjacent social club, hotel
and art gallery is sited between the main road and railway routes, affording access to
Chester and Liverpool. The factory is separately zoned away from the houses which are
arranged in short rows and crescents with their own rear gardens. A central green
boulevard runs through the site, an idea used later by Louis de Soissons at Welwyn. The
large proportion of open space and numbers of trees give a rural atmosphere to what is
actually an industrial suburb. (*U.M.L. Ltd.*)

hotel, social club, bowling greens, swimming pools and a now famous art gallery.
The entire 130 acre site was completed just before the First World War and the low
density semi-rural or 'garden city' layout of only seven houses to the acre set new
standards for urban housing. It bore obvious fruit in terms of the health of the
inhabitants, as Table 9.1 indicates.

1907	Death rate per 1000 of population	Infant mortality rate per 1000
England and Wales	16	119
Liverpool	20	140
Port Sunlight	9	70

Table 9.1. Death rates and infant mortality rates, 1907

Whilst such new housing schemes directly benefited the employees' individual cases, their spread was limited by their dependence upon entrepreneurial generosity and a general belief that they could not be financially self-supporting. It needed an economist to argue the case for large-scale new development and dispersal to begin a genuine widespread zeal for a new form of settlement.

2. Middle-class suburbs

As we have already seen in Chapter 3, the increased mobility of the nineteenth-century businessman and tradesman, brought about by the development of the cycle, tram and horse bus, encouraged an increased dispersal of homes from workplaces and the growth of suburbs. Villages within easy reach of the city by public transport became rapidly transformed into parts of the built-up area, and removal to these new districts became a mark of social distinction, echoed in the ringing names which adorn streets of this period: Burlington, Montague, Addington, Melbourne, Devonshire, and Bedford. The aspiring middle classes were enabled to buy their new, healthier homes by the growth of building societies, which developed out of the small banks and friendly societies of Northern England, and by the setting up of freehold housing estates by entrepreneurs who bought large plots of farmland for subsequent resale. The possession of a freehold plot was a mark of status, carrying with it voting rights at elections.

Whilst many suburbs were built at high densities, often in rows of three-storey terraced houses (perhaps with cramped quarters for a maid at the back), there were notable experiments in planning in the private sector. Sir Henry Calthorpe's estate at Edgbaston, Birmingham, or Bedford Park, West London, designed by the influential architect Norman Shaw in 1877, were two such schemes. These developments are of the standard of the great eighteenth-century spa towns, although there was usually great emphasis on the individual rather than the unified nature of the houses' design, as befitted the spirit of the early Victorian age (see Plate 9.3).

These experiments in urban design were in part inspired by the revival of interest in Gothic rather than Classical architectural forms, and by early socialist ideas on the value of labour and craftsmanship which ultimately found expression in the writings of Ruskin and the designs of William Morris. Collectively referred to as the 'Arts and Crafts Movement', this had great influence on one of the period's most practical thinkers: Ebenezer Howard.

3. Howard and the Garden City movement

Ebenezer Howard's Garden Cities of Tomorrow [1] was published in 1898 and revised in 1902. His argument was that high city land values and rents encouraged over-

Plate 9.3   Nineteenth-century villas. Whilst some of the medium sized Victorian semi-detached houses have been retained in single family occupancy, many have been subdivided for letting to single people or small families. As these areas now form the fringe of central business districts, traffic problems and congestion have speeded the decay of formerly attractive streets. *(Author's photograph)*

crowded high density building, and discouraged the provision of social amenities. On the other hand rural life, despite the advantages of clean air and spaciousness, was lacking in transport, employment and housing. Why not combine the advantages of both environments in the 'garden city'? (see Fig. 9.1.)

Howard considered 30 000 people as the optimum town-estate size and that further growth would be by planned decentralization to new centres grouped around and linked to the central city. It is of interest to note that although he was probably unaware of the work of Von Thünen, and Christaller's ideas on Central Place were published much later, Howard's diagrammatic representation combined aspects of the Von Thünen principle of economic rent with the Christaller theory of central places and market areas.[2] (See Fig. 9.2.)

The features emphasized in Howard's proposals were:

(a)   The town would be built on agricultural land acquired at a low cost.

(b)   All land would be held in trust by 'gentlemen of undoubted probity and honour'.

(c)   The town would contain 30 000 people and have a wide range of facilities and employment opportunities.

(d)   The town estate would incorporate agricultural activities (farms, cow pastures and allotments). These would utilize the refuse of the town.

(e)   The process of growth would be by establishing another new town near to the original town and directly connected by rail and road links.

Howard stressed the need for links between established and new settlements and the need for balanced economic growth rather than mere rehousing, '. . . after being

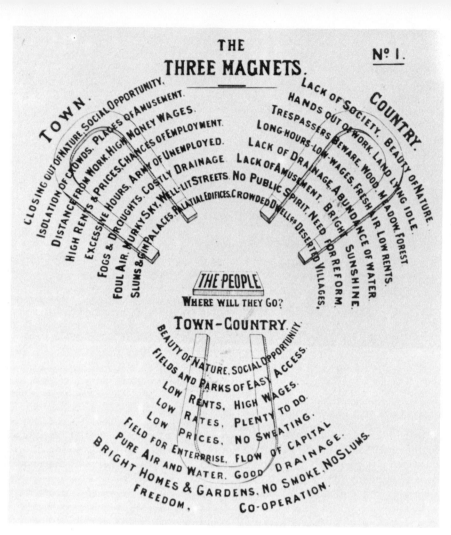

Fig. 9.1   Howard's magnet diagram. *(Hertfordshire County Council)*

once started it ought to be self supporting for the cost of carriage . . . would be less than the saving made in rent. [There would be] much passive resistance at first. Ultimately all would gain, but most the landowners and the rail-roads connected with the colony.'[3] The basic ideas which Howard enumerated have been instrumental in formulating British policy on New Town development, although some time elapsed before Government did recognize the need for it.

In 1901 the Garden City Association, now the Town and Country Planning Association, was established. Two years later with a capital sum of £300 000 the company started work on its first town, Letchworth. In 1920 the second town, Welwyn, was begun. By 1935 the government's Marley Committee reported in favour of the movement, and advocated the 'fullest adoption' of New Towns as an alternative to the suburban sprawl and ribbon development so characteristic of the inter-war period. No action was taken because of the Second World War, but in

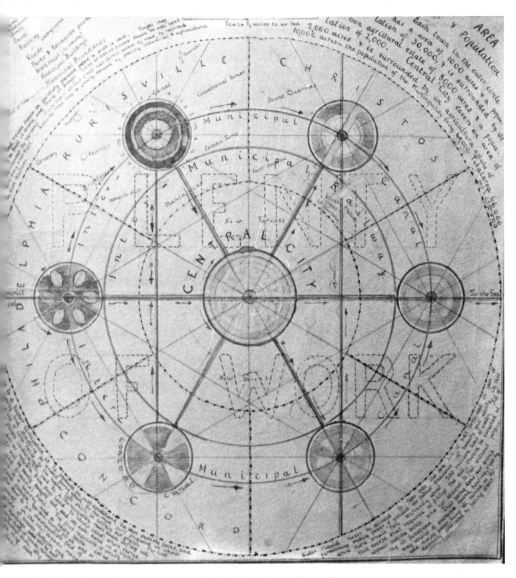

Fig. 9.2   Howard's grand design. *(Hertfordshire County Council)*

1944, Abercrombie's Greater London Plan proposed a constraining Green Belt around London and the overspill of employment and population to ten New Towns to be built 30–50 kilometres from central London. In 1946 a New Town Scheme for Glasgow was advocated and in the same year the New Towns Act was made law.

4. New Town concepts

Howard's principles regarding New Towns came to be expressed as a series of guiding concepts which have since shaped urban design. These may be summarized as follows:

(a) The towns should grow rapidly to an optimum or ideal size from a small initial base population

Hence there must be controls on the size of the settlement, but paradoxically in the early years there must be incentives for people to move there. The New Towns Committee in 1946 were not dogmatic about the optimum size of New Towns but suggested from 20 000 to 60 000 people. The Committee considered that constraints to size included: (i) the need for dwellings to be within walking or cycling distance of work; (ii) that contact with countryside was essential for the whole community; (iii) that it was difficult to attain a sense of civic consciousness in very large towns; and (iv) that smaller units could be built more quickly.

During the period up to the early 1950s the concept of small, dispersed, concentrically planned towns isolated by green belts became a familiar and popular one. However, by 1955 projections of future population growth indicated a need for larger units, and increasing car ownership cast doubts on the scale of distance which was needed for settlements to be independent. Despite this the New Town lobby led by the writings of F. J. Osborn continued to be favoured. His basic tenets were twofold (although the number and size of towns varied between 1918 and 1946, the dates when his book *New Towns after the War* was first printed and reissued). Osborn argued that (i) a town should be large enough for efficient industrial organization and full social activity but no larger, and (ii) the whole of the land both urban and rural should be owned and administered in the interest of the community.[4] Populations of around 40 000 and areas of 2000 acres were envisaged. This philosophy was coupled to Howard's ideas that:

(b) The towns should be comprehensively planned by a development agency

Under the 1946 Act the Minister for Town and Country Planning could designate the site of a proposed New Town and establish a development corporation to implement the proposal. Under the Act the development corporations have the powers to: 'acquire, hold, manage and dispose of land and other property, to carry out building and other operations, to provide water, electricity, gas, sewerage and other services, to carry on any business or undertaking in or for the purposes of the New Town, and generally to do anything necessary or expedient for the purposes of the New Town'. A third principle was that:

(c) The town should be spatially separate from the parent city and be built on land which has been acquired at lower cost than has that at the periphery of the built-up area.

Land values decrease with distance from the city centre and eventually level off where land is in agricultural use. This means that land some distance from the edge of the built-up area is cheaper than land adjacent to the built-up area. The First Garden City Co. Ltd. was able to purchase land at a distance of fifty-six kilometres from central London from fifteen different owners at an average cost of only £42 per acre.

Even today the development agency of a New Town has the right to acquire land compulsorily at the price that would have applied if the New Town did *not* exist. This is necessary because there will have been much public discussion of the plans for the New Town and without such provision land prices in the designated area and surrounding area would rocket upwards in anticipation of the growth of the town.

(d) A large proportion of the property in the town should remain in the ownership of a non-profit-making public body

Ebenezer Howard envisaged that all property in the town would be rented. In fact in New Towns present building can be sold or let. Note that for the first two decades after the passing of the New Towns Act in 1946, only one in five dwellings in New Towns could be sold for owner occupation. But the current policy is to sell 50 per cent of all houses built, i.e. to put New Towns in line with national average of owner-occupation. Most of the industrial and commercial property is also owned by the development corporation and leased to the occupiers.

(e) New Towns should be self-contained

The adjective self-contained is taken to have three meanings:
   (i) describing the physical form of the town. New Towns were in part a reaction against inter-war ribbon development and other forms of suburban sprawl. Also their sites were chosen to avoid as far as possible high quality agricultural land.
   (ii) relating to the provision of facilities. Ideally the town should be self-contained for its requirements of shopping, schools, hospitals, entertainment, and so on.
   (iii) having a sociological definition. New Towns were built some distance from overspill cities in the expectation of their residents becoming independent of their old home bases, and setting up new community groups.

Finally, it was intended that:

(f) New Towns should be socially balanced

They should have a range of age, income and social groups within them – a point made initially by Richardson over a century ago.

The conflicting aims of these principles – optimum size versus self-sufficiency, social balance versus full employment and the provision of public housing, have led to a variety of practical problems which we will consider in a later section.

ASSIGNMENTS
1.   *Howard's ideas of how New Towns should be designed were based upon philosophical perceptions of what towns are for: their purpose for social activity. What in your opinion are the purposes of towns today? What influences should these purposes have on new urban designs such as housing estates, shopping centres and industrial areas?*
2.   *What were the advantages and disadvantages of relying upon private enterprise for the designing of the first New Towns?*
3.   *Explain what is meant by the description of Howard's and Osborn's proposals as 'systems'. Draw a diagram to illustrate the systems relationships within the town and between a New Town and its parent city.*
4.   *Referring to Howard's diagram of the idealized grouping of New Towns around a parent city, select an area of Britain covered by an O.S. 1:100 000 or 1:200 000 map and adapt the pattern to take account of terrain, existing settlements and communications to build your own New Town landscape.*
     On tracing overlays draw the resultant pattern. Choose two or more

*contrasting areas in which to attempt this exercise; preferably areas not too
heavily populated already and of differing physical type.
Explain how and why your landscape differs from Howard's model.*

B. The Building of the British New Towns

1. The early years

Between 1946 and 1949, eight New Towns were designated for the Greater London
area: Stevenage, Crawley, Hemel Hempstead, Harlow, Hatfield, Welwyn, Basildon
and Bracknell (see Fig. 9.3). Subsequently, Corby (1950), Newton Aycliffe (1947) and
Peterlee (1948) were added in the provinces. Scotland had East Kilbride (1947) and
Glenrothes (1948), and Wales had Cwmbran (1949). The designs of the 'Mark I' New
Towns were conceived in terms of low density housing and neighbourhood structure. Eighteen more towns were designated between 1955 and 1970. Of larger size,
they were zoned strictly and based upon the neighbourhood principle; built around
schools and community facilities but at higher densities and often to a cellular
pattern. Some were built on green field sites, others were designed to be extensions
to already existing communities. Most incorporated schemes for pedestrian precincts, traffic segregation in residential areas and modern industrial estates. Almost
all faced local opposition and involved transferring large numbers of people from
other areas. However in positive terms the achievement was an important one:

> 15 towns almost built, a dozen more started. Nearly 175 000 new houses,
> hundreds of new industries in 35 million sq. ft. of factories, 350 new
> schools with 150 000 places, 4 million sq. ft. of office space, 100 new pubs,
> scores of churches and public buildings, several thousand acres of park,
> playing field and open space.[6]

2. The later pattern

The New Towns of Britain kept pace with urban population growth and the desire of
successive governments to solve the problems of inner cities in the post-war period
by rehousing the people in new surroundings. By 1971 the twenty-eight New
Towns in Britain contained 1.61 million people, an increase of 87 per cent in twenty
years for their areas, or eight times the national growth rate. As might be expected
they have higher than the national average of young families and fewer older
residents. One way of comparing these towns is in terms of their stages of development.[7]

Group A. Towns designated pre-1950 and substantially 'filled' by 1960 (Crawley,
 Hatfield, Hemel Hempstead, Welwyn).
Group B. Designated pre-1950, but population still growing after 1960 (Aycliffe,
 Basildon, Bracknell, Corby, Cwmbran, East Kilbride, Glenrothes,
 Harlow, Peterlee, Stevenage).
Group C. Designated 1955–62, most population growth post-1961
 (Cumbernauld, Livingston, Skelmersdale).
Group D. Designated in later 1960s; attached to existing settlements (Irvine,
 Milton Keynes, Redditch, Runcorn, Telford, Washington).

Fig. 9.3 The location of New Towns in Britain.

Group E. Designated in late 1960s and early 1970s with large initial existing populations (Central Lancashire, Newtown, Northampton, Peterborough, Warrington).

The variation among groups is shown in the rate of population growth (Table 9.2). Group A towns grew fastest in the 1950s. Group B showed a more slow and even rate

Table 9.2. Population growth in British New Towns, 1951–71. (Source: Town and Country Planning Association, 1975.)

New Town Group	Population 1951	1951–61 increase	per cent	1961–71 increase	per cent	1951–71 increase	per cent
A	60 743	103 953	171.1	39 335	23.9	143 288	235.9
B	82 726	225 287	272.3	171 069	55.5	396 354	479.1
C	14 478	2 853	19.7	54 532	314.7	57 385	396.4
D	183 025	23 065	12.6	60 855	29.5	83 920	45.9
E	520 212	29 726	5.7	38 405	7.0	78 131	15.0
All New Towns	861 184	384 884	44.7	364 196	29.2	749 078	87.0
Great Britain	48 854 303	2 429 589	5.0	2 694 646	5.3	5 124 235	10.5

Table 9.3. Age structure of British New Towns, 1971. (Source: Town and Country Planning Association, 1975.)

New Town Group	Percentage in each age group						
	0–9	10–19	20–29	30–39	40–49	50–59	60+
A	17.6	18.2	13.6	12.5	15.6	11.1	11.3
B	21.8	18.2	15.3	13.9	13.6	8.6	8.7
C	27.1	15.0	18.9	15.1	10.2	6.5	7.2
D	19.8	14.9	15.6	12.7	12.3	10.5	14.2
E	17.4	14.4	13.6	11.8	12.6	11.8	18.7
All New Towns	19.5	16.1	14.7	12.7	13.1	10.3	13.5
Great Britain	16.5	14.4	14.1	11.6	12.4	12.0	18.9

Table 9.4. Household size and activity rates in British New Towns, 1971. (Source: Town and Country Planning Association, 1975.)

New Town Group	Average household size	1- and 2-person households	Economic Activity rates	
			Males	Females
	persons per household	per cent of all households	per cent	per cent
A	3.20	38.6	87.3	54.2
B	3.32	35.3	88.4	50.1
C	3.44	32.2	90.1	46.1
D	3.08	42.7	85.2	44.1
E	2.90	49.2	83.0	45.3
All New Towns	3.11	42.3	85.8	47.6
Great Britain	2.88	49.8	n.a.	n.a.

of growth, and Group C grew fastest in the 1960s. In other words early town growth is rapid and often unbalanced in age structure. The towns all show (Table 9.3) the effect of this imbalance but it is most clearly evident at different age levels in different stages of development. Thus the newest towns (Group E) have a higher than average population of under 10 years of age, and over 60 per cent of the population is in the under 30 years age group in towns such as Cumbernauld, Livingston and Skelmersdale.

The group of New Towns which was established earliest (A) has the most marked imbalances in its population structure, showing a deficit of people aged 25–34 and 55–59 years.

A consequence of the youthful age of the New Towns' population is the costly but short term need for child welfare, nursery, and school provision. Conversely, expenditure on social facilities for the elderly can be relatively low. A further characteristic of these towns is the relatively large size of households – and the demand for four-bedroomed or larger houses (see Table 9.4). In the long term, there may be problems of redundant schools and housing stock, and a demand for different facilities to be financed from a declining rate base. Moreover the tendency to 'fill' the towns' target for residents so rapidly may lead to severe shortages for housing and jobs for second and third generation inhabitants.

3. The siting of new settlements

As we have already noted, British New Towns have frequently been designed as 'satellites' to larger metropolitan centres. Development has been on relatively cheap, publicly controlled land by a non-profit-making corporation, and has been designed as a comprehensive scheme, with the aim of producing self-contained and balanced communities for work and living. These twin objectives of social balance and economic self-containment are the most difficult to achieve, especially as mobility, labour costs, site advantages and industrial inputs are all variable in the long term, so that a once ideal site may eventually become superseded and derelict (e.g. New Lanark). The choice of location is thus crucial to long term success. Factors such as cost, accessibility from existing centres, the presence of existing infrastructures (roads, water, schools, small communities to act as growth nodes), are amongst the most significant.

At the small scale, Letchworth was provided with 3800 acres of land at an average cost of £42 per acre, though only fifty-six kilometres from London. Milton Keynes, with a target population of 250 000, will cost about £700 million at present prices, invested over twenty-five years, and this represents the largest development to date. An important factor is that under the 1961 Land Compensation Act, the development agency is empowered to acquire land compulsorily at the price it would fetch if the town had not been designated.

The satellite nature of many New Towns was encouraged until recently because of the agreements that existed between the metropolitan centres which exported population and New Towns which received them. A list of the major schemes is given (see Tables 9.5, 9.6). With the decline in central area populations, many New Towns are no longer to receive further quotas of newcomers and will have to fill their housing stocks with local people. The return of industries to central London and other major cities has impoverished the opportunities in some of the satellite centres

Table 9.5. Satellite new towns in the United Kingdom, 1973. (Source: Town and Country Planning Association, 1973.)

	Year of designation	Population at time of designation	Population 1972	Ultimate population
London's new towns:		(thousands)	(thousands)	(thousands)
Stevenage	1946	7	73	100–105
Crawley	1947	9	69	85
Hemel Hempstead	1947	21	73	80
Harlow	1947	5	80	undecided
Welwyn Garden City	1948	19	42	50
Hatfield	1948	9	26	30
Basildon	1949	25	82	134
Bracknell	1949	5	38	60
Milton Keynes	1967	40	50	250
Peterborough	1967	81	91	187
Northampton	1968	131	138	260
Total London's new towns		352	762	1 200 (approx.)
Glasgow's new towns:				
East Kilbride	1947	2	67	90–100
Cumbernauld	1955	2	35	100
Livingston	1962	2	18	100
Irvine	1966	35	44	120
Total Glasgow's new towns		42	164	410–430
Liverpool's new towns:				
Skelmersdale	1961	10	34	80
Runcorn	1964	30	44	100
Birmingham's new towns:				
Redditch	1964	32	44	90
Telford	1968	73	87	250
Belfast's new towns:				
Craigavon	1965	61	73	180
Antrim	1966	33	40	74
Ballymena	1967	48	50	96
Grand total		680	1 298	2 500 (approx.)

and produced long distance commuting, and problems of unemployed rehoused families unable to pay rents in their new homes.

4. Employment and social structure

The original aim that New Towns should be more than dormitories for the populations which filled them from existing overcrowded centres, meant that an adequate range of social and employment opportunities had to be provided. It was not sufficient that the towns be of an adequate size – and what this should be has been established by the costly method of trial and error – but that they should rapidly achieve a range of facilities that have taken generations to establish in other towns. However, whilst the development corporations of the New Towns accept as an

Table 9.6. Selected town expansion schemes of a satellite character in England, 1973. (Source: Town and Country Planning Association, 1973.)

	Exporting/Receiving authority	Completed by 30.6.72	Dwellings for letting. To be built	Total
London's schemes:	Andover MB	1974	4026	6000
	Ashford UD	1953	2297	4250
	Aylesbury MB	2182	1518	3700
	Basingstoke MB	5428	3822	9250
	Bletchley UD	4240	760	5000
	Bury St Edmunds MB	1204	1796	3000
	Haverhill UD	2517	1983	4500
	Kings Lynn MB	1324	2176	3500
	Swindon	7915	585	8500
	Thetford MB	2590	410	3000
	Wellingborough UD	2204	7796	10000
	Witham UD	1747	1253	3000
Birmingham's schemes:	Daventry	1529	3746	5275
	Tamworth MB	2804	3696	6500
Liverpool's schemes:	Ellesmere Port MB	2383	3117	5500
	Widnes MB	853	3307	4160
	Winsford UD	2627	4039	6666
Manchester's schemes:	Burnley CB	14	2686	2700
	Crewe MB	43	3957	4000
Newcastle upon Tyne's schemes:	Seaton Valley UD (Cramlington)	892	5608	6500
	Longbenton UD (Killingworth)	1360	2657	4017

Notes: 1. This table covers expansion schemes agreed in accordance with the 1952 Town Development Act where the development is managed by agreement between the exporting and receiving authority. The table covers most agreements involving the construction of 3000 or more dwellings for letting. There is often a substantial amount of house construction for sale also associated with most of these schemes but the local authority does not usually play any special role in this area.
2. Burnley also had agreements with Liverpool and London for 2200 and 700 dwellings respectively.

objective the standards for shops, schools, health and cultural amenities per head of the population proposed in the New Towns Committee Reports, there is no requirement for them to provide these. This responsibility rests with the local authority within whose area the town is built and, in turn, in the provision of commercial facilities, the local authority has to await planning applications from retailers and others. Although the provision of schools and hospitals has kept pace with demand, the building of shops, cinemas, pubs and other amenities which add to the character and variety of the urban area has lagged behind the provision of housing – because these rely on proved rather than projected demand for their success and profitable operation. For example, Stevenage (population 70 000) had no cinema in 1973, and Newton Aycliffe had no youth centre before its population reached 18 000 in 1967. It seems that the normal economic interplay of 'threshold' and 'range' is eventually achieved in the New Towns, but that demand has to precede and exceed supply. The time lag is often a cause of dissatisfaction and unrest, so that some newcomers decide to move back to their original homes.

ASSIGNMENT
Imagine that you are responsible for the forward planning of new branches of a major retailing chain. Justify to your board the decision to either locate or not locate in a New Town of 30 000 people, designed to grow to 100 000 in ten years.

C. Problems of New Towns

In theory the problems of New Towns should be less than those of haphazardly planned, older settlements. However, the advantages of lower land values, an absence of pollution and new methods of control and servicing have not always been sufficient to offset the problems involved in producing whole new communities from drawing board to bricks and mortar. In general, the speed with which the New Town has had to assimilate its population and acquire people's loyalty, to achieve an individual character and traditions and to cope with the ever changing technology of industry and transport has placed severe strains upon these new urban centres. Moreover some of the concepts fundamental to New Town design carry with them attendant problems: in particular the objectives of self-containment and social mixing.

1. The problem of self-sufficiency

Self-containment implies that the New Town will provide all the necessary services for its population – the objective is that if people do more things in a place they will feel they 'belong' to it more strongly. But certain difficulties arise in the implementation of this policy:
(a) The provision of most kinds of local authority facilities is the responsibility of the county councils, most of whose ratepayers do not live in the New Town. In the early years New Town development imposes a significant extra burden on the rates, especially for services such as health and education.
(b) In the case of facilities provided by private enterprise it is impossible to ensure provision in advance of demand. They will only come in when there is a sufficient threshold population. When shops do come they enjoy a fairly monopolistic position and residents in New Towns often complain of high prices and lack of choice.

Self-containment was considered to be an essential factor in helping to create the identity of places; the fear was that unless New Towns were balanced for housing and employment and people were encouraged to live and work in the same place, they would become dormitories for neighbouring employment centres. Rather than become dormitories, the New Towns serving London should themselves become centres for their surrounding areas.

But there are grounds for supposing that New Towns may become relatively less self-contained in the future.

As the New Towns become more established, more of the initial immigrants will change either their place of work or place of residence. In addition, as more houses are owner-occupied New Town Corporations will have less control over who lives in them, for they may be sold to people who have jobs outside the town.

Another reason for the breakdown of the concept of self-containment or self-sufficiency is the great increase in personal mobility. When the New Town concept was formulated, only one household in twenty was car-owning – today the proportion would be thirteen or fourteen in twenty. The implication for the policy of self-containment will be obvious – New Town populations overspill increasingly into adjacent countryside – and also add to the commuter flows back to the established centres in searching for a range of employment opportunities. Two alternatives present themselves:

(a) If social and occupational facilities are limited the town becomes a suburb.
(b) If they are more attractive than those of neighbouring centres, the town finds itself subsidizing the needs of 'extra-mural' users. The results of the conflict between self-containment and the trends of mobility can be calculated by comparing the growth of journeys *within* the towns with the growth of journeys *to and from* them.

There is little that a development corporation can do to ensure self-containment. The corporation can have only an indirect influence on decisions made by individuals as to whether they use facilities within the town or travel elsewhere. But a development corporation can make self-containment possible by, for example, matching levels of employment and population and by providing the environment and amenities which will induce people who work in the town to live there also. The Index of Commuting Independence provides a measure of the employment self-containment of a town.

To calculate this index we need to know the number of two sorts of journeys being made by people living and working in the New Town:

1. Journeys *within* the town are local journeys.

2. Journeys *to and from* the town are crossing journeys.

The ratio of (1) to (2) is the *index of commuting independence* (independence index). The higher the value the more self-contained the town,

$$\text{Independence Index} = \frac{\text{internal journeys to work}}{\text{commuting in} + \text{commuting out}}$$

But it is not only in the field of industry that obtaining adequate facilities is difficult. In 1969 Ray Thomas[8] reported to the Political and Economic Planning Group on the degree of self-containment of the New Towns around London and in the provinces. His comments upon Newton Aycliffe in County Durham succinctly express the problems facing the town:

> . . . The fact that Newton Aycliffe started from scratch means a complete absence of community facilities. Every other new town had some start, even if it was only a couple of public houses as at Peterlee, but Aycliffe's only asset was its proximity to Darlington. By 1954 the population was nearly 5000 but there were still no public buildings or community facilities. The Corporation reviewed the needs for social facilities and sent a list to the Ministry. In first place came a youth centre, and in second place a town

assembly hall. At that time the population was just under 11 000. Newton Aycliffe did not get its youth centre until 1967 when the population was 18 000.

With regard to the previously mentioned problem of the towns failing to contain their workers, he had this to say:

> The flow of commuting in and out of the new towns is influenced by a variety of factors. The flow depends upon the proximity of the town to other urban concentrations, and it depends upon the availability of transport facilities of all kinds – cars and roads, trains, buses and bicycles. The nearer a town to other centres of employment, and the easier it is to travel, the greater the likelihood that residents will take work outside. The nearer the town to other residential areas the easier it is for people to work in the town without living in it.

Table 9.7. Job ratios in London's New Towns in 1951, 1961 and 1966. (Source: R. Thomas & P. Cresswell, *The New Town Idea*, Open University Press, 1973.)

Town	1951	1961	1966
	(ratio of employment to residents in employment as a percentage)		
Bracknell	108	115	126
Basildon	37	82	107
Crawley	112	101	111
Hatfield RD	123	107	96
Harlow	98	86	97
Hemel Hempstead MB	101	96	97
Stevenage	124	109	112
Welwyn Garden City	124	125	122
Average (weighted)	100	100	107

As a contrast, Stevenage provides an example of a highly self-contained New Town. In 1966 there were 26 000 'residents in employment.' Of these only 4000 worked outside the town. There were 29 000 jobs in the town; so some 7000 were moving in each day to work, thus implying a job surplus in the town. Of course, similar situations exist in the industrial suburbs of other cities with large employers, e.g. Boots at Beeston near Nottingham. The measure of employment relative to the population is the *job ratio* expressed as a percentage of the number of jobs in a town divided by the number of workers resident there. A surplus of employment gives a ratio of over 100 – a deficit gives a ratio of under 100. Of course a perfect balance may not exist even if the ratio is exactly 100 – the *kind* of jobs may not match the kind of skills of the residents. There may be a shortage of part-time jobs or a lack of local management skill. The study by Ray Thomas for the Political and Economic Planning Group in 1969 showed, however, that the New Towns around London were more self-contained than other centres at similar distances – so to some extent the policy has been successful.

Table 9.7 above gives the indices for London's New Towns over the period 1951–66. You will see that there is a considerable difference between 1951–61 and 1961–66. The relative rate of external movement has decreased in most cases.

The employment situation in any town is not static. As well as national trends, local influences operate. People move house or change jobs – move into private rather than rented property or seek promotion. In the early stages of New Town growth their relative independence was achieved by planning control – allocating houses only to those who had a job locally. Once the corporations begin to sell rather than rent houses, or to relax their controls, the structure of the town may alter – even causing congestion and commuting as people move into these new urban centres. In the long term 'artificial' controls such as industrial development certificates, or housing regulations can succeed only if the natural growth of the young town is healthy.

2. The problem of social mixing

Another aspect of the problems associated with building a New Town or greatly increasing the size of an older nucleus is the balance of occupations which are provided. It is often difficult to persuade employers with heavy capital investment to relocate in New Towns. So that although their industrial estates may be clean and quiet, they may also be occupied only by light or processing industries which are not a sufficiently stable base for employment in a large community. Similarly the skills required may cause a social imbalance, with few managerial or professional employees (see Tables 9.8 and 9.9). Ray Thomas has attempted to analyse the socio-economic groups within some of the New Towns and concluded:
(a) there is an under-representation of unskilled manual workers.
(b) professional and white collar workers are proportionately over represented in the New Towns around London, but this group chooses to live outside the towns in which they work and often their absence impoverishes the social mix of these centres.

Table 9.8. Employment structure of selected New Towns, compared with Britain as a whole. (Source: R. Thomas & P. Cresswell, *The New Town Idea*, Open University Press, 1973.)

| Industry | INDUSTRIAL STRUCTURE | | | |
| | Crawley | Glenrothes | Harlow | Great Britain |
	(percentage of total employment)			
Primary	0.3	1.3	0.2	5.5
Manufacture of engineering and electrical goods	31.8	35.6	30.0	9.0
All other manufacturing	21.2	17.9	22.9	25.8
Construction	6.3	19.5	8.7	7.8
Gas, electricity and water	0.6	0.0	0.8	1.7
Transport and communication	5.0	1.4	2.8	6.7
Distribution	10.5	6.7	10.2	13.4
Insurance, banking and finance	2.8	2.0	1.0	2.7
Professional and scientific services	10.3	9.8	14.4	10.3
Miscellaneous services	7.9	4.3	5.6	10.9
Public administration	2.8	1.4	3.2	5.8

Table 9.9. Percentage of persons working in five of London's New Towns but living outside (by socio-economic groups), 1966. (Source: R. Thomson & P. Cresswell, *The New Town Idea*, Open University Press, 1973.)

Socio-economic groups	Living and working in the town (per cent)	Working in the town but living outside (per cent)	Total numbers represented
1.2 Managers	62	38	10 650
3.4 Professional workers	51	49	8 620
5.6 Other non-manual workers	74	26	47 310
9.10.11 Manual workers	79	21	65 700
7.8.12.17 Other groups e.g. service			
industry workers	85	15	13 640
All socio-economic groups	75	25	146 120

(c) in their desire to attract employers the development corporations have not paid any great attention to the socio-economic 'mix' generated by particular industries in their recruitment.

(d) the neighbourhood principle does not achieve much socio-economic mixing – some areas become favoured, others not and segregation takes place quite rapidly.

(e) the unemployed and the unemployable – perhaps those members of society who should be receiving a priority in their treatment and rehousing – are unlikely to gain a foothold in the New Towns as the 'no job, no house' requirement has been fairly rigorously enforced.

The objective of producing a balance of social groups was implicit in the brief given to Development Corporations as early as 1946, and was spelt out in that the aim for Crawley New Town was to achieve a similar balance to that of England and Wales in the local (new town) population. This aim was linked to the post-war belief that the mixing of different class groups would promote greater interaction and understanding between them. Two types of social balance were envisaged: (i) relating to the town as a whole and (ii) the attainment of local or neighbourhood balance.

(i) *In the town as a whole*. A problem here is that rents are relatively high even with subsidies, so that unskilled workers or the elderly are unlikely to be able to live in the new houses. This may be attributable to the fact that in housing provision, as indeed in all other areas, the development corporation is allowed to borrow money only from the Government and the corporation returns to the central government any profits it should make. On the other hand, Howard had envisaged a trust, with profits directly benefiting poorer members of the New Town community.

Another reason for imbalance is that industrial structure and the resulting pattern of employment is a major factor in determining the social class structure of a town. Most of the New Towns have a bias towards firms in the engineering industry which employ an above average proportion of professionally qualified or skilled people. Moreover, as Thomas discovered, the professional and managerial group, who regard house ownership as an investment, have tended to buy houses *outside* the New Towns, where there is a wider choice, and to commute long distances to work.

(ii) *In the neighbourhoods*. Ideally, neighbourhoods should not differ radically from one another – otherwise New Towns would begin to resemble older communities in which the classes, whilst living in the same town, inhabit different areas. Thus the aim was to provide a variety of dwellings within the neighbourhood. But the aim is difficult to achieve. Pursuing the example of Crawley, if it is to reflect class structures of England and Wales as in 1951, the town should cater for 20 per cent middle-class households and 80 per cent working-class. As each neighbourhood would contain approximately 2500 dwellings this would mean the 'dilution' of only 500 middle-class families in an otherwise working-class area.

The solution suggested was the clustering of families of similar social class in sub-units of between 100–300 families within the neighbourhood. Actual social mixing in the neighbourhood was to be achieved by central facilities which would be used by the households, e.g. the Community Centre, a primary school and a neighbourhood shopping centre, and this small scale approach has proved satisfactory. Whatever the effort the development corporation makes in trying to achieve social mix in different parts of the town, some will achieve a reputation for being 'better' than others. This in turn will encourage families to move to areas more in keeping with their class or class aspirations and the net effect of this is likely to be increasing social segregation. In later New Towns such as Milton Keynes the neighbourhood idea has been rejected and it may be that this indicates an acceptance of a certain degree of social segregation by class as inevitable.

3. Design misconceptions of the New Towns

Most of the British towns designated since 1945 have had to face 'teething troubles'. Typical problems have been the rapid rate of growth envisaged in planning, the under-provision of retail and social facilities, the imbalance of the age and employment structure of the population, and the general lack of established resources and 'rawness' of the urban landscape. Similarly the early or 'Mark I' towns were overcentralized in retail services, employment sites were too small and too close to London for self-sufficiency, and the towns were divided into impersonal neighbourhoods. Larger, later generation towns have adopted a grid or cell pattern which allows a more organic growth (see Fig. 9.4) by permitting individual areas to be fully developed without the expense of providing services for the whole town at one time.

The problems of these settlements have been augmented by some misconceptions in their design, for example, the lack of provision for the private car and the difficulties of organizing public transport.

A major problem in modern low density towns is the volume of traffic generated by the physical separation of homes from workplaces. It is costly in terms of passenger kilometres to pick up commuters and shoppers by public transport when they live in suburban areas. The more stops public transit vehicles make, the slower the operation of the whole system and the less popular it becomes. A few high speed systems have been developed, for example in the Bay area of San Francisco, and the recently completed Victoria Line in London, but in the New Towns the emphasis has tended to be upon providing large car parks around the pedestrianized shopping centres and factories, relying upon private cars to transport the population. The difficulties of the non-car-owner, and the inconvenience of congestion have

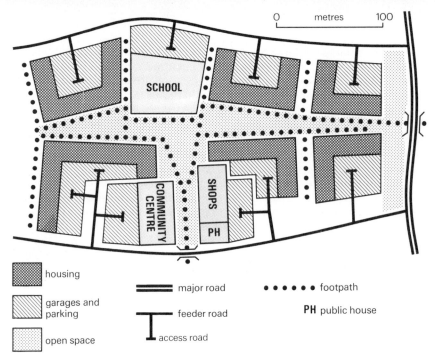

Fig. 9.4   The layout of a modern residential neighbourhood. (Source: after R. F. Reekie, *Design in the Built Environment*, Edward Arnold, 1972, p.71)

caused planners to revise their plans, and now 'dial-a-bus' and 'park-and-ride' schemes are being introduced in many cases. The articles from *The Guardian* of 1972, quoted below, describe the recent proposal for mono-rail systems which would provide quick passenger traffic movement in a flexible form. Unfortunately, the monorail proposed for Milton Keynes was not built, but the dial-a-bus system is operating successfully.

Call for tramline transport
New forms of public transport, especially automatic track-following 'autotaxis' and minitrams, should be introduced to test public reaction, a group of scientists says.

The suggestion comes in evidence to the Greater London development plan inquiry by the British Society for Social Responsibility in Science. The society says that such forms of transport, already known in America, would be safer, easier to use and less damaging to the environment than present systems.

Autotaxis normally have four seats and travel to fixed stations. Minitrams are larger, carry more passengers, but give less individual service. The society says that an advantage of both systems is that they can be used by anyone, including the disabled.

The Guardian 16 March 1972

By any other name . . .
The day of the tram is at hand again – or at least the 'segregated track vehicle,' as Mr John Peyton, Minister for Transport Industries, called it yesterday.

The Minister disclosed this revolution in anti-technology in the Commons when Mr David Stoddart, Labour M.P. for Swindon, predicted a world oil shortage and said it was the greatest mistake ever made to get rid of the trolley-bus.

Mr Peyton said: 'Well, I'm not sure that the day will not come when we reinvent the tram. My department has a programme of studies on new or improved systems of urban transport, including vehicles on segregated tracks.'

The programme is now rattling away at the Road Research Laboratory, where the Government has already invested £250 000 in the development of the mini-tram to carry 10 to 20 passengers.

The last word in 'segregated track' travel will be a four-seat tramcar now being developed at the R.R.L., which will be presented as a rival to the private car. It will run on a fine network of tracks.

The Guardian 16 November 1972

Dial for a bus service
The first trial of a public door-to-door taxi-type bus service begins in Maidstone, Kent, today.

It will provide the public with a 'moderate cost service which is receiving close scrutiny from many local authorities', the Ford motor company, which pioneered the system, said.

The dial-a-ride's service in Maidstone follows a restricted form of service – two days a week – at Abingdon, Berkshire, since June.

British Rail is considering a similar service in Bristol, and interest has been shown in the service at Chelmsford, Harlow, East Kilbride, Seale and Eastbourne, according to Ford. It also goes into operation in Harrogate on September 25.

The Maidstone scheme is being run by a local taxi operator, Mr Denis Freeman. 'The service meets all sorts of personal transport needs. It offers real door-to-door service, and all at a very reasonable cost,' he said. 'Fares in Maidstone are set at a flat rate of 20p compared with an equivalent taxi fare of £1 over similar distances', Ford said.

The buses will answer a customer's telephone call, which is processed by the local dial-a-ride control centre, and drop him at his destination.

The Guardian 30 August 1972

Table 9.10. The purpose of passenger travel, 1964. (Source: National Travel Survey.)

Purpose	Journey stages	Mileage
	(per cent)	(per cent)
To and from work	38.0	30.5
In course of work	4.0	7.9
To and from school or college	8.8	5.1
Shopping and personal business	17.5	13.1
Entertainment, sport, eating and drinking	8.8	8.3
Personal social travel	14.6	19.5
Other personal travel (holidays, pleasure, etc.)	8.3	15.5
	100.0	99.9

As Table 9.10 indicates, passenger traffic is for highly specific purposes which can cause problems of 'peaking' of demand for the service. By failing to reduce the actual journey distances involved between home and work, shops and schools, New Town designers have often exacerbated these problems by their low density and functionally segregated urban layouts.

Similarly, with the exception of the Open University – an institution of a dispersed character – none of the two dozen universities built since the Second World War has been located in one of the New Towns. As Walter Bor, one of the designers of Milton Keynes, has pointed out:

> Surprisingly few New Towns have experimented with their educational, health or social services or indeed in the physical environment, in spite of their potentially favourable conditions. While it is true that housing and working conditions are a considerable advance on existing towns – the quality of urban life as such is in some respects inferior to that existing towns can offer.[9]

The lack of any but modern buildings, the limited variety of occupation, the large scale of the developments, will tend to rob the new environments of the character that their occupants have previously experienced. Additionally, there is often animosity between established residents of villages submerged in the New Town and the newcomers, and little sense of identity on the part of inhabitants whose allegiances are often with relatives and friends in their previous towns.

4. The future of New Town development

The problems of New Town growth have not been lessened by the downturn of the British economy and coincidentally of the birthrate in the 1970s. Hence we find that by 1978 there was no longer an excess of live births over deaths (see Fig. 3.14, page 74). Allied to this, the attempts to reduce immigration into Britain have led to doubts as to the possibility of continued expansion of New Towns. In 1976 the Secretary of State for the Environment, Peter Shore, predicted the cessation of the New Town building programme. It has not quite come to that, but the changes in policy brought about by rising unemployment and decreased rates of population growth are significant. In brief, the situation is one where inner city areas, having lost their active population to the New Towns, now wish to recoup some of the employment which has gone with them. Simultaneously, firms which were encouraged by Government and by an expanding economy to relocate are now anxious to withdraw from the more expensively located sites in the regions. Increased oil and transport costs are instrumental in this; as is the often poor record of labour relations in the areas to which the firms moved. Other difficulties involve the problems of cost involved in building the necessary infrastructure of services to support large new communities. The question inevitably arose as to whether large new schemes could not be replaced by revitalization of the city centres – 'urban renewal' – and by grafting any necessary new building onto existing large centres.

Hence a policy of 'town development' or expansion has replaced large New Town designation. John Williams of the Greater London Council describes how this procedure has operated.

A town development scheme requires the close co-operation of several authorities to provide the many necessary services where and when required. The district council (the receiving authority) is responsible for providing housing, tenants' meeting halls, group practice surgeries, recreation areas, swimming pools, etc., and also for ensuring that in planning the area suitable sites are earmarked for the shops, churches, public houses, etc. which will be needed. The county council provides schools, libraries, highways and social services, and the area health authorities provide the community health and hospital services. [10]

5. Urban renewal or overspill?

As the rate of population growth has declined and as the problems of inner cities have increased, even the policy of relocating city dwellers in established centres such as Northampton, Peterborough and Telford has been revised. The cities have cleared their central areas and replaced their slums during the breathing space created by New Town expansion. Now they are anxious to re-attract residents. The effect of this on the New Towns has been very significant – especially on towns like Skelmersdale – where expansion has been effectively stopped by Central Government. Pat Blake of the Town and Country Planning Association, reviewing a statement by the Government in 1978, describes it thus:

> Milton Keynes and Northampton lost 50 000 people from their original targets. Peterborough lost 20 000, Warrington 35 000, Telford 70 000 and Central Lancashire over 100 000.
> These developments, together with national population trends and a sluggish economy, have led to a continuing fall in the overall rate of growth. Capital expenditure fell from £299m in 1976 to £282m in 1977 and the number of new dwellings fell from about 28 343 in 1976 to 27 316 in 1977. New population fell from 59 937 in 1976 to 15 665 in 1977 and there has been a corresponding decrease in industrial and commercial development. [11]

Urban renewal schemes range in size and success. Many mistakes were made in large high density redevelopments, either in construction as at Ronan Point (Plate 9.4), or in design, as at Hulme, Manchester (Plate 9.5). Some schemes, however, have provided a new focus for city life and increased the proportion of residents in previously wholly commercial areas (Fig. 9.5). Schemes such as the Barbican development are often costly, but more modest plans for rehabilitation of existing houses have proved popular and caused a minimum of displacement. Future New Town growth is likely to be on a small scale and, profiting by past mistakes, strictly regulated in design and quality of its buildings. The foremost current (1978) example is the scheme by Essex County Council to develop a community of 18 000 people at South Woodham Ferrers (see Fig. 9.6). The surviving exception to the return to the small-scale approach to renewal is Britain's largest New Town or rather new city, Milton Keynes.

6. The case of Milton Keynes

Having briefly considered the role of New Town development in urban planning

Plate 9.4   Ronan Point. In 1968 a gas cooker exploded in one of the flats, causing the entire south east corner of this 23-storey block to collapse, killing several people. The structural weakness of this sort of system building was demonstrated and there was great public outcry, particularly as these were council flats in Canning Town, London. The future of high-rise blocks then under construction began to be seriously questioned and councils subsequently abandoned this solution to housing shortage problems. (*Keystone Press Agency*)

policies, we will conclude with a consideration of Britain's largest new urban area, which exemplifies much that has been learned about New Town policy in the last twenty-five years. Comparison of this city with earlier attempts in Stevenage indicate that Milton Keynes has achieved low densities and reasonable journeys to work, though with less accessible retail and social facilities than in the smaller, earlier towns. The constraints imposed by building very large centres are, as previously suggested, beginning to strain the fundamental advantages sought in the 'garden city' movement. The plan for Milton Keynes was published in 1970 by Richard Llewelyn-Davies and Walter Bor. The site is located about 80 kilometres

Plate 9.5   Hulme Flats, Manchester. Council housing on a monolithic scale, which has proved a social failure. The uncompromisingly stark buildings and the long corridors and balcony walkways have encouraged vandalism and the council's housing policy and building standards have also been criticized. Building 'streets in the air' seemed a good solution to housing shortages at the time of construction. (*Manchester Public Libraries*)

Fig 9.5   A sketch of the Barbican development in the City of London. (*Chamberlin, Powell & Bon (Barbican), Architects*)

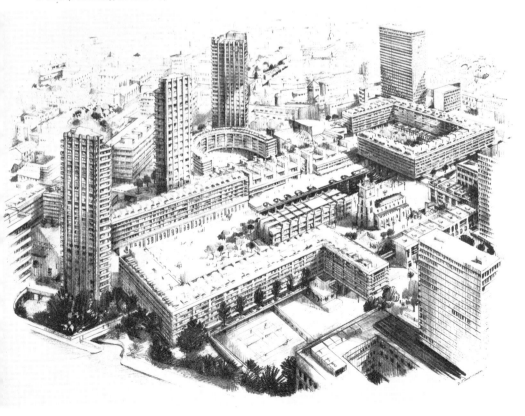

SOUTH WOODHAM FERRERS

A new Country Town on
the River Crouch,
eventual population 17,500. Sites
for industry, workshops, offices,
shops and housing still available

Enquires to:

Essex County Council,
Development Office,
Fenn Farm,Wickford Rd.,
South Woodham Ferrers,
Essex.
Tel:Chelmsford 320168

Fig. 9.6   An advertisement for South Woodham Ferrers. *(Essex County Council)*

north west of London, half way between London and Birmingham along the A5 – Britain's oldest 'intercity' routeway. The original plan had been for a new urban area between Wolverton and Bletchley (see Fig. 9.7), but the later proposal envisaged provision for a quarter of a million people, currently revised to 200 000.

Criteria for planning the city were based on the assumptions of a doubling in real income by A.D. 2000 and the need to provide for highest and lowest income groups – a problem largely unsolved in other New Towns. Walter Bor defines the main planning goals as being:

1. Opportunity (jobs, education, housing, shopping) and freedom of choice.
2. Easy movement and access (including public transport).
3. Balance and variety (simultaneous provision of houses, workplaces and amenities) within the urban landscape, and a distinct 'local' character within the city.
4. An attractive city (both in terms of the car traveller and the pedestrian).

268

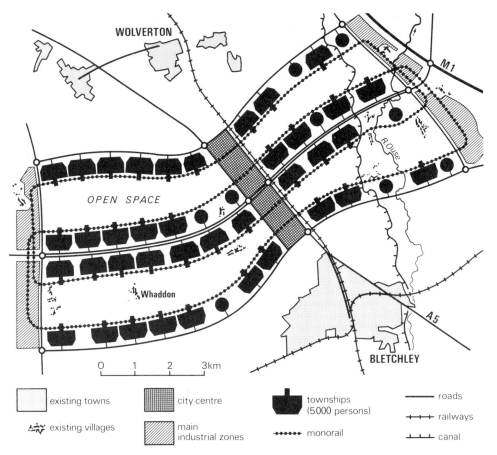

WOLVERTON

M1

R. Ouse

OPEN SPACE

Whaddon

A5

BLETCHLEY

0	1	2 3km

☐ existing towns	▦ city centre
⚡ existing villages	▨ main industrial zones
⬢ townships (5000 persons)	•••••• monorail
—— roads	+++ railways
⊥⊥⊥ canal	

Fig. 9.7   The original design for Milton Keynes. *(Buckinghamshire County Council Department of Architecture and Planning)*

5.   The encouragement of the public to participate in the planning and organization of their local community.
6.   Efficient and imaginative use of resources (quality of management and administration).[12]

The proposals for the city, which contains four existing towns (Bletchley, Stony Stratford, Wolverton and New Bradwell) and thirteen villages, rely on *dispersed* industrial and transport development, and are based on a *network* of dual carriageway roads about 1 kilometre apart, giving eight access points per kilometre square (see Fig. 9.8). This road system is linked to the M1 motorway via three interchanges. The employment areas are sited on the periphery with a large city centre accessible by three-lane highways between the present A5 and M1. The route of a previous transport era, the Grand Union Canal, is to become a linear park.

For social services the planning unit is 30 000 people – the number occupying a small 'traditional' town. Each unit is to have three secondary schools, a health centre and a 'resources' centre incorporating library, swimming pools and so on. The Open University and Milton Keynes College are designed to serve the tertiary education sector. The main hospital is also centrally based. Where pedestrian routes cross major traffic roads, 'local activity centres' – shops, schools, clinic, bus stops – are to

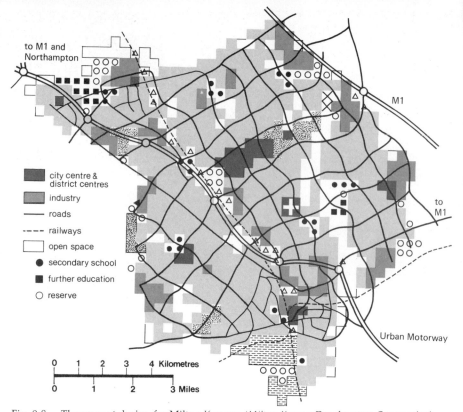

Fig. 9.8 The present design for Milton Keynes. (*Milton Keynes Development Corporation*)

be located. It is hoped to focus local residential areas on intersections rather than inward to the centre of their 'squares'.

The new city centre is designed to serve the whole city and provides a shopping mall together with 'traditional' pedestrian shopping streets and squares (see Plate 9.6). Obviously the concept of the city depends on high mobility and this is to be encouraged and served by a 'dial-a-bus' system. The city should provide regional facilities for recreation, entertainment, and sports. It is hoped that journeys to work will average fifteen minutes by car and twenty minutes by bus.

While Milton Keynes is a far cry from the pioneer garden city as envisaged by Howard, it still retains basic concepts of privacy, space, mobility, balance and self-containment. Whether these can be achieved at such a greatly advanced scale remains to be seen.

ASSIGNMENTS

1. *Consider the images portrayed by the advertisements for New Towns. At what sort of people are they aimed?*

2. *It has been suggested that there are 'code words' or phrases in New Town publicity e.g. community, prosperity, integrated, planned, exciting, balanced environment, choice, home.[13] Discuss the use of these terms and their implications in relation to New Towns. Do they have an application in old-established settlements?*

3. *Why is Milton Keynes likely to be the last large-scale New Town?*

270

Plate 9.6   Milton Keynes Shopping Centre. The neighbourhood principle of shopping facilities located near housing estates has been supplemented by the building of a large centre. The importance of private car transport is shown by the presence of car parks and road access points, and the distance at which residential areas (upper right of photograph) are located precludes walking into town. In some ways this resembles the out-of-town hypermarket centre but office and cultural facilities will also be located here, although the density is far lower than in older cities. *(Milton Keynes Development Corporation)*

4. *Why do New Towns have difficulty in attracting and accommodating members of (a) very low and (b) very high income groups? What disadvantages does this have?*

5. *Why have the 'optimum sizes' of New Towns been continuously revised upwards since the Second World War?*

6. *How does Government encourage industrial relocation within New Towns, and what factors operate against this policy?*

D. Planning in Rural Areas

So far we have considered how planners and government agencies have tried to solve the problems of urban communities, but this is only part of the picture. In this section we will turn our attention to what has happened in the villages and hamlets.

Despite the growing area and population of urban settlements, 80 per cent of contemporary Britain is still rural land – farm, marsh, moor, mountain or shoreline – and 25 per cent of the country's population still lives in rural areas. Whether many of these people have a direct connection with the land is doubtful – often villages have experienced the change to satellite dormitories for neighbouring towns, and with increasing mobility the prospect of a long daily journey to work has often been outweighed by the advantages of rural residence. However, the general decline in demand for rural labour has meant the growth of a new rural commuting population, whose demands for transport, shops and entertainment are identical with those of the urban dwellers. The problems generated by New Town development on green field sites, and by retirement and second home ownership, all bring change to the countryside and its villages. In concluding our review of the development of rural settlement, the ways in which planning policy has attempted to deal with the changes in village communities are considered. It is expected that you will have access to local materials, which should exemplify the processes taking place.

1. Changes in population distribution

The Town and Country Planning Act of 1947 was the first piece of national legislation to require local authorities to prepare plans of development in their areas. Previously there had been local initiatives to stabilize village population and prevent a drift to the towns – the replacement of tied cottages by council houses, the provision of water, gas and electricity and the subsidizing of local bus services to encourage and sustain villages. But whereas before and during the Second World War the population in rural areas had continued to decline, in the post-war period it has grown as urban dwellers appreciate the attractions of rural life. Between 1951 and 1971 the rural population increased by around 25 per cent, some 2.5 million people. At the same time, increasing private car ownership and the economies of scale which favour larger enterprises have seen the loss of local shops, the closure of village schools and the phasing out of cottage hospitals, so that the amenities in rural areas have been reduced. The effect of this on the non-mobile rural population has been largely overlooked, although a recent survey by the Standing Conference of Rural Community Councils entitled *The Decline of Rural Services* has highlighted the problems. Of course this broad generalization requires qualification and it is possible to distinguish several processes taking place. Brian Woodruffe has devised a six-fold classification of rural districts on the basis of what has happened to their population:
  (i) Districts where the post-war decrease in population has become more rapid or accelerated.
 (ii) Districts where the decrease has slackened or reduced.
(iii) Districts where population decrease up to 1961 has been reversed and increase has now begun to take place.
 (iv) Districts where population increase up to 1961 has now fallen away again – their growth has been reversed.
  (v) Districts where the population, though still increasing, is slowing down in its growth, or being reduced.
 (vi) Districts of continuing and accelerated growth of population.[14]

2. The role of government

During the last thirty years the Government has taken an active hand in attempting to influence population distribution in Britain, and in matching the provision of services to that population. In the early County Plans, town and country were treated separately, and the quality of rural services depended very largely upon the amount of cash left over from urban rates. Since 1970 and local government reorganization, the new functional areas often include more than one major urban and surrounding rural area, and indeed may contain more than one 'old county'. The Structure Plans for these new administrative regions are developed by the successors to the County authorities. Detailed considerations, often including the designation of conservation areas, the provision of rural public transport, or the development of housing in villages, are the responsibility of District Authorities replacing the old boroughs and rural districts.

In many of the early development plans, a hierarchy of settlement was established. Levels of service centre and population thresholds developed in quite close accordance with Central Place theory, and especially the work of its English practitioners, Dickinson (1947) and Bracey (1953), to whom we referred in Chapter 8.

On the basis of the data collected, local authorities formulated plans designed to combat rural problems such as lack of drainage, or poor transport, and to encourage the process of local service centre development. The attempt was to 'order' the landscape to provide a compromise between efficient administration and social need. 'Key settlements' were to be identified and developed and, it was silently conceded, less important ones were to be allowed to decline by refusing to allow building, new industry, or improved social services to develop in them. Hence during the 1950s and 1960s the overall pattern of village and small town growth was determined by local government selection of those settlements which were to expand and the concentration of resources into them. By the careful vetting of planning applications it was possible to influence private building, to prevent sprawl and to encourage infilling of empty land. By the early 1960s most Counties' Five Year Plans had a classification of villages on a five-point basis which was similar to the following:

   (i) Villages where expansion is unlikely (remote, poor services) and/or to be discouraged.
   (ii) Villages where limited and controlled expansion is possible (having regard to natural beauty, good farmland).
   (iii) Villages where expansion is to be deferred (new road or sewer proposed).
   (iv) Villages suitable for minor expansion (limited by services available – e.g. size of school, water supply or amount of non-agricultural land).
   (v) Villages suitable for major expansion (close to growing town, having much spoiled land suitable for housing, needing new growth for social mix).

In other words by this time the local authority had moved away from merely allocating land for future development and applying restrictive measures to prevent the loss of farmland or pollution, to the role of active settlement policy. This active role was further developed in the 1970s when major structure plans were developed. These plans included the choice of strategies for the growth of population, the diversion of money into recreation, schools, roads or industry, and the competing demands for resources from health, education, transport, and social services. Frequently, simplified versions of possible alternatives have been presented to the general public in an effort to involve them in participation. The resulting 'preferred strategy' is then published and forms the blueprint against which proposals for new roads or schools, housing estates and factory sites are tested. The settlements scheduled for development or decline are named and the pattern of policy made evident. Whilst this procedure is superficially democratic, it is arguable whether the authorities' responsibility for public accountability can be resolved by putting on a planning exhibition in the local town library.

3. Planning at the local level

Whilst general policy for what happens to villages is given in Development and Structure Plans, in many cases individual plans have been produced for particular villages. These may be villages where there are buildings of great architectural value, or villages which are scheduled for expansion, or renewal, or new 'planned' villages (see Plate 9.7). Occasionally the impetus may come from local residents' associations or parish councils rather than from Government. It seems possible to distinguish five approaches in formulating village plans although these are often combined.[15]

(a) Outline structure approach

Instead of concentrating on infilling land to compact the shape of the village, development is permitted only in character with the historical morphology (linear,

Plate 9.7   Goldsworth Park, Woking – a New Ideal Homes' development. This aerial view shows the layout of a modern planned village where houses, shops, schools and leisure facilities have been planned, along with roads, in an attempt to improve upon the speculative estates characteristic of much suburban development in England. (*Photography by Dawson Strange Photography Ltd,. Cobham, Surrey. © New Ideal Homes Ltd.*)

circular) of the village. This has been tried in north east England where the traditional linear pattern is very strong. In Essex, design guides to ensure that new development is in keeping not only in materials and styles but also in form with the old, have been introduced. There are obvious cost problems in the wholesale application of this approach, but often the inclusion of village greens and traditional patterns helps overcome the raw newness of housing estates.

(b) Capacity approach

The question of how to limit the village is a vexed one, and probably local rather than general answers are more appropriate. In the open framework of hamlets which is characteristic of parts of the south Midlands, the village may have no focus, but consist of half a dozen or more 'ends' which bear a common linkage of name and lanes, whereas the compact, narrow-streeted sheep villages of the old West Riding of Yorkshire have a much more definite 'edge'. However, the designing of an arbitrary limit to development, an 'envelope', is often used to indicate what are acceptable limits for growth. This may be on the basis of physical area, or the capacity of the village services.

(c) Visual appraisal approach

This is a fairly subjective method, but one which is gaining popularity. The appropriateness of new building, or demolition, to the appearance of the existing village, and the evaluation of the physical appearance of hedges, walls and street signs is involved. You may like to refer to Gerald Burke's *Townscape*,[16] or the *Art and the Built Environment Project 16–19*[17] for examples of evaluation of buildings. This method has obviously been most commonly used in areas of particular character – the Cotswolds, Kent and Cambridgeshire.

(d) Policy area approach

The method here has been to isolate the various components of the village either in functional or character terms and then decide which ones are to be altered or extended. This approach lends itself more to villages which are large, or contain a variety of clearly defined zones or periods of construction, or to new villages where it is desired to develop the character of individual neighbourhoods.

(e) Conservation area approach

Perhaps the most commonly thought of method of controlling village growth is the designation (under the 1967 Civic Amenities Act) of conservation areas where, because of the particular interest of a group of buildings or streets, the scale of change is strictly limited. A village green, or belt of trees, may also be included. Some 4000 of these areas have been established in the last decade and it is likely that many more will be, especially as more old village centres are bypassed by new roads.

Conservation is a subject which is still young, and the variety of approaches and subjective values of its practitioners illustrate that there is as yet little consensus over the objectives and methods that should be adopted if we wish to retain the quality of our landscape and its resources. However, it seems certain that the pressure of geographers and others interested in the environment will grow in the future, in the effort to ensure that planners do not adopt cheap, short-term solutions to settlement problems.

1. At this point you should read the reprint of the Bedfordshire County Council publicity leaflet issued as part of their public consultation procedure, and Christopher Hall's article from the Guardian handbook Places for people. Attempt to evaluate the arguments put forward in them. See Appendix, page 278.

2. Choose a village within reach of your own locality and prepare a village plan for conservation based on one or more of the approaches described in the previous section. Reference to examples produced by your local authority should make this task easier.

Key Ideas

A. *Principles of New Town development*
1. The New Town movement has its base in nineteenth-century industrial philanthropy.
2. Certain fundamental principles of social equality and harmony guided the early movement and its creations.
3. Since 1945, Government social policy has guided design, location and functioning of New Towns, and this has presented some problems in the conflict of aims and their realization.

B. *The building of British New Towns*
1. Post-war British new towns grew rapidly with an incursion of population drafted into them from their parent cities. The towns were seen primarily as a means of accommodating metropolitan growth.
2. Later new towns have marked concentrations of populations of particular age and occupational groups: this has particular implications for employment and social service provision.
3. The siting of the new towns has been determined by economic constraints and the needs of Government in providing centres for industrial activity and population growth in the provinces and rural areas.
4. Commercial services are often reluctant to establish themselves in new towns until they are sure of the economic viability of such a move.

C. *Problems of New Towns*
1. The New Towns have experienced particular problems because of the social role which they have been required to play, the relatively narrow age and class bands of their residents, and the general decline in Britain's post-war economic boom.
2. Not all New Towns have achieved self-sufficiency of residence or employment.
3. The policy of providing a mixture of social classes within the towns has proved difficult, especially when jobs and housing are scarce.
4. The rawness of the urban landscape and the need to create all forms of cultural and social infrastructure from nothing is often an inhibitor to the community's development.

5. In future, with the exception of existing commitments, the process of urban renewal is likely to supersede that of New Town designation as an attempt to solve urban problems.
6. The largest scheme for New Town development, that at Milton Keynes, presents a special case because of the size of the undertaking and the concept of high mobility which underlies its planning.

D. *Planning in rural areas*
1. Rural planning is constrained by the need to sustain village life and preserve the landscape on the one hand, and to provide services and homes at economic prices on the other, a problem which increased concern for the environment makes difficult.
2. At regional level, planning of rural communities and facilities is undertaken as part of major structure plans and at local level, the economies of service provision means that conservation is often restricted to limiting new developments, rather than arresting decay.

Additional Activities

Try to visit one or more New Towns, or failing that, new estates in your own area. Attempt to devise criteria for evaluating them in terms of their building standards, aesthetic appeal and functional efficiency, and apply these to the examples that you study. There are many sources to help you, but you may find the Schools Council *Art and the Built Environment Project* and the Essex County Council Design Guides[18] useful. Consider the means available for displaying your comparison: photographs, checklists, slide tape sequences etc.

Reading

A. CHERRY, G. *Urban Change and Planning*. Foulis, 1972. Chapters 5, 6.
B. MERLIN, P., *New Towns*, Methuen, 1971.
    CHERRY, G., *op. cit.*, Chapters 7, 8.
C. THOMAS, R. & CRESSWELL, P., *The New Town Idea*, Open University, 1973.
D. WOODRUFFE, B. J., *Rural Settlement Policies and Plans*, O.U.P., 1976.

Villages~Out in the Cold?

Village character preserved.

Farming needs and the avoidance of all unnecessary building come first in the countryside.

Village growth
Many villages will gain new housing through schemes already agreed but, after this, most new building will be concentrated in the towns. In the rural parts of the Districts a few villages will have room for a little more housing. These will be:—

- North Bedfordshire:
  Sharnbrook, Wilstead
  Wootton

- Mid Bedfordshire:
  Shefford, Arlesey, Cranfield

- South Bedfordshire:
  Barton, Eaton Bray
  Toddington

Away from these places there will be little new building in villages and in between villages but old buildings will be replaced by new ones and a few remaining plots here and there will be found. Apart from that – virtually nothing.

Tough choice

For people living in the villages this may seem unfair but it cannot be any other way if the priorities and aims set by the County Council are to be met.

- If villages go on growing they take vital farmland
- If villages go on growing they grow into each other and lose their individual identity
- Many villagers will, in fact, be happy to see little change in their surroundings, but there will be problems:

No extra jobs

As for jobs in rural areas, the answer will be the same – very little change at all. Existing establishments such as research laboratories and agricultural colleges may expand. Agricultural jobs will not be affected.

There will be no deliberate dispersal of employment to country areas.

Increased food production is a national priority. Hence the important place of farmers. They, together with the mineral excavators will remain the principal employers in the countryside. Their interests are safeguarded, although farming must not mean undue damage to fine countryside.

Smaller villages

The policy of restricted growth in the rural areas may mean that services in some villages may be depleted:

- There may not be enough children in the smaller villages to keep the school going.
- Village shops may find it difficult to stay profitable with custom remaining static.
- Community spirit may be affected as children grow up and seek the attractions of the towns.

Of course, there is the other side of the coin. Many people choose to live in isolated villages rather than the faster pace of the towns. These rural policies will not please everyone but, in the countryside, the County Council puts farmers first.

(from Bedfordshire County Council publicity leaflet, prepared during consultation on the Structure Plan.)

Changing Lifestyles in the Village

The only choice for most of the 5000 villages in England and Wales today is whether to become suburbs in the fields or upper middle class museum pieces. Originally most villages housed the people who worked on the land. Today, even in rural areas, barely three per cent of the working population are in agriculture. But the villages remain and in recent decades the proportion of people living in the countryside has been rising – from 21 per cent in 1951 to 27.7 per cent in 1971.

The impact of this reverse flow to the countryside is evident in the villages selected by planning authorities for expansion. New speculative estates sprawl around the older village core. They house the commuters – often newly-weds for whom such a home is a better buy than its urban equivalent. In the old centre are more commuters, retired people or week-enders – all people able to afford the maintenance of desirable properties now beyond the purse of indigenous villagers. The latter are likely to be living on the council estate at the edge of the old village.

This is a crude picture drawn with a necessarily broad brush, but it is recognisably true of many villages which planners have selected for growth in order to concentrate as cost-effectively as possible the services and facilities which are expensive to provide among small, dispersed communities. In these 'key' or 'selected' villages – the jargon varies – there will be a primary school, enough passengers to justify subsidy for a bus and enough customers to keep the local shops and post office alive.

Here ought to be also the ingredients of a thriving community. But, unless expansion has been gradual and on a scale the existing village community can cope with, and unless the local authority has taken exceptional care to get the resulting social mix right, expanding villages are likely to suffer an 'us and them' divide between the indigenous and incoming families. Estate-based residents' associations rival the parish council. Economic and social differences between the wholly white collar spec-estates and mostly manual council houses are acutely obvious in the confined area of a village.[1]

But integration can happen. Studying Walkington, north of Hull, David Neave found that integration of the old and new had occurred because growth in the village had been relatively slow and because the post-war council estate in the village had had time to develop its own confidence which found expression in a vigorous welcome policy towards the newcomers. Yet it was in this village that a woman wrote to the local newsletter 'Before the new estates were built everyone knew everyone and always spoke or waved a hand in acknowledgement when passing each other in the street.'

Conservationists have usually welcomed the selection of certain villages for growth, because it enables strict preservationist policies to be followed for those not selected. They rarely ask who lives under the expensively maintained thatch and behind the roses rambling over the porches of these physically static settlements.

Non-selection means no – or very few – new houses thus forcing the younger indigenous population away. Strict conservation means no site for even the smallest workshop or light industry. The school population declines until the children have to be bussed to a village or town perhaps miles away. An hour and a half a day in the school bus is a common experience of village schoolchildren today.

As the indigenous villages go, so do the transport and shops they supported. In 1974 Beckley, near Oxford, lost its post office-cum-shop forcing old people to take the bus to get their pensions. Last year the bus went too. The net result is a few more pretty cottages for Oxford dons and British Leyland executives to tart up.

The villages which the planners – thinking physically – see as static are in fact in social flux. Their native population is gradually exchanged for those affluent enough to be able to afford the upkeep of old houses and the cost of living – two cars essential – remote from shops and services. These changes, amounting to a large scale piece of social engineering, have never been consciously willed by the planners – still less by the villagers themselves. They are the unforeseen consequence of concentrating growth in selected settlements.

Such a policy may be sound local authority book-keeping, but does it make social sense? A Hampshire Council of Community Service study last year noted that in Basingstoke the proportion of children taken into care was six times that ruling in four neighbouring villages. The juvenile offence rate in the town was three times and the probation rate five times that of the villages. The village, just because it is a small and partly self-regulating community, is a more law-abiding place than a town.

The extreme wing of the environmental movement holds that a sustainable life-style demands a mass return to living in small agrarian communes. There is no need to go so far in order to see that village life holds certain measurable pluses for society as a whole.

It would be pleasant if we could tell the world that the rural policies of our government – central and local – recognise the advantages of village life and are designed to maintain and revivify these communities. But on present evidence this would not be true.

Christoper Hall
Christopher Hall is Director of the Council for the Protection of Rural England.

(from the Guardian *handbook*, Places for People.)

References

Chapter 1

1. PATTISON, W., 'The Four Traditions in Geography' in BALE, J., GRAVES, N. & WALFORD, R., *Perspectives in Geographical Education*, Oliver & Boyd, 1973.
2. CHORLEY, R. & HAGGETT, P., *Models in Geography*, Methuen, 1967.
3. MINSHULL, R., *An Introduction to Models in Geography*, Longman, 1975.
4. FITZGERALD, B. P., *Developments in Geographical Method*, Oxford University Press, 1974.
5. PRED, A., *Behavior and Location*, Gleerup, 2 vols., 1967 and 1969.
6. POCOCK, D. & HUDSON, R., *Images of the Urban Environment*, Macmillan, 1978.
7. FIREY, W., 'Sentiment and Symbolism as Ecological Variables', *American Sociological Review*, **10**, 1945. Reprinted in JONES, E., *Readings in Social Geography*, OUP, 1975.
8. BUTTIMER, A., 'Social Space in Interdisciplinary Perspective', *Geographical Review*, **59**, 1969.
9. GOODEY, B., *Perception of the Urban Environment*, University of Birmingham, Centre for Urban and Research Studies, Occasional Paper 17, 1971.
10. HARVEY, D., *Social Justice and the City*, Arnold, 1973.

Chapter 2

1. CHISHOLM, M., *Rural Settlement and Land Use*, Hutchinson, 1966, Chapter 2.
2. ORWIN, C. S., *The Open Fields*, Clarendon Press, 1954.
3. LIVELY, P., *The Presence of the Past*, Collins, 1976, page 112.
4. ORWIN, C. S., *op.cit.*
5. HOSKINS, W. G., *The Making of the English Landscape*, Hodder, 1977.
6. ASHTON, T. S., *The Industrial Revolution, 1760–1830*, OUP, 1968.
7. BURKE, G., *Townscapes*, Penguin Books, 1976.
8. HOSKINS, W. G., *op.cit.*, page 53.
9. DARBY, H. C., *New Historical Geography of England before 1600*, Cambridge University Press, 1976.
10. SAWYER, P. H., *Medieval Settlement*, Arnold, 1976.
11. LIVELY, P., *op.cit.*
12. RUSSELL, J. C., *Medieval Regions and their Cities*, David & Charles, 1973, page 124.
13. WRIGLEY, B. A., *Population and History*, Weidenfeld, 1969.
14. DARBY, H. C., *op.cit.*, page 396.
15. MILLS, D., 'Has historical geography changed?', *New Trends in Geography*, Open University Press, 1972, pages 70–75.

Chapter 3

1. BURKE, G., *Towns in the Making*, Arnold, 1975 edition, page 63.
2. JONES, E. & VAN ZANDT, E., *The City, Yesterday, Today and Tomorrow*, Aldus Books, 1974, page 51.
3. CONZEN, M. R. G., 'The Use of Town Plans in the Study of Urban History', in DYOS, H. J., (ed.), *The Study of Urban History*, Arnold, 1968, pages 127–130.
4. HOSKINS, W. G., *The Making of the English Landscape*, Penguin Books, 1970, page 272.
5. BERESFORD, M., *New Towns of the Middle Ages*, Lutterworth Press, 1967, page 340.
6. BURKE, G., *op.cit.*, page 105.
7. HOSKINS, W. G., *op. cit.*, page 282.
8. SULLEY, P., *History of Birkenhead*, 1888, page 308.
9. BURKE, G., *op.cit.*, page 127.
10. BURKE, G., *op.cit.*, page 130.
11. TAYLOR, I. C., 'The Court and Cellar Dwellings: the Eighteenth Century origin of the Liverpool slum', *Trans. of the Hist. Soc. of Lancashire and Cheshire*, **122**, page 67.
12. MORRISON, A., *A Child of the Jago*, Methuen, 1897, page 1–2.
13. WHITE, B. D., *A History of the Liverpool Corporation, 1835–1914*, Liverpool University Press, 1951, pages 30–45.

14. TREBLE, J. H., 'Liverpool Working Class Housing 1801–51,' in CHAPMAN, S. D., (ed.), *A History of Working Class Housing: A Symposium*, David & Charles, 1971, pages 167–220.
15. WHITE, B. D., *op.cit.*, page 64.
16. WHITE, B. D., *op.cit.*, page 136.
17. WHITE, B. D., *op.cit.*, page 140.
18. ENGELS, F., *The Condition of the Working Class in England*, Panther, 1969, page 80, (first published in German in 1845, in English in 1892).
19. PRICE, S. J., *Building Societies, Their Origins and History*, 1958, pages 59–62.
20. DYOS, H. J., *Victorian Suburb, A study of the growth of Camberwell*, Leicester University Press, 1966, page 67.
21. *Ibid.*, page 69.
22. OLSEN, D. J., *The Growth of Victorian London*, Batsford, 1976, page 321.
23. *Ibid.*, page 314.
24. DYOS, H. J., *op.cit.*, page 28.
25. *Ibid.*, page 78.
26. *Ibid.*, page 59.
27. MORTIMORE, W. W., *History of the Hundred of Wirral*, Whittaker & Co., London, 1847, page 413.
28. STRACHAN, A., 'The Planning Framework for Modern Urban Growth: the example of Great Britain', Chapter 4 in JOHNSON, J. H., (ed.), *Suburban Growth, The Geographical Processes at the edge of the Western City*, Wiley, 1974.
29. City of Liverpool, Architectural and Housing Dept., *Housing Progress 1864–1951*, Liverpool Corporation, 1951, page 8.
30. BURKE, G., *op.cit.*, page 157.
31. WILLIAMS, N., *Population problems of New Estates, with special reference to Norris Green*, Liverpool University Social Science Dept., Statistics Division, Liverpool University Press, 1939.
32. City of Liverpool, *op.cit.*, page 24.
33. STRACHAN, A., *op.cit.*
34. Public Relations Office of the City of Liverpool, *Liverpool Rebuilds, 1945–1966*, Liverpool Corporation, 1967, page 27.
35. *Report to the Slum Clearance and Rehousing Progress Sub-Committee on Manchester's Housing Needs and Resources, 1970–78*, 1970.
36. *The City's Housing Requirements*. Report of the Policy and Finance Committee of Liverpool Corporation, 1970.
37. CONNELL, J., 'The Metropolitan Village. Spatial and Social Processes in Discontinuous Suburbs,' Chapter 5 in JOHNSON, J. H., (ed.), *op.cit.*, pages 77–100.
38. MILLS, D., *Spread of Cities*, Unit 24, Open University, 1973, pages 67–68.

Chapter 4

1. ENGELS, F., *The Condition of the Working Class in England*, Panther, 1969, page 79.
2. BURGESS, E. W. , 'The growth of the city: an introduction to a research project', in PARK, R. E., BURGESS, E. W. & MCKENZIE, D. (eds.), *The City*, University of Chicago Press, 1925, page 47.
3. HERBERT, D. T., *Urban Geography: A Social Perspective*, David & Charles, 1972, page 70.
4. CARTER, H., *The Study of Urban Geography*, Edward Arnold, 1976, page 170.
5. HOYT, H., 'Recent Distortions of the classical models of urban structure', *Land Economics*, **40**, in L. S. BOURNE (ed.), *Internal Structure of the City*, OUP, 1971, page 95.
6. SJOBERG, G., *The pre-industrial city past and present*, Free Press, 1960.
7. QUINN, J. A., *Human Ecology*, Prentice-Hall, 1950.
8. SCHNØRE, J. F., 'On the spatial structure of cities in the two Americas,' Chapter 10 in HAUSER, P. M. & SCHNØRE, J. F. (eds.), *The Study of Urbanization*, John Wiley, 1965.
9. HOYT, H., *The structure and growth of residential neighbourhoods; in American cities*, Federal Housing Administration, 1939.
10. *Ibid.*
11. HERBERT, D. T., *op.cit.*, page 72.
12. MORRILL, R. L., *The spatial organisation of society*, Duxbury Press, 1970, page 165.

13. HARRIS, C. D. & ULLMAN, E. L., 'The nature of cities', *Annals of the American Academy of Political and Social Science*, **242**, 1945, pages 7–17.
14. MANN, P. H., *An Approach to Urban Sociology*, Routledge and Kegan Paul, 1965.
15. ROBSON, B. T., *Urban Social Areas*, OUP, 1975, pages 26–27.
16. REES, P., 'Problems of defining the metropolis'; in BERRY, B. J. L. & HORTON, F. E., *Geographic Perspectives on the Urban System*, Prentice Hall, 1970, pages 308–311.
17. LAWTON, R., 'An Age of Great Cities', *Town Planning Review*, **43**, 1973, page 217.
18. *Ibid.*, page 220.
19. HERBERT, D. T., *op.cit.*, page 73.
20. ROBSON, B. T., *Urban Analysis: a study of city structure with special reference to Sunderland*, CUP, 1975, page 97.
21. HURD, R. M., *Principles of city land values, the Record and Guide*, 1903.
22. RATCLIFFE, R. V., *Urban Land Economics*, **369**, 1947.
23. ALONSO, W., 'The historic and structural theories of urban form: their implications for urban renewal, *Land Economics*, **40**, 1964, pages 227–31.
24. CLARK, C., 'Urban population densities,' *Journal of the Royal Statistical Society*, Series A, **114**, pages 490–496.
25. BERRY, B. J. L., SIMMONS, J. W. & TENNANT, R. J., 'Urban population densities: structure and change'; *Geographical Review*, **53**, pages 389–405.

Chapter 5

1. SHEPHERD, WESTWAY & LEE, *A Social Atlas of London*, OUP, 1974, page 26.
2. HERBERT, D. T., *Urban Geography, A Social Perspective*, David & Charles, 1972, page 121.
3. *Ibid*, page 130.
4. ROBSON, B. T., *Urban Analysis. A Study of City Structure*, Cambridge University Press, 1975, pages 8–14.
5. REES, P. H., 'Concepts of Social Space. Towards an Urban Social Geography'; Chapter 10 in BERRY, B. J. L. & HORTON, F. E., (eds.), *Geographic Perspectives in Urban Systems*, Prentice-Hall, 1970, pages 314–317.
6. HERBERT, D. T., *op.cit.*, page 146.
7. *Ibid*, page 146.
8. McELRATH, D. C., 'The social areas of Rome: a comparative analysis'; in *American Sociological Review*, XXVII, 1962, pages 376–91.
9. REES, P. H., *op.cit.*, pages 326–7.
10. ROBSON, B. T., *op.cit.*, page 160.
11. BURGESS, E. W., 'The growth of the city: an introduction to a research project,' in PARK, R. E. & BURGESS, E. W. (eds.), *The City*, University of Chicago Press, 1925, page 47.
12. *Ibid.*
13. FIREY, W., 'Sentiment and Symbolism as Ecological Variables', *American Sociological Review*, **10**, 1945, pages 140–148.
14. JONES, E. & EYLES, J., *An Introduction to Social Geography*, OUP, 1977, page 34.
15 HERBERT, D. T., *op.cit.*, page 253.
16. POCOCK, D. & HUDSON, R., *Images of the Urban Environment*, Macmillan, 1978, pages 64–67.
17. ORLEANS, P., 'Differential cognition of urban residents: effects of social scale on mapping'; in DOWNS, R. M. & STEAD, D. (eds.), *Image and Environment*, Aldine Publishing Co., Chicago, 1973, pages 115–130.
18. LYNCH, K., *The Image of the City*, MIT Press, 1960, pages 47–48.
19. JONES, E. & EYLES, J., *op.cit.*, page 62.
20. GLASS, R., *The Social background of a plan: a study of Middlesbrough*, Routledge & Kegan Paul, 1948.
21. BLOWERS, A., 'The Neighbourhood: exploration of a concept'; in *The City as a Social System*, Open University, DT 201, Unit 7, page 56.
22. YOUNG, M. & WILLMOTT, P., *Family and Kinship in East London*, Penguin Books, 1962, pages 112–3.
23. *Ibid.*
24. POCOCK, D. & HUDSON, R., *op.cit.*, page 86.
25. HERBERT, D. T., *op.cit.*, page 227.
26. JONES, E. & EYLES, J., *op.cit.*, page 169.

27. *Ibid.*, page 173.
28. BOAL, F. W., 'Ethnic Residential Segregation'; in HERBERT, D. T. & JOHNSTON, R. J., (eds.), *Social Areas in Cities, Vol. 1. Spatial Process and Form,* J. Wiley, 1976, page 52.
29. KEARSLEY, G. W. & SRIVASTEVA, S. R., 'The spatial evolution in Glasgow's Asian Community', *Scottish Geographical Magazine,* **90,** 1974, pages 110–124.
30. JONES, P. N., 'Some aspects in the changing distribution of coloured immigrants in Birmingham, 1961—66'; in *Trans. I.B.G.,* **50,** 1970, pages 199–218 and reprinted in JONES, E. (ed.), *Readings in Social Geography,* OUP, 1975.
31. JONES, E. & EYLES, J., *op.cit.,* page 177.
32. BOAL, F. W., *op.cit.,* pages 45–50.
33. *Ibid.,* page 57.
34. BOAL, F. W., 'Social space in the Belfast urban area'; in *Irish Geographical Studies,* 1970, pages 373–93 and reprinted in JONES, E., *op.cit.*
35. BOAL, F. W., 'Territoriality in the Shankill Road-Falls Divide', *Irish Geography,* **6,** 1970, pages 30–60.
36. KING, R., 'Bedford: The Italian Connection'; in *Geographical Magazine,* April, 1977, pages 442–449.
37. BROWN, J., *The Un-Melting Pot,* Macmillan, 1970, pages 84–5.
38. ADAMS, J. S. & GILDER, K. A., 'Household location and intra-urban migration'; in HERBERT, D. T. & JOHNSTON, R. J., *op.cit.* pages 159–192.
39. BACKLER, A. L., *A Behavioural Study of Locational Change in Upper Class Residential Areas: The Detroit Example,* Indiana University Press 1974, page 49.
40. ROBSON, B. T., *Urban Social Areas,* OUP, 1975, page 41.
41. HERBERT, D. T., *op.cit.,* page 251.
42. ROBSON, B. T., *Urban Social Areas, op.cit.,* page 35.
43. HERBERT, D. T., *op.cit.,* pages 253–256.
44. ROBSON, B. T., *Urban Social Areas, op.cit.,* page 23.

Chapter 6

1. CARTER, H., *The Study of Urban Geography,* Arnold, 1976, page 193.
2. MURPHY, R. E., *The Central Business District,* Longman, 1972, page 2.
3. RANNELLS, J., *The Core of the City,* New York 1956, page 151.
4. CARTER, H., *op.cit.,* page 232.
5. JOHNSON, J. H., *Urban Geography: An Introductory Analysis,* Pergamon, 1972, page 121.
6. CARTER, H., *op.cit.,* page 217.
7. MURPHY, R. E., *op.cit.,* pages 10–12.
8. MURPHY, R. E. & VANCE, J. E., 'Delimiting the CBD'; in *Econ.Geog.* **30,** 1954, pages 189–222.
9. MURPHY, R. E., *op.cit.,* page 34.
10. DAVIES, D. H., 'The hard core of Cape Town's Central Business District: An Attempt at Delimitation'; in *Econ.Geog.* **36,** 1960, pages 53–69.
11. HORWOOD, E. M., & BOYCE, R. R., *Studies of the Central Business District and Urban Freeway Development,* University of Washington Press, Seattle, 1959, Chapter 2.
12. GRIFFIN, D. W. & PRESTON, R. E., 'The Zone in Transition: a study of urban land use patterns'; in *Econ. Geog.* **42,** 1966, pages 236–60.
13. GOODEY, B., 'City scene: An exploration into the image of Central Birmingham as seen by area residents,' *Research Memorandum No. 10, Birmingham, Centre for Urban and Regional Studies,* 1971.
14. DAVIES, D. H., *op.cit.*
15. CARTER, H., & ROWLEY, G., 'The Morphology of the Central Business District of Cardiff'; in *Trans. Inst. Br. Geogr.* **38,** 1966, pages 119–34.
16. CARTER, H., & ROWLEY, G., *op.cit.,* page 216.
17. MARSDEN, W. E., *Changing Environments in Britain. 1. Towns and Cities,* Oliver & Boyd, 1974, pages 65–67.
18. *Liverpool City Centre Plan Review,* City Planning Dept., 1972.
19. The National Economic Development Office, *The future pattern of shopping,* HMSO, 1971.
20. PARKER, A. J., 'Hypermarkets: the changing pattern of retailing'; in *Geography,* **60,** part 2, April 1975.

Chapter 7
1. CHRISTALLER, W., *Central Places in Southern Germany*, Jena, Fischer, 1933.
2. SKINNER, G. W., 'Marketing and Social Structure in Rural China'; in *Journal of Asian Studies*, **34,** 1964.
3. IZARD, W., *Location and Space Economy*, Yale University Press, 1956.
4. JOHNSON, J. H., *Urban Geography*, Pergamon, 1965, page 76.
5. BALE, J., 'The Weber Model' in *The Location of Manufacturing Industry*, Oliver & Boyd.
6. PRED, A., 'Initial Advantage and American Metropolitan Growth'; in *Geographical Review*, **55,** 2, pages 158–185.
7. JOHNSON, J. H., *op.cit.*, page 79.
8. ZIPF, G. K., *National Unity and Disunity*, Principia Press, (USA), 1941.
9. BUNGE, W., *'Theoretical Geography,'* Lund Series in Geography; cited in BLUNDEN, J. R., *'Spatial Aspects of Society'*, Open University Press, 1971, page 107.
10. BERRY, B. J. L., *Geography of Market Centres and Retail Distribution*, Prentice Hall, 1967.

Chapter 8
1. GREEN, P. H. W., 'Urban Hinterlands in England and Wales: An analysis of bus services'; in *Geographical Journal*, **166,** 1950.
2. SMAILES, A. E., *The Geography of Towns*, Hutchinson, 1953.
3. JOHNSON, J. H., *Urban Geography*, Pergamon, 1969.
4. NORCLIFFE, G. B., *Inferential Statistics for the Geographer*, Hutchinson, 1977, pages 27–29.
5. BRACEY, H. E., 'Towns as rural service centres'; in *Transactions of the Institute of British Geographers*, **19,** 1953.
6. REILLY, W. J., *Theory of Retail Gravitation*, University of Texas, 1930.
7. CARTER, H., *Study of Urban Geography*, Arnold, 1976, Chapter 6.
8. PAHL, R. E., *Whose City? and other essays*, Penguin Books, 1966.
9. MAYER, H., in COHEN, S. B. (ed.), *Geography and the American Environment*, Voice of America, 1968.
10. PAHL, R. E., *op.cit.*
11. CARTER, H., *op.cit.*, Chapter 12.
12. COLEMAN, A., 'Is Planning Really Necessary?'; in *Geographical Journal*, **142,** Nov. 1976.
13. COLEMAN, A., *op.cit.*

Chapter 9
1. HOWARD, E., *Garden Cities of Tomorrow*, Faber, 1902.
2. CHRISTALLER, W., *Central Places in Southern Germany*, Jena, Fischer, 1933.
3. HOWARD, E., *The Housing of the London Poor*, 1884.
4. OSBORN, F., *New Towns after the War*, Dent, 1942.
5. OSBORN, F., *Green Belt Cities*, Evelyn, Adams and McKay 1969.
6. SCHAFER, F., *New Town Story*, Paladin, 1972.
7. CHAMPION, A. G., 'New Towns Special'; in *Town and Country Planning*, February 1975.
8. THOMAS, R., *London's New Towns*, and *Aycliffe to Cumbernauld*, P.E.P.G., 1969.
9. BOR, W., *The Making of Cities*, Leonard Hill, 1972.
10. WILLIAMS, J., 'Town development, how it works'; in *Town and Country Planning*, September 1977.
11. BLAKE, P., 'Britain's New Towns: facts and figures'; in *Town and Country Planning*, February 1978.
12. BOR, W., *op.cit.*, 1972.
13. ALONSO, W., 'What are New Towns For?'; in *Urban Studies*, **7,** 1, 1970, pages 37–55.
14. WOODRUFFE, B. J., *Rural Settlement Policies and Plans*, OUP, 1976.
15. *Ibid.*
16. BURKE, G., *Townscapes*, Penguin Books, 1976.
17. WARD, C., et al: 'Art and the Built Environment Project 16–19', *Bulletin of Environmental Education*, Spring, 1976.
18. JENNINGS SMITH, D., *A Design Guide for Residential Areas*, Essex County Council, 1973.

Appendix
1. Bedfordshire County Council Publicity Leaflet, 1977.
2. *The Guardian*, 1 March 1976, page 12.

Index